Reactive Risk
and
Rational Action

California Series on
Social Choice and Political Economy

Edited by Brian Barry and Samuel L. Popkin

REACTIVE RISK
AND
RATIONAL ACTION
Managing Moral Hazard
in Insurance Contracts

Carol A. Heimer

UNIVERSITY OF CALIFORNIA PRESS

Berkeley   Los Angeles   London

University of California Press
Berkeley and Los Angeles, California
University of California Press, Ltd.
London, England

© 1985 by
The Regents of the University of California
First Paperback Printing 1989

Library of Congress Cataloging in Publication Data
Heimer, Carol Anne, 1951-
  Reactive risk and rational action.

  (California series on social choice and political
economy)
  Bibliography: p.
  Includes index.
  1. Risk (Insurance). 2. Insurance. I. Title.
II. Title: Moral hazard in insurance contracts.
III. Series.
HG8054.5.H45 1985   368   84-8466
ISBN 0-520-06756-8

1 2 3 4 5 6 7 8 9

Contents

Preface

This book has gone through a tortuous evolution from what I first wanted it to be, a book about how and with what consequences insurance organizations assumed responsibility for the management of risks associated with variations in individual trustworthiness. Now it is a book about how insurers can carry on their business when many of the risks they cover are controlled by policyholders whose motivation to control losses is greatly reduced by insurance coverage. I now conceive the book mainly as a contribution to the literature on markets and organizations, and I hope that it will influence others to investigate how organizations and individuals actually behave.

The evolution of the book occurred partly for sound intellectual reasons and partly because of my discovery of my own naiveté about both social science and insurance. When I started out, I had hoped that insurance would be like the enclosure movement—that its history would be well documented and that I could make my contribution by reanalyzing identified and partially analyzed materials. I still do not understand why insurance has been so much neglected by social scientists other than economists. My second misconception was that since insurers base their rates on statistical analyses, the raw material of some of these analyses might be available to me, perhaps in all those yearbooks or in the reports for the state insurance commissioners. As it turns out, the annual reports concern the solvency of the insurance companies, and all of the interesting statistics are proprietary information. Despite these setbacks, I still found myself with some interesting things that I wanted to write about. But the research was carried out on a graduate student budget that did not permit as many trips as one might wish to the crucial libraries and offices of Wall Street.

What this means is that this work is not the product of a perfect marriage of theory and data but is instead the result of a lengthy affair between the two. For me, at least, the book took shape as a love child—ill planned, perhaps, but well loved. It is my hope that my affection for the work has somehow compensated for my earlier naiveté.

Work on this book was interrupted by the usual sorts of events— marriages, divorces, moves, births. Some of these hindered the work, some helped, most delayed it. For whatever it is worth, I would like to go on record on the side of those who believe that it is possible to make both babies and books and that sacrifices in career advancement do not necessarily translate into corresponding sacrifices in intellectual development. One of the advantages of having a child in the middle of a big project is that an infant will not negotiate about its demands. This means that one necessarily keeps one's work in perspective, and this is as often because a beaming baby comes over and begs to be picked up as because he has to be changed or fed. When the person who is asking for your time feels so unambivalent about taking you away from your work, a few moments of play can bring a lot of joy. But all this depends on arranging a work life that permits a lot of flexibility in scheduling.

A number of institutions and people have made important contributions to this work. My dissertation committee at the University of Chicago (including at various times Charles Bidwell, Edward Laumann, Paul Hirsch, Donald Levine, and Michael Schudson) did me a favor in giving me a "hunting license" rather than turning down my admittedly vague proposal. I believe that I am a hard person to supervise, and I appreciated the fact that they let me get by without too much supervision. When the dissertation was completed, Samuel Popkin gave me an enthusiastic response, seeing what I hope has turned out to be virtue in a rough piece of work. He was an excellent broker, introducing me to ideas and people I otherwise might have missed. Among the latter, Nathaniel Beck and Robert Bates provided comments that guided the main revision, and Beck read and commented on the next draft as well. (I dare not praise Nathaniel Beck's generosity and intelligence further lest he be flooded with manuscripts to read.) The sociology of science literature contains much speculation about the effects of rewards at various career stages. Robert Bates and Aaron Wildavsky, besides giving useful comments, praised me in ways that not only made me happy but also made me try to make the manuscript more worthy. Jonathan Bendor and Charles Bidwell gave me comments that reminded me that there was still more work to be done.

Besides those who commented on the whole manuscript, many others commented on individual chapters. Howard Becker, Peter Cowhey, Mary Douglas, Mary Jo Neitz, Kim Scheppele, Max Stinchcombe, and Christopher Winship gave suggestions for revisions. I also received help from members of the organizations and politics seminar at Stanford, both as a result of a session devoted to a piece of this book and in other discussions throughout my year of research leave. Serge Taylor, Martha Feldman, and John Ferejohn were especially important to my thinking.

Because of my peripatetic lifestyle, I had the privilege of being supported by several institutions while I was doing this work. The Sociology Department at the University of Arizona, the Mellon Foundation and the Graduate School of Business at Stanford University, and the Sociology Department at Northwestern University all provided office space and secretarial support, as well as a salary for me. At Stanford I had a ten-month research visit in a very stimulating intellectual environment. I would also like to recommend James G. March as a boss sympathetic to the needs of parents. Northwestern University, where I am now employed, has generously given me a reduced teaching load for my first year, and this had made it just barely possible for me to finish the last revision. Jo Migliara typed the first draft of the manuscript at the University of Arizona, meeting the exacting standards of the University of Chicago dissertation secretary. Mary Johnson typed the second draft at Stanford, and Ruth Ellis and Nancy Klein have produced the final draft at Northwestern. Nancy Klein's intelligence and flexibility have helped to decrease my anxiety in the last few weeks. Robert Sterbank has cheerfully scurried around correcting the bibliography, proofreading, collecting books, and making sensible judgments about which portions to photocopy when the books were unavailable.

Finally, my husband, Arthur Stinchcombe, deserves my gratitude. He cooked and cleaned, made pots of tea, cared for Kai, told people to leave me alone so I could work, fed dimes to a copying machine in the library of the American College of Insurance, believed that it would be a good piece of work if only I would get it done, and provided comments on each new piece in turn. Over the years I have learned not to be intimidated by his questions about the intellectual point of a piece of work, and this book is certainly richer for his criticism.

Now that I have detailed the faults and virtues of the project itself and of some of the people associated with it, let me cheerfully accept full responsibility for the remaining errors but urge the reader to look for some virtues.

1

Reactive Risk, Market Failure, and Insurance Institutions

Insurance and Theories of Rational Action

In theory, insurers should be able to calculate the odds of loss from a specified cause, such as fire, and then set insurance rates appropriately and sell coverage. But although it is true that insurance is bought and sold in a market, market activity is not all there is to insurance. Two facts indicate that the market is imperfect here: (1) some kinds of insurance (such as divorce insurance) are not available for purchase; and (2) insurers clearly try to alter and constrain the behavior of policyholders as well as to sell them insurance. Arrow (1971) correctly identifies the general problem: it is not possible to transfer risk from a policyholder to an insurer without altering the incentives of the policyholder.[1] When the policyholder's incentives

---

1. According to Arrow, "The problem is that the insurer, or more broadly, the risk-bearer cannot completely define his risks; in most circumstances he only observes a result which is a mixture of the unavoidable risk, against which he is willing to insure, and human decision. If the motives of the insured for decision are to reduce loss, then the insurance company has little problem. But the insurance policy may, as we have seen, lead to a motive for increased loss, and then the insurer or risk-bearer is bearing socially unnecessary costs" (1971:142–43).

Arrow argues that the problem of moral hazard, the change in policyholder incentives and therefore in the probabilities of loss, will prevent an optimal shifting of risks. This is unfortunate because unless risks are shifted, many high-risk but potentially beneficial ventures, such as engaging in research or starting a new business, will not be undertaken. At the same time, if risk is shifted completely, incentives for success will be dulled since benefits will also be shifted to the risk-bearer. Arrow elaborates

change, the odds of loss change, and the insurer has difficulty calculating likely losses and setting prices. In this book we will assume that both insurers and policyholders are rational actors, trying to maximize their expected profits. We will focus mainly on the actions of insurers that attempt to take policyholders' interests and behavior into account.

One of the most important limitations on rational action and decision making is risk. Rational action is easier when everything is known (including the ends that the actor in question wishes to pursue) and when nothing will change than when there are many unknowns. A major modification introduced into the model of the rational actor, then, has been an adjustment of the model to account for imperfect information. Those pursuing this line of work have developed numerous models in which actors choose their courses of action using different decision rules. An actor might, for example, choose a course of action (1) that would lead to the highest expected payoff (a decision rule maximizing expected utility), (2) that would minimize the biggest possible loss (a minimax decision rule), or (3) that would minimize the difference between the best possible outcome that could have been achieved with advance information and the outcome from the alternative that was actually chosen (a minimax regret decision rule).[2]

These models assume that although there may be a probabilistic relation between action and outcome, this probabilistic relation does not change once a course of action has been chosen. When this assumption cannot be made, these models do not tell us what a rational actor might do. This problem typically arises when there is a time lag between action and outcome and when the outcome is controlled by a second actor whose incentives are modified by the behavior of the first. "There is," Simon argues, "really a serious circularity here.

---

this general argument by analyzing its application to insurance itself as well as to other problems such as the provision of medical care and investment in invention. He argues that we should expect systematic underinvestment in invention and research (and greater underinvestment in more basic research) because research does not predictably lead to results and because the benefits of research, when they occur, do not accrue only to those who invested. But it is also true that if a company can appropriate the benefits of its research investments, then that information will not be used as fully as it could be, and a loss to society will result.

2. See Lave and March (1975) or Frolich and Oppenheimer (1978) for an introduction to this literature.

Before A can rationally choose his strategy he must know which strategy B has chosen; and before B can choose his strategy he must know A's" (1976:71; see also 1976:70–71, 105, and 243). The problem is that one can only make sensible decisions when the consequences are fixed (though perhaps they are only fixed probabilities). But when the consequences depend on the actions of others, one cannot regard them as fixed, since the actors will respond to each other's decisions. As Simon comments: "Only when the behaviors of others are taken as 'constants'—that is, when expectations are formed regarding their behaviors—does the problem of choice take on a determinate form" (1976:105).

Clearly, actors are not completely paralyzed by this circularity, however. Though the calculations that must be made are different when the outcome is controlled by a force to which they are "not only *exposed* but also *opposed*" (Goffman 1969:92), still they manage to decide what to do.

In this book I try to extend the model of rational action to include those cases in which risk is *reactive*—that is, when the odds of loss or gain shift once an actor has decided what to do. But rather than outlining a model of choice under reactive risk, I have studied a field in which this problem is faced, and I have tried to outline the strategies used to make decisions in the face of reactive, as opposed to fixed, risks. In insurance the problem of reactive risk is usually discussed as the problem of moral or morale hazard.

I will argue that when actors find that they cannot use the usual decision-making procedures and that a problem cannot be solved by collecting information, calculating the odds, and choosing the best course of action, they instead engage in strategic interaction, with the basic purpose of transforming reactive risks into fixed risks so that it will once again be possible to use conventional decision procedures.

Reactive risk therefore poses not only a decision problem but also a strategic problem. In economic terms, this means that the outcomes generated by the behavior of other actors are *not* taken parametrically. Because the probabilities of various outcomes are not fixed, since they depend both on exogenous variables and on endogenous factors such as the actor's *own* behavior, actors cannot treat them as parameters in a decision-making problem. The economic environment is thus not a market but a game. The rational decision-maker will therefore not only invest in information but will also behave strategically and try to alter and constrain the behavior of others. Social interaction and strategically devised patterns of interdependence thus emerge in what is seemingly a market situation. People do not merely buy and sell insurance; instead, they write building codes, check social backgrounds of potential clients, inspect safety equipment, audit books, and supervise the construction of buildings and the hiring of employees. In short, they substitute hierarchies and organizations for markets, building these hierarchies and organizations into the insurance contract. Institutions, then, are being built by actors who should presumably be acting as rational, individual agents.

But it is important to do more than just point out that we also find hierarchical elements where we had expected to find markets. In addition, I want to show the relation between these hierarchical elements and the existence of insurance markets. I will argue that the main function of these hierarchical elements is to make the market possible.

Insurance is, after all, bought and sold in a market. (In fact, one could argue that insurance necessarily involves a market because its main function is to spread risk widely.) Given my earlier arguments about why insurers might have trouble pricing their product, we should not take the existence of an insurance market for granted. It is not a trivial matter to set prices when the likelihood of loss changes after the insurance contract is signed. The question we want to ask, then, is what is it that makes an insurance market possible? More specifically, which features of hierarchy are required in order for a market to function smoothly, and what exactly do they do? In answering these questions, I want to go beyond the usual discussion of noncontractual elements of contracts (such as common culture) to elaborate the mechanisms used by one party to the insurance contract to make the other party meet the conditions required for a market transaction. My basic concern is how imperfect information affects decision making and how hierarchical elements transform the decision problem.

This concern with imperfect information is hardly new to social science. Some authors (e.g., Luce and Raiffa 1957, and others in the same theoretical tradition) concerned with this problem have focused on the consequences for individual actors, outlining decision strategies that might be appropriate under various assumptions about actors and their preferences. Others (e.g., Akerlof 1970, Rothschild and Stiglitz 1976, and Arrow 1963) have examined systemic consequences of information asymmetries, arguing that under a wide variety of circumstances markets theoretically cannot exist. In many of the cases described in this literature, the markets "unravel": in the used-car market, only "lemons" are offered for sale because owners of "peaches" have no convincing way to convey the information that their cars are better than average (Akerlof 1970); in insurance, low-risk policyholders leave the market because the price is too high, and the price is then adjusted upward to take account of the higher average risk, with the result that the next-lowest-risk policyholders withdraw (Rothschild and Stiglitz 1976).[3] The point is not so much that markets will cease to exist but that when markets get thin (when only low-quality goods are offered for sale or only high-risk policyholders want to buy insurance) they will have to be bolstered in various ways.[4]

3. Similar issues are discussed by Greene (1974) and Williams (1974).

4. For a market to work properly, buyers must know what they are buying (and in particular whether or not a competitor is selling the same thing), sellers must know the cost of producing the goods or services, and the knowledge needed for a firm or individual to compete with another seller (or buyer) must be accessible to enough people to maintain competition.

As Akerlof (1970) points out, the seller of a used car typically knows more about its condition than the buyer does. Because only the owner knows whether it is in good shape, there is not much reason to try to make price variations reflect anything but variations in such observable traits as condition of the body, cleanliness, and odometer reading. Owners of especially good cars cannot sell them for what they are really worth and thus should be motivated to keep them out of the market. Alternatively, owners should be motivated to sell "lemons," especially good-looking ones with low mileage. In the long run, then, buyers should be willing to pay only for what they expect to get—cars that are worse than they appear to be. Similarly, buyers of health insurance policies should have more information about their own health than the insurance company does. This suggests that they will tend to buy health insurance only when their health is worse than the insurance company has any reason to expect, and that insurance payments will always be more than the insurer estimated at the time it set the price for the insurance coverage. In these cases market failure is due to differential knowledge about the actual state of the commodity being bought or sold.

Markets can also fail because competitors do not have access to the information necessary to compete. This might happen, for example, when only the defense contractor that developed a weapon has the shop drawings necessary to produce the weapon efficiently (Scherer 1964:108–9). That is, information asymmetries in which buyers know more than sellers, or vice versa, may prevent the formation of stable prices because one or the other cannot tell exactly what is being sold. Information asymmetries between competitors may cause market failure because competition does not produce equilibrium prices.

Two other bodies of literature suggest what alternatives will fill the void when pure markets are not possible. Those writing in the markets-and-hierarchies tradition (e.g., Williamson 1975 and 1981) try to specify more exactly the conditions under which market failures occur, and attempt to say what features of hierarchies are functional under what conditions.[5] Those writing about the relations between principals and agents (e.g., Ross 1973; Holmström 1979, 1982a, and 1982b; Rogerson 1982; Shapiro and Stiglitz 1982; and Townsend 1980) ask how to provide optimal incentives for agents to act in the interests of principals, given that principals, for example, lack information about the character and abilities of agents, cannot directly observe their behavior, and so cannot tell whether an appropriate amount of effort is being expended. In both of these traditions, a central question is what kinds of institutions and patterns of behavior emerge to compensate for the deficiencies of the market mecha-

5. The general problem here is that sometimes it costs more to trade in a simple market than to trade within an organization. Which of these forms will be chosen depends on the magnitude and nature of the transaction costs. For instance, when it is easy to discover and agree on prices, we would expect to find simple market transactions. But when it costs a lot to determine prices, as when several people's contributions to a product's assembly cannot be measured (and therefore priced) separately, we would expect complex contracts and firms to supersede markets, since the contributions of individual workers do not have to be separately assessed in an organization. Cheung (1983) discusses the role of transaction costs, especially the costs of pricing, in the formation of firms and analyzes piece-rates as an intermediate form between markets and complex contracts. Okun (1981) discusses the range of variation in labor markets, product markets, and asset markets. Williamson (1975) analyzes some of the advantages and disadvantages of markets and organizations or hierarchies as alternative contracting modes; he considers organizational failures as well as market failures.

This transaction-cost justification for the existence of contracts and organizations is an alternative to the argument that organizations are formed to manage risks and uncertainties and that profit is justified by the entrepreneur's willingness to bear these risks (Knight 1971). Barzel (1983) argues that Knight's analysis of the role of uncertainty and risk in the formation of the firm has been misinterpreted (because Knight abandoned the concept of moral hazard at crucial points) and that, when correctly understood, it provides an explanation of the role of risk in the formation of the firm that is consistent with the transaction-cost explanation. In particular, Barzel argues that when two or more parties join together to make a product or sell a service, the one whose contribution is most difficult to measure (and therefore to price) will become the employer. This arrangement decreases the likelihood of morally hazardous behavior like shirking by making the employer's income directly dependent on his or her own contribution. What is required is not organization in the form of a firm, but only that the party most able to affect the income of the joint effort be the one who receives the residual (the income left over after wages and other costs) rather than a fixed wage. The entrepreneur thus bears the overall risk in order to eliminate his or her own incentive to generate risk.

nism under conditions of imperfect information. Hierarchical relations facilitate the collection of additional information, but they also make behavior more predictable by making the interests of the two parties more congruent. When a principal provides appropriate incentives, the behavior of the agent should become more predictable even when there are information asymmetries.

In some senses, my work brings these intellectual traditions (decision theory, market failures) back together again by focusing on the relation between market failure and decision-making strategies. The question is, given this instance of possible market failure due to strategic behavior of the policyholder and to the fact that the insurer must still make pricing decisions that depend on policyholder behavior, what makes it possible for a market to continue to exist? There is an insurance market, and both insurers and policyholders engage in market transactions, *but* they also build institutions. The questions, then, are how these two kinds of behavior—market and nonmarket— are related, what functions the nonmarket behavior serves, and under what conditions it occurs.

Stated another way, I am concerned with the implications of opportunism for decision making. According to Williamson and Ouchi (1981:349), bounded rationality (due to the inability of actors to collect and process all of the relevant information) and opportunism (guileful calculation, especially when two actors are interdependent because of previous contractual agreements) are the main human causes of market failure. But while those studying market failure have examined the implications of opportunism for organizational structure, I will instead be asking what problems it poses for *calculation* and how hierarchical features in the insurance contract help overcome these problems. And while decision theorists have had much to say about bounded rationality and the way it affects calculation, they have written less about the effects of opportunism. Different kinds of uncertainty have different effects on decision making, and they must be dealt with in different ways.

The Insurance Contract as Strategic Interaction

The literature on insurance for the most part asserts that insurers are faced with an "actuarial" problem of making decisions under risk. Insurance is about calculating the odds of various kinds of accidents and the magnitudes of the losses associated with them, setting rates that take into account both the expected losses and the uncertainty about those expectations, and selecting good risks rather than bad ones. All this suggests that insurers are facing a decision problem under fixed risk. In fact, though, insurers quite often behave as if they were instead engaged in strategic interactions with their policyholders. Such strategic interactions for the most part take the form of contract conditions rather than of actuarial calculations, and I will argue that the main effect of such contract conditions is to make actuarial calculation possible. By manipulating contractual conditions, the insurer engages in strategic interaction with the policyholder in an attempt to transform the insurance relation into a much more tractable decision problem.

Decision making under risk requires that the actor be able to estimate the likelihood of a series of outcomes. If insurance works by pooling the loss experience of many people and providing compensation for the few who actually have accidents, then what is required is that the losses really be due to accidents.

But the losses covered by insurance are only partly accidental. Though some of the losses covered by insurance are "acts of God," others are partly due to human failings of one sort or another. Though a warehouse fire might be started by lightning, it could also be started by arsonists, and the magnitude of the losses in either case might depend on whether the owner of the warehouse had inspected and repaired the sprinkler system. A ship might sink in a storm simply because of bad weather, but if the shipowner had failed to make needed repairs, or if the captain had sailed from port even though a storm was predicted, or if the shipowner had ordered the captain to cast away the vessel, the loss might not be accidental. And employee thefts are rarely accidents: employees presumably control their own behavior, and employers can also control employees to some degree through screening procedures, internal control systems, and selective firings for misbehavior.

What is especially worrisome is that policyholders' behavior may change as a direct result of having coverage. Unless the insurance company is very careful, the likelihood of loss may actually rise when a person or an organization purchases insurance. A person who is not going to lose much if there is an accident has less reason to take pains to avoid the accident, and there will be times when an "accident" will be financially beneficial. Such changes in behavior after insurance coverage has been arranged, called moral or morale hazard, make it very difficult for insurers to compute expected losses.

In general, the problem is whether risks are reactive or fixed.[6] By this I mean when the (fixed) risks do not respond to the decisions taken by an actor (in this case, the relevant decision is the insurer's decision to grant coverage), it is safe for the actor simply to make decisions and to implement them. But whenever the (reactive) risk is affected by the decision of an actor—whenever the likelihood of loss (or gain) either increases or decreases as a result of the actor's decisions—the actor must engage in strategic interaction with the other parties involved.

Insofar as losses are caused by truly accidental factors such as lightning or storms at sea, insurers are faced with fixed risks and a decision problem. Information on the frequency of loss-causing events and the extent of losses can be used to set rates, and insurers can sell insurance without much anxiety about whether losses will be higher than anticipated. The odds of hail storms are not affected by a farmer's purchase of insurance; storms at sea do not become more likely when an insurer agrees to cover associated marine losses.

But when losses are partly or entirely the policyholder's fault, as when the policyholder smokes in bed, overloads a ship, or fails to complete a contract, insurers are faced with reactive risks and cannot use standard decision-making techniques. Since policyholders, their agents, or other people can do various things to increase or decrease the likelihood of loss, insurers cannot just compute expected losses, set rates, sell the insurance to selected applicants, and leave it at that. Insurers must also make sure that actual losses do not regularly exceed expected losses. Ideally the insurer wants the policyholder to engage in a wide variety of loss-prevention activities, and not to defraud the insurance company. Thus the insurer will engage in strategic interaction to alter the incentive structure of the policyholder to make it resemble that of the insurer (or of the "prudent uninsured owner"). The policyholder must be induced to engage in loss-

6. In fact, reactivity is a continuous variable, not a dichotomous one, since a policyholder (in this case) can have anything between no control and complete control over losses.

prevention activities, even though the insurance company will cover the losses. Once the incentive structures of the actors (policyholder and insurer, or perhaps policyholder, insurer, and agents of policyholder) are similar and fixed, the insurer is again faced with a more simple decision problem. The only remaining uncertainties are whether this particular policyholder will experience a loss, what the magnitude of the loss will be, and when it will occur.

What we want to discover, then, is how insurers are able to set rates and sell insurance when they cannot really tell what the losses will be because policyholders act differently when they are covered by insurance than when they are not. The general answer, as I have outlined above, is that if insurance contracts and pricing systems can be designed to provide incentives for policyholders to reduce or prevent losses, just as they would if they were not insured, then risks will not increase as a result of insurance coverage, and it will be possible for insurers to calculate the odds of loss. That is, insurers must transform reactive risks into fixed ones if they wish to employ the usual decision-making techniques in setting rates and marketing insurance.[7] In the next section, I will outline the main kinds of solutions used by insurers.

7. It may seem that insurers should be interested in *decreasing* the odds of loss rather than in simply *fixing* those odds at precontractual levels. In general, though, it is much easier for insurers to deal with large losses than with unpredictable ones. Premiums can always be set high to cover high but predictable losses. (And, in fact, high premiums and high losses can be preferable to low premiums and low losses if insurance company profits come mainly from returns on invested premium income.) But if an insurance company cannot predict its losses, it may sell coverage at less than the cost of providing insurance. When losses are under human control, changes in incentives can lead to substantial changes in losses. As we shall see, insurance institutions are designed to curb the more routine changes in incentives following insurance coverage. But incentives may change dramatically with changes in the business cycle, with technical advances that decrease the value of obsolete property below its insured value, or with other shifts in social conditions. Because many policyholders are affected in the same way by these shifts in social conditions, the swings in the loss experience of an insurance company can be quite large. Thus insurers are much more concerned that the likelihood of loss be fixed than that it be low.

In general, if the odds of loss go down throughout a class of risks, as might happen for example with new building code regulations about fire protection in electrical wiring, then all the insurance companies that sell coverage for that class of risks will be forced by competitive pressure to lower their premiums. An insurance company only benefits from decreases in the likelihood of loss if such decreases are confined to its own policyholders.

Institutionalized Strategies
in Insurance Practice

Though insurers must take account of particulars such as
the frequency of losses, characteristics of their customers, and administrative costs associated with alternative arrangements,[8] four
general principles govern the management of reactive risk: (1) reactivity varies inversely with distance between the policyholder and the
person who controls losses, as well as with the extent of volitional
control over the loss-producing action, and contractual arrangements
must vary accordingly; (2) policyholders can be made to behave like
prudent uninsured owners by making them participate in losses and
gains; (3) control of important loss-prevention activities can be
placed in the hands of other parties when it is difficult to motivate
policyholders; and (4) frequent renegotiation of insurance contracts
is necessary to guarantee that the value of the property is reflected in
the policy so policyholders will not be motivated to cause losses to
collect insurance money. Insurer strategies are based on these principles, each of which involves some deviation from simple market
transactions.

Whether risks are reactive or fixed depends to a large extent on
whether the loss-causing events are under human control. But there
are cases in which insurers can treat risks as fixed even though the
losses are caused by controllable human action. From the point of
view of the insurer risks are fixed if there is sufficient distance between the policyholder, whose motivations will be affected by coverage, and the person controlling the event so that changes in the
policyholder's incentives will not substantially alter those of the
policyholder's agent or employee. Policyholders can only influence
those relatively close to them; we do not usually develop elaborate
plans to influence the actions of people with whom we are only indirectly linked.

Policyholders often form organizations to increase their control

---

8. See Calabresi (1970) on the relationship between such practical considerations
and more lofty goals in the rational design of institutions. In analyzing systems of
accident law, Calabresi discusses the match between various proposed and existing
systems of allocating accident costs and the deterrence of accidents, reduction of accident costs, and reduction of administrative costs.

over the supply and quality of important goods and services. But precisely because this organizational solution *increases* predictability for the policyholder it will *decrease* predictability for the insurer *if the policyholder's incentives change*. The more market-like the relation between the policyholder and the person who controls the loss-causing event, the less that person will be affected by the changes in the policyholder's motives; the closer the bond between policyholder and loss-causer the more likely it is that changes in motive will be transmitted. This should hold true for incentives to avoid loss as well, and many features of insurance contracts either require that policyholders influence their own agents or employees or, more rarely, involve direct insurer penetration of policyholder organizations.

This observation that the reactivity of risk depends on the distance between the policyholder and the potential loss-causer suggests a guideline for insurers. Briefly, it is safe to grant insurance coverage to some parties (those distant from the potential loss-causer) but not to others. In later chapters we will see how insurers have used this principle. Because cargo owners can do little to influence the behavior of the crews of ships on which their cargos are carried, insurers grant them insurance for pilferage. Insurers need not worry that losses will increase substantially if cargo owners give up their attempts to control pilferage losses. Similarly, insurance of fidelity losses becomes possible when the person buying the policy and receiving the benefit is distant from the one whose dishonest behavior is covered. Because the owner of a large business has little influence on the behavior of low-level clerks, bonding companies are not worried that fidelity losses will increase if the owner's incentives change when clerks are bonded.

Distance should be regarded as a continuous, rather than a dichotomous, variable. The greater the distance between the insurer and the policyholder, on the one hand, and the potential loss-causer, on the other, the less reactive the risk, and therefore the less uncertainty there will be in the insurer's calculation of expected losses. The insurer can control the reactivity of risk by refusing coverage except when changes in the incentives of the policyholder have little or no influence on the likelihood of loss (even though losses are under human control). The first principle governing the management of reactive risk, then, has to do with the relationship between the incentives of the policyholder and those of the potential loss-causer.

Other principles for the management of reactive risks have to do with the *manipulation* of incentives. The second principle involves the incentives of the policyholder. By making the outcomes of policy-holders dependent on their actions, insurers create a community of fate between the insurer and policyholder and in this way encourage policyholders to continue to behave like "prudent uninsured own-ers." Though the main risk of a large, unanticipated loss is trans-ferred to the insurer, the policyholders' outcomes still vary with their behavior. There are many ways this community of fate can be ar-ranged. In those cases in which insurers know some of the main causes of loss and have developed effective loss-prevention programs, coverage and rates are made contingent on use of loss-prevention equipment or techniques. Both policyholders' and insurers' out-comes then depend on such activity—insurers' because they cover the losses and policyholders' because of these contractual arrange-ments. Fire insurers might, for example, refuse to give coverage to businesses without sprinkler systems and fire drills. Marine insur-ance policies include clauses requiring that safer routes be taken, thus requiring loss prevention for the insurance to be valid.

But it is often the case that insurers do not know exactly how to keep losses low, find it too cumbersome to list all the required pre-cautions, or want the standard of behavior to change as standard practices are modified to incorporate new information. In such cases they cannot prescribe a specific course of action but must instead motivate the policyholder to do whatever necessary to keep losses low. This is usually accomplished by making the policyholders' fi-nancial outcomes dependent on their success in avoiding losses. Co-insurance arrangements, deductibles, and experience rating all force the policyholder to bear some of the financial burden of losses.

These schemes to join policyholder and insurer in a community of fate bear some resemblance to the systems of incentives proposed by those writing about the relations between principals and agents. For instance, Holmström (1979) discusses the motivational value of de-ductibles and Townsend (1980) discusses the role of longer contracts in inducing honest reporting by agents.

Note, though, that these schemes are only intended to further un-balance incentives in a situation in which the insurers have selected policyholders whose incentives are already skewed against loss. In-surers do not want to cover policyholders who are indifferent to losses, and they assume that insurance compensation for losses will only make up for *financial* losses (and perhaps not all of those) and that their policyholders will also experience frustration at the interruption of regular activities, lose customers, and so forth. But just in case the balance shifts so that policyholders are no longer so motivated to avoid losses, insurers want to make their financial outcomes contingent on loss experience as well.

From the point of view of the insurer, not all loss-prevention activities should be under the control of the policyholder. This brings us to the third principle for managing reactive risk, in which loss-prevention activities are put under the control of a third party whose incentives are more manipulable. It is usually the case that the policyholder will have mixed reactions to loss prevention, being interested in loss-prevention activity only as long as it does not divert too much time and energy from other, more rewarding activities. Fire drills are a good thing, but the manager of a manufacturing firm will be strongly tempted to postpone training programs for the company fire brigade when there is a backlog of orders. Because the municipal fire department's main business is preventing and putting out fires, it will not be nearly so tempted to defer training and practice. By encouraging the relocation of loss-prevention activities to organizations that do not benefit from neglecting them, insurers increase the likelihood that these activities will actually be carried out.

There are other reasons why someone besides the policyholder should control loss-prevention activities. In most cases the insurer cannot induce any single policyholder to do research about causes of loss, to develop and enforce standards for performance, or to purchase especially expensive loss-prevention equipment (testing equipment or water works, for example). The returns for such activity are just too small, especially when many of the benefits of reduced losses accrue to insurers rather than policyholders. In these cases the insurer or a group of insurers needs to encourage collective action. Research and inspection organizations such as the marine classification societies can provide relatively cheap information about how to prevent losses. Insurers can make certain that such public goods are provided by requiring policyholders to have their vessels inspected periodically by these societies. While individual policyholders might fail to band together to provide these public goods (though many "public goods" are actually public services), insurance companies guarantee the provision of some public goods by directly supporting them or by making coverage contingent on policyholder support of these institutions.[9]

So when policyholder motivation to engage in loss prevention is weak or mixed, or when loss-prevention activities can be carried out more efficiently by a central organization but the problems of collective action make outcomes unpredictable, insurers can increase the predictability of outcomes by locating loss prevention in a third-party organization or by requiring policyholders to invest in one. Because such organizations have purer incentives (at least vis-à-vis loss prevention), loss prevention is less likely to be neglected and the reactivity of risk is reduced. It makes no difference if the policyholders' interest in avoiding losses is decreased with insurance coverage when

9. Olson's (1971) analysis of the conditions under which groups will provide themselves with collective (or public) goods is relevant here. The basic problem is that when a benefit is shared by all members of the group (many *collective* goods can be made *divisible* through conditions of access, just as many *divisible* goods can be provided *collectively*), the individual may be tempted to share the benefit without sharing the costs. The concern here is not so much with the unfairness of such free riding, as it is called, but instead with the outcome for the group. When benefits are automatically shared, while costs are not, no one is motivated to bear the costs to provide the collective good. In the best of circumstances (when the marginal benefit to some individual is larger than that individual's marginal cost), a sub-optimal amount of the good will be provided; in less favorable situations (when marginal cost exceeds marginal benefit for all group members), none of the good will be provided. There are several ways around this dilemma: (1) to find a way to force people to share marginal costs; (2) to provide individual incentives (divisible and contingent benefits) for participation in the provision of collective goods; or, more problematically, (3) to make each individual believe that his or her contribution is crucial to the group effort.

For example, Popkin (1981) applies this framework to rural agricultural relations to show why plot consolidation and insurance schemes often fail and why in a canal cleaning or digging project villagers might be assigned specific sections of the canal or required to work all on the same day.

This analysis of collective goods is relevant to my argument in two ways. First, the problem of reactive risk is a negative variant of Olson's public goods problem since what is collectivized is the *loss*. Individuals have little incentive to fail to provide something bad that is shared by all. If the individual is fully compensated for the accident, then his or her share of the loss (an increased premium) will likely not be adequate to deter him or her from conferring the collective bad, especially since the connection between the provision of the collective bad and any effect for the individual is likely to be indirect and to occur only after a time lapse. The question, then, is what sorts of individualized incentives can be provided to deter the provision of collective losses. Rather than worrying about *inducing* the provision of collective benefits, insurers must worry about *deterring* the provision of pooled losses. Strategies for doing this include making it possible for the policyholder to share the marginal benefit of

important loss-prevention activities have been removed from policy-holder control anyway.[10]

The fourth and final principle for the management of reactive risk follows from the recognition that incentives change as the values of property covered by the insurance policy change. When insurance contracts are made, insurers take great pains to see that policy-holders have no incentive to cause losses. The insurance literature is filled with explanations of the indemnity principle, which states that policyholders should never receive more in compensation than they lost. When a fidelity loss occurs, the employer cannot collect more from the insurance company than was stolen by the employee. When a ship sinks the owner should not receive more money than the ship was worth. Otherwise there would be an incentive for the employer to convince the employee to steal and for the shipowner to collude with the captain in scuttling the ship.

But while insurance contracts are carefully designed to strike an appropriate balance between the value of property and the possible insurance compensation at the time the contract is signed, if the value of the property changes dramatically, policyholder incentives may shift. In such cases policyholders may succumb to the temptation to destroy property and submit fraudulent claims. The problem here is not so much that the policyholder made the contract in bad

---

failing to cause a loss (through experience rating, for example), providing divisible costs for causing losses (through deductibles, for example), and presumably, convincing each policyholder that he or she plays an important role in causing the current level of collective loss (as in small mutuals).

But the theory of public goods is also relevant in a positive sense. An important issue in insurance is how to arrange for collective loss prevention when this is more efficient than individual loss prevention. This problem was especially important in the early history of fire insurance when information about the causation of fires led to substantial decreases in fire losses. But for some time no one was motivated to pay for the research. Policyholders were unwilling to do the research because most of the benefits accrued to insurers; individual insurers were unwilling to pay for the research because their competitors would be able to use the information without paying for it. This and other examples of dilemmas in the provision of collective loss prevention will be discussed in later chapters.

10. Quite often this loss-preventing activity takes the form of supervising the policyholder's activities, inspecting equipment, or checking records. Such practices are especially significant because, as Holmström (1979) demonstrates for a set of speci-fied conditions, any additional information allows a more accurate judgment about the agent's (in this case the policyholder's) performance, providing an incentive for effort with less loss of risk-sharing benefits.

faith as that the incentives for good conduct changed as the value of property changed.

In this case the reactivity of risk is not so much due to the effects of granting coverage as to the effects of changes (decreases) in the value of property when insured value remains constant. In order to fix risks in these situations insurers must renegotiate insurance contracts frequently to keep insured value equal to actual value.

Variations in Reactive Risk: Fire Insurance, Marine Insurance, and Surety Bonding

To flesh out this description of insurers' strategies I have studied fire insurance, marine insurance, and fidelity and surety bonding in order to learn what insurers in each of these fields do to control reactive risk and avert market failures. In this section I will discuss, first, why we should study insurance in order to learn how reactive risk limits rational decision making and how such limits are overcome and, second, why these three lines of insurance are strategic ones to examine.

Although in the first section of this chapter I asserted that this book is about limits on rational action and how institutions help overcome the problems of opportunism and reactive risk and so make markets possible, in fact this book is not primarily about how people plan to achieve their goals, or how they cope with the fact that their abilities to scheme are limited by the unpredictability of other actors, by ignorance, and so forth. Instead it is about how *insurers*, actors who are paid to assume some of the risks of their policyholders, think about risk and design insurance agreements so that they come out ahead. This means that this book provides little information about how a risk-management strategy is coordinated with an attempt to achieve other goals. What it mainly discusses is how people and organizations who make their livings making judgments about risks think about risk.

Though this study has the limits outlined above, it has the virtue of being based on the distillation of many experiences with risk. While we might assume that small business owners succeed because they have the right ideas at the right times rather than because they are good risk managers, we are less likely to believe that the success of insurance companies is accidental (especially when we also know something about their failures when they miscalculate). If we study risk-management techniques by studying the behavior of insurers, then, we are more certain that we have isolated a body of successful risk-management techniques than we would be if we tried to study some other sample of risk-management techniques.

A second advantage to studying insurance is that the insurers have predigested the evidence for us. Their rate tables, major classifications, exclusions from lists of covered perils, contract conditions, and so forth, tell us what matters—which risks are hard to predict or control, which are subject to the control of the policyholder, and how insurers believe they can keep losses under control.

Finally, and most importantly, insurers do distinguish between reactive and fixed risks. Reactive risks are important in insurance at two levels. First, certain reactive risks are included as perils (causes of loss) covered by the insurance policy. In some lines of insurance very few reactive risks are included among the covered perils, while in others very few fixed risks are included in the list. For example, fidelity bonding is concerned almost entirely with reactive risk, the risk of an employee stealing from an employer. At the other extreme is fire insurance, in which few of the covered perils involve human action. We would not expect fire insurers to be too much concerned with reactive risk. In between is marine insurance, in which pilferage and barratrous acts (such as the captain and crew taking over the ship for their own purposes) are among the covered perils.

But reactive risk is important at a second level as well. Insurers recognize that though policyholders may not be able to prevent losses due to physical perils, they can often reduce losses, and they can deliberately cause them. People can keep their ships in good shape so that they can weather storms; they can also cast them away when the insurance is greater than the market value of the ship. These sorts of risks, referred to in insurance literature as "morale hazard" and "moral hazard," are analogous to fidelity risks faced by an employer (as opposed to fidelity risks faced by the insurer on the employer's behalf). That is, *when we look at the problems of moral and morale hazard, we are no longer really seeing insurers as managers of other people's risks, but instead as actors managing their own risks.* A comparison between techniques for managing fidelity risks of others and for managing moral hazards can tell us something about how risk changes as one's relation to it changes and as one's control over the behavior of others increases or decreases.

By studying the behavior of the insurer as a risk-management specialist, then, this book tries to answer the following questions: (1) how do insurers adjust their techniques (rate-setting methods, underwriting methods, contract conditions) when they are covering reactive risks rather than fixed ones, and (2) how do the techniques for managing the reactive risks that policyholders face differ from those for managing reactive risks experienced firsthand (that is, those due to the policyholder's behavior)?

One can begin to answer such questions by outlining the ways in which losses occur in any line of insurance, tracing back to find the points at which crucial events were under the control of other actors. That is, one must begin by determining the extent to which the uncertainty is due to the fact that other actors control crucial events (where the risks are reactive ones) or due to fluctuations in nature (where the risks are primarily fixed). This is not as easy as one might think, though, since we are often blind to the fact that people can affect the likelihood of accidents. For example, we do not usually think of people as having much control over whether or not they have fires, but people do, after all, have some control over how they store gasoline, whether they install sprinkler systems, and whether or not they smoke. Human control is considerably easier to detect in marine insurance and in fidelity and surety bonding. We have no trouble seeing that losses are likely to be lower if the captain is competent, if the crew is well trained, and if the ship is kept in good repair. And we have little trouble seeing that losses due to employee theft are contingent on the actions of certain key employees.

Having laid out the chain of events that might lead to a particular kind of loss, one must then begin to ask about the relations of crucial actors to the loss-causing event. In insurance, the important question is how directly the policyholder controls the loss-causing event. If the policyholder directly controls the loss-causing event, then he or she usually cannot get insurance coverage for it. The answer to this question, then, determines whether or not a particular peril will be covered by insurance. Fire insurance does not cover arson when the arsonist is the owner of the property being burned; marine insurance does not cover losses due to the negligence of the shipowner; fidelity companies do not compensate losses due to thefts arranged by the beneficiary of the policy. As control becomes more indirect or less complete, losses are more likely to be compensated. In marine insurance, for example, it is easier to get coverage for losses due to negligence (except of the owner) than due to intentional actions. Coverage of losses due to intentional acts is more likely the greater the distance between the policyholder and the potential loss-causer. What this says is that insurers are more willing to provide insurance coverage when the reactive risks resemble fixed ones because the distance between the policyholder and the potential loss-causer is sufficiently large that the policyholder really cannot do anything to decrease (or increase) the odds of loss.

After one has determined which reactive risks are covered by insurance and which are not, one can next study the rating scheme to see which situational factors increase or decrease the odds of loss. The rating scheme used in a line of insurance is helpful because it provides clues about which variations in the characteristics of policyholders are sufficiently strongly correlated with variations in loss experience to warrant insurer attention. Some of these characteristics will be related to the behavior of the policyholders and their employees, others will not. For example, marine insurance rates vary with a vessel's trade, which is probably not much related to behavior, but also with the loss record of that shipping company, which probably depends quite heavily on behavior. In fidelity bonding, rates vary with the type of business (churches have lower rates than drugstores), with supervisory structure, with the number of employees, and so on, and most of these variables are related to behavior.

Insurance rates and coverage vary with the reactive risks faced by the policyholders and with their ability to control these risks. But policyholders may or may not choose to control the reactive risks with which they are confronted. This is a reactive risk that the *insurer* must manage. At this stage insurers use three different kinds of techniques. First, they gather as much information as possible about potential policyholders so that they can decide which ones are good bets and which are not. This is the job of the underwriter. Secondly, insurers provide contractual incentives for good behavior. That is, they try to alter the payoff structure for the policyholders so that they will be motivated to exercise whatever control is possible. For example, insurance companies can do this by making rates contingent on loss experience through experience rating, or they can insist that the insurance agreement include a large deductible when the policy-holder has a particularly bad record. Such arrangements have two functions: first, they permit the insurance company to avoid lots of small losses when it thinks these are very likely, but secondly, they also alter the incentive structure for the policyholders by forcing them to share all losses that they fail to prevent. And when it is too difficult to manipulate the incentives of policyholders, insurers will support institutions (e.g., fire departments) in which control of important loss-reducing activities is in the hands of other actors.

After analyzing how insurers deal with reactive and fixed risks, one must still make the connection back to the rest of life. This book is not primarily about insurers as organizations, so one cannot extend the analysis to other empirical settings simply by arguing that since insurers are typical organizations facing typical problems, we should be able to make a simple mapping to these other settings. Similarly, since insurers cover only selected kinds of risks, we cannot argue that the risks they cover are representative of all risks. Instead we have to take the contrasts between reactive and fixed risks discussed in the book and ask where else these contrasts can be found. That is, we can claim to say something about how people (or organizations) will adjust their behavior when confronted with reactive rather than fixed risks or when they have varying degrees of control over the outcomes. In an afterword, I analyze the role of reactive risk in sexual relationships, asking for instance how a woman can protect her reputation, and in tort law, asking what incentives there are for manufacturers, sellers, and service-providers to avoid making mistakes.

In order to answer the above questions, I have drawn on an assortment of documents about insurance, including rate books, texts for insurance students, newspaper articles, pamphlets urging courts to require that corporate sureties (i.e., insurance companies) be used to back fiduciaries, and diatribes by mutual company spokesmen against stock companies. These documents have a varying relation to actual insurance practice, so in some cases I am really discussing what insurers believe they should do, in other cases what they do or say they do (e.g., it is never clear how faithfully they follow rate manuals), and in still other cases what they claim to have done or what others charge them with having done. Though what emerges is perhaps a view of the mountains through the mist rather than on a clear day, one can still get a sense of the main shape of the range.

This is partly because the differences in techniques for managing reactive and fixed risks show up time and time again in the accounts (by whatever party) of any single line of insurance, but also partly because the accounts in one line of insurance tend to be supported by the evidence from other lines.

In order to get sufficient variation in setting, and sufficient redundancy in the problems as well, I have examined insurance practices in three different areas. The core of the book is contained in chapters 3, 4, and 5, which discuss fire insurance, marine insurance, and fidelity and surety bonding respectively. In each of these three chapters I ask, first, what role reactive risk plays and, second, what the insurers have done to manage reactive risk and whether they have been successful.

Fire insurance is a useful example because it covers relatively few perils in which the causes of loss are human actions. This means that fire insurers faced the question of reactive risk only after discovering that risks were not fixed after all. In addition, fire insurance is purchased not just by commercial customers but by private individuals. This means that many of the techniques typically used to control reactive risks cannot be used because they are too expensive when compared with the premium paid by the policyholder. Fires are also relatively rare, so it is not possible to peg rates to loss experience and then offer an incentive for loss-prevention efforts. Finally, fire insurance is interesting because moral hazard is an important problem—the values of homes and business property fluctuate, providing incentives to destroy property.

Many more of the perils covered by marine insurance involve human control over losses than do those covered by fire insurance. There is also considerable variation in the policyholder's control over these reactive risks. Since ships and cargos are physically separated from their owners for long periods of time, the owners (the policyholders) have only indirect control over their property. This means that even though the loss-causing events are partly under human control, they are likely not to be under the direct control of the policyholder. Marine insurance therefore provides a good case for studying the way in which reactive risk changes with physical and social distance or with other factors that decrease control. Moral hazard and morale hazard are also very important because shipping markets change and because ships must be maintained if accident rates are not to increase substantially.

Finally, fidelity and surety bonding are useful cases to study because they are almost pure cases of reactive risk. Fidelity bonds cover mainly honesty, while surety bonds cover contract performance. Insurance contract arrangements are a bit different in fidelity and surety bonding than in other lines of insurance. Traditionally, the person whose behavior was covered by the contract was the one who bought the insurance, but the beneficiary was another person who would suffer if the policyholder did not meet his or her obligations. Fidelity contracts have evolved in recent periods so that they are more like standard insurance contracts. This means that fidelity bonds are now really dishonesty insurance, and the reactive risks covered in this line of insurance are treated more as if they were fixed risks because the person who purchases the insurance does not directly control the loss-causing events.

In addition to these three core chapters about the lines of insurance, I have included a chapter (chapter 2) discussing the relations between reactive risk, moral hazard, and morale hazard; a concluding chapter (chapter 6) outlining the principles that govern the management of reactive risk; and an afterword applying these principles to the management of reactive risk in sexual relationships and products liability.

Insurers' Models of
Individuals and Organizations:
A Methodological Note

Throughout this book I will discuss the relation between policyholders and insurers as if each were an individual.[11] Rather clearly neither is an individual in many, perhaps most, of the cases that I will discuss. Part of the reason for perpetuating this fiction is that I am analyzing the risk-management techniques of insurers, and the insurers and insurance specialists usually write as if both the policyholders and the insurers were individuals. In this section I will discuss the question of whether serious biases are introduced by making the assumption that, if the insurer and the policyholder are

.

11. Though it is quite common to treat organizations as if they function like human individuals, not everyone agrees that this is useful. For recent critiques of this simplifying assumption, see March and Shapira (1982), Bendor (1985), and Hogarth (1982).

not actually individuals, they nevertheless can be expected to behave as rational, calculating, economically motivated individuals would.

Let me begin by noting that insurers do sometimes recognize that their policyholders are not individuals but are instead organizations. They do not carry this recognition through consistently, but they do sometimes talk about the distinction between the policyholders and their agents, thus recognizing that the problem is often not just one of motivating an individual but instead a chain of individuals. This problem is discussed most explicitly in marine insurance, where insurers argue about whether or not a shipowner should be allowed to recover for pilferage as well as for theft; whether a shipowner should be allowed to recover for losses due to mutinous acts of the captain and crew; and whether or not cargo owners should be allowed to recover for pilferage, since this will decrease their motivation to pack goods properly and also to select carriers carefully. But though the insurers recognize that they must motivate not just the policyholder but also the agents of the policyholder, they never discuss the question of whether or how it is possible to motivate a policyholder who is not an individual but a corporation.

As the insurer sees it, then, the problem is to motivate the policyholders (assumed to be individuals or some entities that calculate as individuals do) to exercise whatever control is possible over their agents. But insurers recognize that if one is to exert control over agents this is usually not so much a matter of providing incentives for individual action as it is a matter of developing organizational routines and standard operating procedures. For example, though the surety and fidelity bonding companies are certainly interested in providing incentives to discourage stealing, they are also interested in encouraging their policyholders to establish *routines* that will make theft difficult. The fidelity and surety companies are especially concerned to institute systems of checks so that several people have to be consulted when money is spent, audits so that the financial records of the company are checked periodically by an outsider, screening procedures for checking on the honesty of new employees, and so on. The insurers recognize that though part of the problem is to introduce incentives for people to behave properly, another part is to establish organizational routines that make it harder to deviate and easier to detect deviations.

Fire and marine insurers also are aware that their policyholders might be heads of organizations rather than isolated individuals. In fire insurance, for example, the insurers are well aware that they must establish routines for checking on the performance of fire-extinguishing devices. Insurers and policyholders will agree on schedules of checks, and the employees of the policyholder are also supposed to fill out forms indicating that they have checked a certain fire-extinguishing device. Valves are wired open so that the employees of the policyholder cannot inadvertently close off crucial supplies of water. Locks are placed on other valves so that someone has to fill out forms in order to turn them on or off. Fire drills are held; company fire fighters are trained. In addition, because the insurers recognize that workers will not always be inclined to be careful with fire or cannot be careful because they must work too quickly, flammable products are separated from work processes involving sparks.

In marine insurance, routines are institutionalized in various ways. Insurers specify that they must be consulted before certain actions (such as abandoning a ship) are taken. They make recovery for losses contingent on "suing and laboring" and therefore provide an incentive for the policyholder to develop routine procedures in this area. Insurers also insist that the vessel not deviate from its specified course. Finally, the training and the rigid hierarchy of the captain and crew make it more likely that routines can be institutionalized.

Organizational routines are important because they translate the good intentions of policyholders into requirements for the policyholders' agents. Offering incentives for policyholders to keep losses down does not necessarily mean that they will manage to transmit these intentions to their agents. One of the reasons that the agents of the policyholder will not always act in the interest of the insurer is that they will not always know what the insurer's interest is, will not perceive that this is a relevant interest to attend to, or will believe that the insurer's interest can surely be sacrificed to more pressing concerns. Good workers will believe that fire drills or the maintenance work on fire-extinguishing equipment can be put off when the company is behind on production. Audits can be put off until a more convenient time. Repairs to a ship can be postponed, and when the ship is behind schedule the captain may decide to sail in stormy weather. (See Perrow 1984 on the role of production pressure in marine accidents.) The establishment of appropriate organizational routines will help to focus the attention of the agents of the policyholder on the insurer's interests or perhaps persuade them to act in the insurer's interest whether they are aware of doing so or not.

Though insurers recognize that their policyholders are *attached* to organizations, they continue to assume that the policyholders *themselves* are individuals rather than organizations. We must therefore ask what difference it makes that the insurer will not be dealing with an individual who owns a ship or business but instead with the insurance specialist representing the corporation that owns the ship or business. This obviously will make some difference since that individual will not actually be comparing the costs of insurance with other costs or choosing whether to use different processes or procedures that might reduce the likelihood of loss and therefore cut the costs of insurance. Within the scope of their authority insurance specialists might be affected by the incentives introduced by the insurer, though. Though they will not lose the money and will not have to pay the premiums, how much is paid for insurance will influence to some degree the possibility of promotions and salary advances. But insurance specialists will not be able to make all of the relevant decisions alone. They will have to bargain with other executives about the feasibility of introducing a new procedure or the possibility of reorganizing the manufacturing plant to segregate sparks from flammable products or about pressuring the captain of the ship to keep a closer eye on crew members suspected of pilfering the cargo. Since these people's outcomes will *not* depend on cutting insurance costs or improving safety records they will very likely not pay too much attention to the insurance specialist.

How much attention is paid to insurance and to safety considerations probably depends on how large a portion of the budget is spent on insurance. Just as the insurance company does not think it makes sense to reward individual policyholders for installing smoke alarms in their homes, so the commercial policyholder will often not think that it makes sense to spend a lot of time and effort cutting insurance premiums (already a small proportion of the budget) by a small amount. The Factory Mutuals (a group of mutual fire insurance companies, discussed in chapter 3, formed specifically to offer reduced premiums to those interested in loss prevention) were worried about overcoming this sort of obstacle, and it is for this reason that a business cannot purchase insurance from the Factory Mutuals without some indication that the policyholder places a high priority on safety and will do whatever possible to keep losses down. That is, the Factory Mutual insurers recognize that their incentives will only work if the policyholder in effect agrees to behave like a rational *individual* (and one concerned about insurance expenses) rather than like a bureaucracy. In other words, the Factory Mutuals insist on establishing a set of routines in which insurance and safety matters are given some attention. They insist on an organizational design in which their incentive system will work.

In summary, whether the insurer's risk-management strategies are effective when the policyholder is an organization or an individual heading an organization depends on several variables. When the policyholder is an individual heading an organization, insurers' risk-management strategies will be more effective if they are translated into organizational routines and standard operating procedures. When the policyholder is a corporation, insurers' risk-management strategies will be more effective when an individual whose fate depends partly on successful risk management links the insurer to the policyholder organization. Finally, the success of insurers' risk-management strategies will depend heavily on how important insurance is to the overall outcome of the organization. In cases in which insurance premiums are a large part of the budget or in which losses occur frequently and are very costly, more attention will be paid to insurance and to loss prevention, and the insurers' systems of incentives will be more likely to be effective. The closer the policyholder comes to meeting these conditions, the more effective the insurer's policies will be.

2

Insurers' Analyses of Moral Hazard

Moral Hazard and Reactive Risk

The problem of incentives shifting once insurance is purchased is usually discussed in both insurance and economics as the problem of moral hazard (Denenberg et al. 1964; Arrow 1971; and Pauly 1974). In order to show more clearly the connection between moral hazard and decision-making problems, I am going to discuss exactly where moral hazard enters the chain of causation leading to insurance losses. Insurers usually think of moral hazard as an independent factor affecting insurance losses at a single point in the causal chain; this assumption leads them to emphasize careful underwriting as a solution. I will argue that moral hazard is the result of an interaction between character and economic incentives, and that insurers must always combine *underwriting* to eliminate the worst characters with *incentive structures* to motivate loss prevention and deter insurance crime. Neither tactic will work alone.

Generally speaking, insurance covers losses from a particular peril or set of perils. A *peril*, such as fire, lightning, wind, a liability judgment, or theft, is simply a source of loss. In theory, the insurer can calculate, largely from past experience, the likelihood that a policyholder in a particular category will experience a loss from a given peril. If this were all that were involved, prices could be set according to expected losses, and insurance could be bought and sold in a market with no further adjustments.

Unfortunately, certain conditions, some of which the policyholder controls, modify the probability of loss. In insurance terminology, these are *hazards*, conditions that increase the probability of loss. Defective wiring and poor housekeeping are both hazards that increase the likelihood of loss from fire; living on the first floor in a bad neighborhood and carelessness in locking one's door are hazards that increase the probability of loss from theft; a surgical practice, strict liability laws, and careless surgery are hazards increasing the likelihood of loss from an unfavorable judgment in a medical malpractice case.

Insurance writers often divide hazards into two categories—physical and moral—and sometimes into three—physical, legal, and moral. Physical hazards arise "from the natural condition of property or from impersonal surroundings" (Denenberg et al. 1964:8). Among the examples cited above, defective wiring, surgical practice, and a first-floor residence in a bad neighborhood are all examples of physical hazards, though they clearly have social elements. Physical hazards also include individual characteristics, such as blindness or advanced age, when these are relevant.

Legal hazards, usually treated as a subset of physical hazards, are laws, contracts, and legal interpretations that modify the likelihood of loss from a covered peril (Page 1970:60). In a malpractice case, for example, the doctor does not suffer the loss, but he or she can be made to share it through legal liability. Stricter liability laws are a legal hazard affecting the probability of loss from an unfavorable decision in a malpractice case. Laws and legal interpretations that redistribute the losses make it more likely that losses not directly experienced by policyholders will later be passed on to them.

Moral hazards are "those conditions that increase the frequency or severity of loss because of the attitude and character of an insured person" (Denenberg et al. 1964:8). Many authors use the term *moral hazard* to describe a tendency toward fraud or, sometimes more mildly, "a departure from the standards of conduct acceptable to society" (Page 1970:64) and use the term *morale hazard* in discussions of increased carelessness or accident-proneness that may result from insurance coverage. Poor housekeeping, carelessness in surgery, and absentmindedness about locking doors are all examples of morale hazard. Lying or shading the truth when applying for insurance is an example of moral hazard. Though the distinction is fuzzy, moral hazard is generally taken to be a character trait existing prior to insurance coverage, while morale hazard is a change in incentives that occurs after coverage. Insurers regard morale hazard as a subtype of moral hazard; economists have devoted their attention exclusively to morale hazard but have called it moral hazard.[1]

Insurers' views of the roles of hazards in modifying the likelihood of insurance losses are summarized in Figure 1. Although the occurrence of a covered peril such as a fire is assumed to be largely unpredictable, some conditions are known to affect the likelihood of such an event. Among these, legal and physical hazards are factors one can calculate about, while moral hazards are not. In this view, legal and physical hazards have a fixed quality that is absent in moral ones. Legal and physical hazards are fixed risks; moral hazards are reactive risks. Doctors do not change from medical practices with low rates of malpractice suits simply because they now have insurance coverage; citizens cannot change the legal climate of the communities in which they live simply because they now have liability insurance coverage; and shipowners do not shift from safe coastal routes to more dangerous ocean routes because they have insurance. Because physical and legal hazards are determined by other factors, such as the nature of a shipowner's trade, they will not be as likely to react to coverage. This means that insurers can safely classify potential policyholders according to the legal and physical hazards they face, and they can expect that these calculations of expected losses will continue to be accurate.

Insurers have long recognized that moral hazard contains an element of choice, that it is reactive. It is for this reason, as I will argue later, that they believed they could not calculate about moral hazard but instead could only eliminate the problem by refusing to give coverage to applicants judged to be moral hazards. If the insurers believed that applicants were likely to be careless about loss prevention, to lie about losses so that they would be covered, and so on, then the insurers would refuse to give them coverage. Once the problem of moral hazard was eliminated, it would be possible to calculate insurance losses since moral hazard was the only reactive risk, the others being fixed.

But this strategy does not work, and insurers have modified their behavior if not their rhetoric. There are two reasons why such a strat-

---

1. In fact, economists are also concerned with the question of how one gets information about character (or ability), but this issue is discussed in the literature on employers learning a worker's "type." See, for example, Spence (1973), Weiss (1981), Harris and Holmström (1982), and Hart (1982).

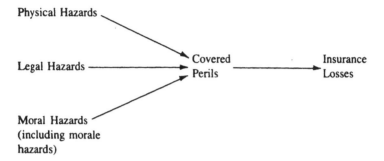

Physical Hazards

Legal Hazards ——————→ Covered ——————————→ Insurance
                        Perils   Losses

Moral Hazards
(including morale
hazards)

Figure 1. *Insurers' view of the role of moral hazard in the causation of insurance losses.*

egy is doomed to failure, having to do, first, with the role of moral hazard in the causation of insurance losses and, second, with the nature of moral hazard itself. In the next section I will take up the first question, arguing that moral hazard affects all of the other steps in the causal sequence rather than affecting only the occurrence of a covered peril. After that I will consider the question of whether moral hazard is a matter of economic rationality or bad character, and therefore whether it is possible to eliminate moral hazard through underwriting alone.

Moral Hazard and the Causation of Insurance Losses

Perhaps it is a mistake to classify moral hazard as a hazard at all since it does not fit neatly into the sequence of condition (hazard) increasing the likelihood of a particular loss-causing event (peril). Sometimes moral hazard leads to the creation of another hazard that increases the likelihood of loss. Knowing that a loss would be covered by the insurance, a shipowner may advise the captain to take a shorter but more dangerous route. Sometimes moral hazard leads directly to the event causing the loss. If a cargo has been damaged in a way that might not be covered by the insurer, the owner might arrange to have it destroyed in an "accident" in order to collect the insurance. And sometimes moral hazard has nothing to do with conditions affecting the probability of loss or even with the loss-causing event, but instead directly affects the losses sustained by the insurance company. A shipowner might inflate expenses incurred in trying to rescue a vessel in distress and request reimbursement for the inflated sum. Ross (1970) asserts that in auto insurance it is quite common to collect even when one's losses are clearly not covered. That is, moral hazard can increase insurance losses by increasing physical or legal hazards or more directly through fraudulent staging of accidents or inflation of insurance claims. Figure 2 summarizes my view of how moral hazard affects insurance losses.

At each of these stages we can see how the policyholder and the insurer react to each other's actions. If a marine insurer sets rates for a particular trade route, but then captains deviate from that route and experience higher losses, the rates for the route will be raised. If only certain kinds of losses are covered, policyholders may try to reclassify their losses by staging "accidents." When these deliberate losses are grouped together with accidental losses, the rates for insurance coverage of a particular class of losses will rise. This process of insurer action, policyholder reaction, insurer reaction, ad infinitum, occurs at each step in the causal sequence, leading not only to an inflation of rates but also to a distortion of the relation between classification schemes and the losses actually attributed to any single category.

Further, in each of these cases moral hazard contains an element of choice. Policyholders react to the fact that they have insurance coverage and adjust their behavior accordingly. While moral hazard does not affect the overall probability of lightning storms in a given location or the legal climate of a particular community, it can affect physical and legal hazards involving an element of choice. The likelihood of installing lightning rods or the likelihood of entering into a given contract may be affected by whether or not the person has insurance that would cover the losses. Since the policyholder has some control over many of the legal and physical hazards that could increase the odds of loss, this means that the insurer cannot calculate exactly what the odds of loss are. The odds of loss are not fixed but change as policyholders adjust their behavior to take into account the fact that many of the losses they might sustain will be repaid by the insurer.

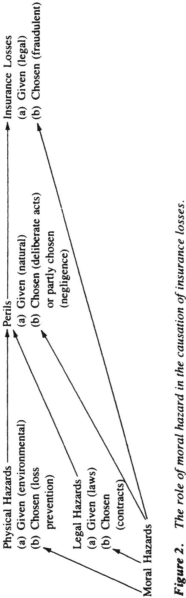

Figure 2. The role of moral hazard in the causation of insurance losses.

Put another way, the probability of a ship being lost in a storm is higher in the North Sea than in the Gulf of Mexico, but it is also higher if the ship is poorly maintained, incompetently sailed, or docked in a harbor not equipped to service ships of its size. There are many variables determining the probabilities of loss, and some of the causes of variation are physical, some legal, some moral. In addition, there are covariance effects, so that general carelessness and the presence of improperly stored combustibles are correlated, and physical and moral causes are confounded. If we think of the causation of loss in this way, we see clearly that moral causes cannot easily be untangled from physical ones. We also avoid the error of classifying losses as *either* due to moral factors *or* to fixed physical or legal ones. A fire can rarely be classified as due *either* to carelessness *or* to combustibles; the loss of a ship can rarely be attributed *either* to a storm *or* to poor maintenance.

The point of this book is to show that it is the reactivity of risk that makes the use of conventional decision procedures impossible. In this section we have seen that there is a reactive component to all insurance risks, and this reactive component is what insurers and economists call moral hazard. (Later I will argue that there are other reactive components as well, since actors other than the policyholder can increase or decrease the likelihood of loss.) What makes the problem especially intractable is that moral hazard can have an effect at any point in the chain of causation.

In classifying moral hazard as a hazard, insurers seem to be assuming that this reactive component works only by increasing the likelihood of an accident. Their assumption that moral hazard can be eliminated by underwriting also seems to be similarly based. If this were the case, then once applicants believed to be moral hazards were eliminated, the insurer could calculate the odds of loss because the rest of the conditions should be either fixed (and could be handled with rating schemes) or entirely accidental.[2] But in fact the policyholder's actions often directly or indirectly change the odds or size of loss. This means, for example, that insurers cannot simply eliminate

---

2. When possible losses are especially large, or when the risk is of a new sort, insurers cannot calculate the odds of loss even if the odds are fixed. See Heimer (1980) for a discussion of this problem in the insurance of the oil-drilling rigs and production platforms in the Norwegian North Sea.

applicants believed to have some tendency toward fraud but must also watch out for those policyholders who become lax about inspecting their sprinkler systems.

Moral Hazard: Bad Character or Economic Rationality?

Insurers need a correct analysis of moral hazard in order to figure out how best to combat it. There seem to be two theories of moral hazard, one of them quite explicit, the other more implicit. In the first, moral hazard is coterminous with bad character; in the second, moral hazard is more like economic rationality.

The insurance literature most often discusses moral hazard as if it were a question of character. If moral hazard is due to bad character, then the solution is better underwriting. Through careful investigation of the habits of potential policyholders, underwriters should be able to exclude hopeless cases and to assign higher rates to doubtful ones. As might be expected, there is some uncertainty in the technology of underwriting. Moral hazard investigations look into some aspects of the person's history that are clearly relevant (such as previous loss experience) and many others that are not so clearly relevant (such as relations with the spouse, whether the home is in a bad or good neighborhood, how recently the potential policyholder immigrated, church attendance, reputation of the wife as a loose woman, and so on).

Though bad character may indeed be one part of the problem of moral hazard, surely another part of it is economic rationality. According to this position, a more fruitful way to think about moral hazard is in terms of the separation of policyholders' incentives to prevent loss from their control over loss prevention. With the purchase of the insurance policy, the economic consequences of a loss pass from the insured to the insurer. This means that the policyholder is no longer so motivated to prevent the occurrence of a loss and, in fact, that it is often economically rational for the policyholder not to invest the additional resources in loss prevention. Sometimes it is even economically rational for the insured to cause a loss—if the policyholder can get away with it. But while the *incentive* to reduce loss passes to the insurance company, much *control* over loss prevention remains in the hands of the policyholder. In this case, the solution is to provide incentives for honesty and loss prevention. There are many ways that the insurance company can affect the incentive structure of the policyholder, and though these are rarely classified as solutions to the problem of moral hazard, they are often used (Doherty [1976] does discuss some of them). Such solutions include large deductibles, coinsurance, experience rating, pricing based on loss-prevention activities, and even making renewal of the policy contingent on loss-prevention activities.

What makes the problem especially complex is that bad character and economic rationality do not operate independently to cause insurance losses. People of bad character probably respond differently to economic incentives than do more moral people. If parents did not kill their infants to collect insurance money, but gangs sometimes did take out policies on acquaintances and then arrange for their deaths after an appropriate time lapse, this was presumably not just because the insurance agreement was arranged properly in one case and not in the other. Instead, character traits probably make people respond differently to economic incentives. The worst characters may deliberately buy insurance to reap the rewards for losses deliberately caused. Intermediately bad characters may buy insurance in good faith, but when external factors alter the incentive structure (e.g., when there is a general recession or the particular business seems likely to fail), they may be persuaded to follow a different course of action. Intermediately good characters may simply become more careless about loss prevention once they are insured. And the best characters may not be economically rational or may calculate differently because they have different ideas about what costs and benefits are.

It is also important to remember that incentive systems designed for one situation will have to be redesigned when the situation changes. Not all relevant incentives can be controlled by insurers, so insurance agreements must be restructured to maintain the balance when external conditions change. Claims rise in the shipping industry when freight prices are down; more big cars are destroyed or stolen when gasoline prices rise; property losses were higher than usual during the Depression; arson rates skyrocketed in the 1970s and seemed to be highly correlated at the individual level with canceled contracts, declines in sales, and other signs of impending business failure (McKinley 1979). This problem of incentive changes in outdated bargains is discussed in more detail in chapter 6.

Techniques for
Reducing Moral Hazard

Let me now turn to the question of how insurers have actually handled the problem of moral hazard. Since moral hazard is some combination of bad character and economic rationality, some combination of two corresponding general strategies is appropriate in combatting it—underwriting, which involves excluding the really bad risks and forming rate classes and setting prices for the others according to expected loss experience; and offering incentives to encourage honesty and to induce policyholders to engage in loss-prevention activities. These two general strategies have usually been embodied in the following four techniques (which have not always been employed with the specific intention of reducing moral hazard): (1) casual or on-the-spot underwriting; (2) more formal data-based rating and underwriting; (3) pricing of the insurance policy; and (4) contract writing, including the refinement and application of important legal principles. I will discuss each of these techniques in turn, but I will be most concerned with contractual mechanisms.

Casual underwriting

By casual or on-the-spot underwriting I mean the rejection of "shady" characters as potential policyholders. This is "casual" underwriting because, as far as I can tell, no statistical data are presented to support the recommendations about either the acceptance or rejection of specific applicants or what *sorts* of people should be accepted or rejected. Usually it is the agents or brokers who decide if someone is a shady character, but underwriting departments often formulate underwriting programs to aid them in this process.[3] An underwriting program includes one list of risks that should never be accepted and another list of risks that cannot be bound (that is, the

---

3. See Sullivan (1950), Upshaw (1933), and Vlachos (1929) for examples of how agents, brokers, and underwriters detect moral hazard.

insurance coverage cannot begin) without prior approval by the insurance company. Any risks that do not appear on the lists can be written freely. One sample list (Page 1970:72) includes "itinerant or transient workers" and "persons with indefinite addresses" as risks that should not be bound without prior approval.

Casual underwriting is a three-step process: the underwriting department formulates a program and distributes this to its agents and brokers; the agents and brokers screen applicants using this program and their own intuitions about shady characters; the underwriters screen applicants who are neither clearly bad nor clearly acceptable risks.

In the third stage of casual underwriting, a moral hazard report is sometimes prepared by an outside firm specializing in this service. One example of what might be included in a moral hazard report on an applicant for auto insurance is given by Page (1970:67).[4] In addition to confirming the accuracy of information given on the application form, the report would include discussions of the following topics:

1. Vehicles—condition of vehicles such as glass, tires, paint, alterations to engine or body, garaging of the vehicle

2. Insured—number of children and ages; net worth and annual income, name of employer, business reputation, job stability, and credit reputation

3. All drivers—personal or driving reputation questionable; any physical or mental impairments; and any questionable drinking habits

4. Environment—criticism of the neighborhood or premises; crime rate of the neighborhood; type of residence in which insured lives.

But as the author emphasizes over and over again,

while collection and scrutiny of the foregoing information are extremely important in the proper underwriting of individual risks, the interpretive judgment which the underwriter applies to such information is by far the most important facet of the selection functions.

(Page 1970:68)

---

4. Burke (1933), Retail Credit Co. (n.d.), and *Eastern Underwriter* (1925) provide information on what is contained in moral hazard reports and how the reports are secured.

When we recall that much of the information that the underwriter is interpreting consists of the judgments of other people (like the producer [broker or agent] and the moral hazard investigator), it begins to seem as if there is little room left for hard evidence. However, this is the method for handling moral hazard advocated by the writers of most insurance texts. Such authors admonish agents, brokers, and underwriters to be constantly on the lookout for people likely to defraud the insurers and to deny coverage to these people. One is constantly reminded to use one's "intuitive judgment" in these matters.[5]

Casual underwriting involves a great deal of technical uncertainty. No one knows very well how to separate the wheat from the chaff. Insurance crime losses indicate that many bad characters are able to get insurance coverage, and there is reason to believe that many good risks are refused insurance coverage, as, for example, when whole communities are redlined and their residents denied fire insurance (Heimer 1982).

Formal rating and underwriting

The second technique, more formal data-based rating and underwriting, is rarely if ever explicitly mentioned as a method of controlling moral hazard. Though data-based rating and underwriting are still techniques concerned primarily with the problem of detecting bad character rather than with that of motivating good behavior, their purpose is to *classify* risks to be insured rather than to *exclude* uninsurable risks. When insurers group policyholders into categories, estimate the loss experience of each category, and assign varying premium rates to the categories, they do not explicitly consider how the variations among categories are affected by variations in moral hazard. But in those lines of insurance where moral hazard is strongly implicated in covered losses, we might expect that the classification scheme would end up reflecting variations in moral hazard even though this was not the express intention of ratemakers and underwriters. It is also possible, though, that when insurers believe that

5. Cialdini's (1984) work suggests that lay theories about who is reliable may not be very good. He provides evidence, for example, that we almost instinctively trust and obey anyone who seems to be an authority. But our methods for judging who is an authority are very crude—we are persuaded by costumes, titles, and other trappings of status.

moral hazard is especially important they will de-emphasize formal classification and rating schemes since they *believe* that people who are moral hazards should be excluded rather than charged steeper rates.

In fidelity and surety bonding the major perils insured against (dishonesty in one case, failure to perform in the other) are closely related to moral hazard. The loss-causing events are largely under human control; consequently reactivity and the detection and control of moral hazard should be important issues. Do surety and fidelity bonders use formal rating and underwriting techniques to classify groups of policyholders (implicitly by variations in moral hazard) and to sort applicants into these categories? The answer seems to depend on the insurers' ideological prejudices about whether the particular line is really insurance or not and on whether some factor besides character (though it may be related to character) can be used as the sorting criterion.

Insurance writers often claim that bonding is not really a form of insurance (though all of them end up discussing it in their texts despite this disclaimer) and that one of the reasons for this is that there is essentially no expectation of loss. This argument is made more forcefully about surety bonding than about fidelity bonding. Surety bonding is not a pooling of losses, the authors argue, but a pledging of credit, and the premium paid to the surety company is only a service fee (Longley-Cook 1970a: 35; Denenberg et al. 1964: 155; Porter 1966: 52).

But surety bonders do have underwriting procedures, and they do calculate rates. It is true that surety underwriting procedures (described in Porter 1966: 53–54) do *seem* to be more concerned with excluding than with categorizing. Though some of the areas for investigation sound as if they would be useful in ratemaking, since the questions and possible responses are simple and specific (whether or not the applicant has the skill, experience, knowledge, and capital necessary for the task to be undertaken; terms under which the surety will have to guarantee the performance; nature and extent of the obligation), many of the others include the more usual vague questions about character. The purpose of underwriting (exclusion versus classification) and the formality of the procedures seem to vary from one type of surety bond to another. In construction contract bonds, for example, underwriting procedures are more formal and provide criteria for the classification of applicants, not just for their exclusion. In public official bonds, in contrast, underwriting procedures are less well developed and provide fewer rating categories. These differences are reflected in the rate manuals (in how detailed they are) and perhaps also in the frequency of revision of rates.[6]

This variation in the formality and purpose of underwriting in different kinds of surety bonds appears to be related to the importance of moral hazard as a determinant of nonperformance. When other factors, such as competence, adequacy of capital, or economic conditions, are also important determinants of nonperformance, underwriting procedures are more formal and more geared to classification of applicants. When moral hazard is the most important determinant of nonperformance (and when nonperformance may also be poorly defined), underwriting procedures are less developed and are oriented to decisions about whether to grant or refuse coverage.

The situation is somewhat different in fidelity bonding, which most authors agree is more like insurance. In this line, the insurers acknowledge in advance the possibility of loss; premiums are more than just service fees; and loss ratios are reviewed much more frequently, sometimes on an annual basis (Longley-Cook 1970a: 35; Denenberg et al. 1964: 155; Porter 1966: 15–28). In fidelity bonding, rating is based on the classification of employees according to supervision of their activities and the extent to which their jobs bring them into contact with money and merchandise. Further, insurers in this field use experience rating and have developed a copyrighted exposure index based on current assets and gross sales (Porter 1966: 25; Beardsley 1965: 826; Surety Association of America n.d., e) to help applicants determine how vulnerable they are to employee dishonesty and how much insurance they need. Note that the question asked by the insurer is no longer "Are this applicant's employees bad characters?" but, instead, "Are their jobs arranged so that it is easy (and therefore perhaps economically rational) for them to steal?" That is, when insurers actually get around to classifying something related to reactive risk, they are more concerned with classifying social situations rather than personalities, and they tend to treat moral hazard as a problem of economic rationality. This does not mean that insurers

6. Longley-Cook (1970a: 35) states that surety rates are revised only every twenty years on the average.

are providing incentives for good behavior; rather they are classifying work situations by the incentives for honesty or dishonesty embedded in them. Businesses that provide incentives for employee honesty pay lower fidelity rates than businesses that do not encourage employee honesty.

Pricing of insurance coverage

Though pricing techniques are often used to encourage loss prevention, insurers rarely discuss these in terms of moral hazard. The idea is quite straightforward: if some activity cuts the insurer's losses, some of this saving should be passed on to the insured in the form of lower premiums; therefore, lower premiums can be offered for engaging in activities known to reduce losses.

This strategy can be implemented in various ways: sometimes insurers collect a great deal of information about how to prevent losses, then agree to reclassify policyholders into new categories with lower rates if they will make the appropriate modifications; sometimes, when a factor makes a big difference in loss experience, the renewal of the insurance policy at the current rate is made contingent on the policyholder making appropriate changes; sometimes insurers charge policyholders a rate appropriate to their rate classification but agree to return part of the premium if policyholders avoid losses (by whatever means). This latter method, known as experience rating, has several variations, depending on whether the rate finally charged is based on the experience during the policy period or during a previous period.

Notice that this strategy of pricing insurance to encourage loss prevention assumes that the problem of moral hazard is primarily a problem of economic rationality. Most of the effort in such pricing schemes goes into figuring out in detail what variables affect losses. Since these factors are *variable*, the policyholder has to be encouraged to purchase safety equipment, maintain safety devices, keep hallways free of debris, keep flammable materials isolated, and so on. Price reductions offer such an incentive and so attempt to counteract the usual change in incentives that occurs when insurance is purchased and losses pass to the insurance company while control remains with the insured. But this policy of pricing to encourage loss prevention assumes that the underwriting department has already eliminated all the bad risks and so has taken care of the other half of moral hazard. The incentive systems will only function properly when the insurance contract is a contract in good faith. As insurers sometimes learn, though, even contracts that are formed in good faith may be broken when external factors alter the incentive structure. This is one of the reasons that thorough inspections covering seemingly irrelevant issues are often coupled with pricing schemes.

Contract provisions

The fourth and final technique for combatting moral hazard is in the writing of the insurance contract. Insurance contracts follow rules developed over the centuries in response to the worst abuses of insurance contracts; these rules are the work of insurance companies, courts, and legislatures. Most of the many substantive rules that make up the two to three important doctrines are derived originally from the principle of indemnity, which is the practice of insuring only against losses rather than providing a chance for gains *or* losses. Although most insurance authors open their discussions of the legal features of contracts by announcing that insurance is a contract of indemnity, this is actually only partly true. As Keeton notes (1971:92-94), there is only a *tendency* toward indemnity; other equally important principles conflict with the indemnity principle at certain points, and compromises must be made. The importance of the principle of indemnity and of the doctrines and rules derived from it thus varies considerably from one line of insurance to another. I would argue, though, that willingness to compromise on the indemnity principle is determined in part by the importance of moral hazard in any given line of insurance and the availability of natural social checks against it.

The purpose of an insurance contract is to transfer loss. This implies that the insurance payment is a reimbursement and that payment is limited to losses actually sustained by the policyholder. According to the indemnity principle insurance contracts are to be interpreted and enforced in a manner consistent with conferring a benefit that is no larger than the loss sustained (though it may be smaller). The indemnity principle has been implemented primarily through its embodiment in the doctrine of insurable interest, in the doctrine of subrogation, and in rules limiting or reducing recovery to the value of the interest insured.

The doctrine of insurable interest is concerned with the question of whether the policyholder has really lost anything when the event insured against occurs. One of the main reasons that this doctrine was developed was that people once took out life insurance policies on strangers and then had them killed in order to collect the benefits. Although one of the major statutes designed to stop this practice was passed in 1774, apparently the problem was not entirely solved at that point; Carr (1975) gives several examples of similar abuses in the 1920s. In life insurance an insurable interest now can be based either on a family relationship or on a monetary interest (a creditor can insure a debtor or a corporation can insure a key employee). And, though this violates the principle of indemnity, in life insurance insurable interest needs to exist only at the time the policy is taken out. This is probably because life insurance policies are not just insurance but also investments, and the requirement that they be canceled when insurable interest ends would mean considerable loss to policyholders.

In property and liability insurance the bases of insurable interest are somewhat broader. Insurable interest can be based on any of the following: (1) a property right; (2) a contract right; (3) legal liability; (4) representative insurable interest; or (5) factual expectation. A property right can be based on ownership, but it can also be based on use. For example, a tenant has an insurable interest in an apartment. A contract right is one in which the insured does not hold the title to the property but still has an economic interest in its preservation. A bank, for example, has an insurable interest in a house on which it holds a mortgage contract. A liability interest exists whenever the occurrence of the event insured against will impose a legal liability on the policyholder. Custodians, for example, may have an insurable interest in loss or damage to property under their care. A representative insurable interest exists when the law allows one person (such as a trustee) to insure the interest of another. There is considerable debate about whether a factual expectation (such as that of an only child in the property of his or her aged father who had drawn up a will passing all the property to that child) is sufficient basis for insurable interest. The majority view, apparently, is that factual expectation does not give rise to an insurable interest. Another important difference between life insurance and property/liability insurance is that in the latter, the insurable interest must exist at the time of loss in order for the contract to be valid and for the insured to collect.

The second major doctrine, that of subrogation, is concerned with the problem of keeping the insured from recovering from both the insurance company and from whoever caused the loss. Under the doctrine of subrogation the legal rights and claims of the insured pass to the insurer when the insurer pays the claim. If anyone is to recover from the actor who caused the loss, then, it is the insurance company. There is quite a bit of difference between the theory and the practice of subrogation, though. One might think that subrogation rights, which imply that the insurance company will attempt to recover from those causing losses, would provide a powerful incentive for loss prevention. In fact, subrogation rights are often implemented as treaties between insurance companies, stipulating automatic payment of claims of some sizes, negotiation of claims of other sizes, and disregard of trivial claims (Wilmot 1976).

Even when the person at fault is not covered by insurance, subrogation is still much more bark than bite. In fidelity bonding, for example, the doctrine of subrogation implies that the insurance company can recoup its losses by recovering from the dishonest employee. But since the suit against the dishonest employee would be a criminal suit rather than a civil one, different standards of proof would apply and the insurance company would be quite unlikely to be able to recover anything (Denenberg et al. 1964:159). So subrogation probably has very little effect in creating an incentive to avoid loss—the insurance company, despite its staff of lawyers, is just not going to bring a suit against the average private citizen unless the loss is huge and the evidence very good. But it still provides an incentive for policyholders to exercise some care on their own behalf since they do not get to recover from both the insurance company and those causing the losses. Many insurance contracts, for example those in marine insurance and in fidelity and surety bonding, also require that the policyholder help the insurance company recover from the loss-causer.

Most of the other rules derived from the indemnity principle have to do with two questions: (1) how is the loss to be evaluated? and (2) when more than one party is liable, how are losses to be divided among them? There is quite a bit of controversy surrounding the first question, which is generally referred to as the question of the measure of recovery. The rules about this are also different in marine insurance than in other fields. Generally, insurers have argued that they should have to pay actual cash value (either market value or replacement value less depreciation). This, they argue, should lessen the incentive to destroy property that is no longer worth so much. But, of course, even with these rules, owners who no longer have any use for the property in question may be inclined to destroy it.

For several good reasons, policyholders have not always approved of these measure-of-recovery rules. First, these rules enable insurers to urge policyholders to take out insurance policies with large face values when they will end up receiving quite small amounts in compensation. One antidote to this has been to require the insurers to pay the difference between the loss and the face value to someone else (say another person injured in the accident). A second objection to these rules is that often actual cash value is a poor measure of how much something is worth to the policyholder, either because market value does not adequately reflect some idiosyncracy of the object that makes it especially useful to the policyholder, or because market value rarely includes a measure of sentimental attachment. Because of these objections, the indemnity principle has lost quite a bit of ground to other principles (such as equity) on the question of measure of recovery.

The question of how losses are to be divided among liable parties is also complicated by the applicability of several principles. In general, when more than one party is liable, each pays on a pro rata basis according to the degree of its financial responsibility. If two insurance companies are liable, each pays the fraction of the loss that is proportional to the fraction of total face value made up by the face value of its policy. But sometimes the question is not how to divide responsibility between insurance companies but how to divide responsibility between the insurance company and the policyholder. Since most losses are small, policyholders are often tempted to take out insurance policies with fairly small face values. Since the odds of having a small accident are so much larger than the odds of having a big accident, this would seem to make sense. But the chances of total loss on such policies are not the same as the chances of total loss when total loss is equivalent to the actual value of the property (in fact, they are higher).

Insurance companies have tried to get around this problem by arguing that when the policyholder chooses to insure only a portion of the value of the property, then the insurance company is only liable for that proportion of the loss. The idea is that the policyholder has elected to self-insure the rest. Since the formulas for calculating all this get complicated, many insurers have argued for insurance to value. That is, they require that the policyholder buy a policy with a face value equal to a very substantial portion (usually at least 80 percent) of the value of whatever is being insured. This requirement is often waived for commercial policyholders, who then have a co-insurance agreement under which the insurance company pays a fixed proportion of the loss and the insured pays the rest (Denenberg et al. 1964:188–89).

A final question of how to divide losses has very little to do with the indemnity principle. This is the question of deductibles, waiting periods, and so on. There are two parts to the insurers' argument here. The first is that insurance is not intended to cover small losses that can be planned for and included in the household or business budget. The extra administrative expense of paying these small but somewhat unexpected losses simply makes insurance a costly way of handling them. Instead, the policyholder should act as a self-insurer for these small losses, and the insurance company should only be brought in to cover larger, more catastrophic ones. Besides this, insurers argue, it also makes sense to have the insured *share* in each loss since this provides some small incentive for him or her to try to prevent loss. It is really this question of incentive that makes deductibles and waiting periods important provisions of insurance contracts; otherwise insurance companies would be quite happy to take people's money for providing the service of planning their budgets.

Let us return now to the question of how these provisions of insurance contracts work to reduce moral hazard. The main virtue of these contractual provisions is that they combat both aspects (bad character and economic rationality) of moral hazard. Insurers recognize that there are some potential policyholders willing to defraud the insurance companies (and in some cases to do serious damage to other people in the process), and the point of these contractual provisions is to discourage these people from buying insurance by reducing the odds that they will be able to collect. These principles and rules attempt to eliminate the possibility of certain kinds of incentives at the point of contract. One of the ways that this is done is to play off one set of interests against another. While the doctrine of insurable interest is primarily an attempt to keep policyholders from recovering more than they have lost (by making sure that they have something to lose), one of the reasons that it works is that it stakes the policyholder's interest in the status quo against his or her interest in the cash to be recovered. By requiring that policyholders have *legitimate* interests in whatever is being insured, the insurance company makes the policyholder's interest in the insured object act as a check on his or her interest in the cash to be recovered in the case of loss. By making sure the policyholder cannot recover more than the value of the loss, the insurance company tries to make sure it is not better than an even trade and so not likely to be worthwhile when the costs of time and trouble are added in. And by making the policyholder bear a small part of each loss the insurance company at least adds a tax when it has somehow miscalculated and the incentives were not quite what it thought.

Only really bad characters (and good ones, of course) should be interested in an insurance contract with the safeguards and incentive systems described in this chapter. Such contracts are certainly not likely to be much use for speculative gain unless one goes to quite a bit of trouble. And, of course, the insurers hope that the really bad risks have already been eliminated by their agents, brokers, and underwriters, who are always watching out for those shady characters.

3

Reactive Risk in Fire Insurance

If we believed that most fires were more or less natural disasters, we would not expect to find much variation in fire losses; what variation we did discover would not seem to have much to do with human action. This would suggest that fire insurance, which covers almost purely accidental losses, would not be a strategic site for an investigation of techniques used to control reactive and fixed risks. Insofar as fire losses are not under human control, changes in incentives due to insurance coverage would have no effect on the risk of fire.

But while it is clearly the case that human behavior does affect fire losses,[1] it is also true that behavior plays a different role in fire insurance than in the other lines of insurance examined in this book. Except in the case of arson for the purpose of collecting insurance money, neither policyholders nor their agents benefit from fires. In most cases, then, human behavior usually functions as a hazard increasing the likelihood of loss rather than as a peril directly causing loss. The insurers' problem is more to motivate loss-prevention ac-

1. *The Fire Protection Handbook* confirms the importance of human acts in fire losses: fire deaths are related to alcohol intake; 56 percent of residential fires are started by cigarettes; some countries have considerably lower death rates from fires than do others (the U.S. had the highest death rate from fires in a list of fifteen industrialized countries); and a list of twenty-seven causes of the spread of conflagrations between 1901 and 1967 includes many factors under human control (e.g., delay in giving alarm, cotton rags stored outside of buildings, dry vegetation adjacent to buildings, riots preventing or hampering fire fighting, and so on; McKinnon and Tower 1976: sec. 1: 5, 7, 8, and 34).

tivity than to deter people from causing losses. In marine insurance and surety bonding, in contrast, others sometimes benefit from causing losses—this is true for the perils of pilferage, barratry, and theft—and insurers must deter these loss-causing acts as well as motivate other loss-prevention activities.

In addition, fire insurers once believed that the role of behavior was relatively trivial and that it was not the insurers' responsibility to motivate policyholders to prevent losses. Fire insurance rates were structured as if the risks were fixed, and insurers refused to give reductions for the installation of safety equipment.

But insurers' practices do not develop in response to a single pressure. In this case, fire insurers have adjusted their practices to provide incentives for policyholders (or at least for commercial policyholders), but they have not modified them as much as we might expect. Because fires are relatively rare events, information about the effectiveness of loss-prevention activity accumulates slowly, and it is not possible to tie premiums too directly to loss experience. Information about loss prevention can also be gathered by inspecting safety equipment and monitoring policyholder behavior, but both of these are expensive. The strategic behavior of fire insurers must be adapted to these practical constraints as well as to the particular way in which the problem of reactivity is manifested.

In fire insurance, then, the problem of reactive risk is discussed mainly in two somewhat independent empirical contexts, those of loss prevention and of valuation. One of the earliest discussions of moral hazard (or reactive risk) occurred in the mutuals' debates about loss prevention. Historically, there have been two rather different traditions in fire insurance, the mutual tradition and the stock company tradition (though the two have tended to converge in recent years). Mutual fire insurance, especially the factory mutual system, has always emphasized loss prevention, excluding policyholders who do not try to prevent losses and offering incentives (both permission to participate and lowered rates) for safety and reduced fire losses. Stock companies, in contrast, have paid considerably less attention to preventing losses and instead have emphasized the "insurance principle" of spreading losses.

Because an agreement to try to prevent losses by adopting safety innovations was often a prerequisite for participation in mutual schemes, the pools of policyholders in the two kinds of insurance were probably somewhat different. Mutual companies believed that their policyholders were more safety-minded than those of stock companies. As a result, mutual fire insurers worried a lot less about both moral and morale hazard, and they did not try to adjust rating schemes to cope with these problems. Their approach was to try to exclude bad risks by specifically selecting policyholders interested in vigorous loss-prevention programs. With less emphasis on loss prevention, the stock companies have attracted a different set of policyholders, and they have had to use other rating and underwriting techniques to cope with the problems of reactive risks. An examination of the methods used by these two different kinds of companies should therefore tell us something about how fire insurers have tried to manage reactive risks and how techniques for managing moral hazard and morale hazard are different from those intended to control physical hazards. In many cases, collective loss prevention is more effective than individual loss prevention, so an additional problem has been how to motivate the provision of public goods.

A second concern of both fire insurers and their customers has been the setting of appropriate face values for fire insurance policies. Interestingly enough the original reason that face values were a focus of disagreement had to do with the dishonesty of the insurance agents. Disreputable insurers once made substantial profits by overvaluing property and selling too much insurance on it, then denying that the property was really worth that much when a loss occurred. In the meantime, the insurer had collected premiums (from which the agent had collected a commission) on the inflated value, and it was not customary to return these excess premiums. In some states, policyholders retaliated by passing valued-policy laws requiring that the insurer pay the entire face value when a total loss occurred. Insurers were incensed at this requirement, arguing (with some justification, since loss rates are considerably higher in valued-policy states) that this provision often gave property holders an incentive to set fire to their homes and businesses in hard times to get the extra cash. Face values have continued to be a touchy issue in fire insurance as arson rates have gone up and as insurers have faced criticism for redlining minority neighborhoods. The face value problem is especially acute in minority neighborhoods because the market value of the property is often considerably below replacement value. If insurance is pegged to market value, compensation will not cover the cost of repairs, but if insurance is pegged to replacement value, an incentive for arson is introduced (Heimer 1982).

Insurers, then, face three chief problems: (1) they must motivate policyholders to continue to try to avoid losses even though these losses will be covered by insurance, and even though such vigilance might conflict with other activities; (2) they must adjust insurance contracts so that the compensation for losses is adequate to replace lost property but does not tempt policyholders to destroy property; and (3) they must arrange for collectivized research, fire departments, building codes, and so on, since these problems are more efficiently solved collectively than individually.

Not all of the principles for managing reactive risk outlined in chapter 1 can be applied in fire insurance. Because fire losses are quite rare, insurers cannot use experience rating to make policyholder outcomes contingent on avoiding losses. But they can and do adjust commercial customers' rates when these policyholders do things that *on the average* reduce losses. Insurers also try to create a community of fate by making policyholders participate in losses through deductibles. And, finally, insurers arrange for frequent renegotiation and detailed adjustment of contracts (for example with separate provisions for compensation for repairs and for total losses), partly to make sure that incentives have not become unbalanced, partly to provide an occasion to check on policyholder behavior and to provide a bureaucratic incentive for vigilance.

Ratemaking in Fire Insurance: Calculating About Rare Events

Fire insurance rates historically have not provided much reward for reducing fire losses, and thus they have not done much to curb the reactivity of risk in fire insurance. This shortcoming, I will argue, is due primarily to two sorts of limitations on fire insurance ratemaking: (1) the inherent difficulty of rewarding good behavior given that fires are rare events, and (2) the high cost of monitoring policyholders, especially in personal fire insurance. In addition, I will argue that fire insurers have not been especially sensitive to the problem of reactivity. Because they believed that fires were accidental events, they did not look for ways to incorporate incentives for good performance into their rates. Later, when the evidence indicated that fire losses could be reduced by loss-prevention programs, many fire insurers continued to maintain that loss prevention was not an appropriate concern for insurers.

There are two different ways in which insurers might take reactivity into consideration in setting insurance rates. Either they can offer incentives to do specific things that they know will decrease losses (such as offering incentives to install sprinkler systems), or they can offer incentives for good loss experience (by doing experience rating). While fire insurers insist that moral and morale hazard are serious problems and that a high premium rate cannot compensate for these problems, they were for many years reluctant to try to incorporate incentives for loss prevention into their rating schemes.

This reluctance was partly a matter of historical precedent, partly a matter of philosophy, and partly a matter of inherent difficulties in fire insurance ratemaking. From the beginning, fire insurance rates were based exclusively on the physical characteristics of the insured property. The first rates (developed in the late 1660s after the Great Fire of London) were based entirely on construction—rates were quoted for brick and stone buildings, and the rates for wooden buildings were twice the quoted rates (Hardy 1926:9). When contents began to be covered by fire insurers, they were rated the same way as the building itself; fire insurance for identical contents cost twice as much in a wooden building as in a stone one (Hardy 1926:8–10, 19). The rates continued to become more complex as contents came to be rated separately from the buildings in which they were housed and as insurers developed long lists of the sorts of commercial and industrial enterprises that should be rated as common, hazardous, extra hazardous, and so forth.

Flat rates such as those described above provided no incentives for loss prevention. Once a business was located in a building of a particular construction and had started work, its fire insurance rate was completely determined. Having extra exits, separating combustibles from ignition sources, or having a good supply of water made no difference in the insurance premium, even though fire losses might be affected by these precautions. Insurers did not believe it was their job to prevent losses; they were in the business of selling insurance and compensating losses when they occurred; and loss prevention was believed to be a separate enterprise. (This view is discussed further in the section on loss prevention below.) But insurers eventually had a change of heart. They came to believe that policyholders really made their own rates in the sense that any person could get a low rate by making the necessary alterations so that the property had more protective appliances and was less susceptible to fire damage (Ketcham and Ketcham-Kirk 1922:274). Schedule rating became common after this change of perspective.

Schedule rating, which first appeared in the rating of American manufacturing plants sometime before 1840, permits more individualized rating (Hardy 1926:37–40, 266). Though schedule rating is based primarily on four components (fire protection class of the city, construction type of the building, occupancy of the building, and exposure to other structures), numerous details about each of these components are noted during an inspection. An inspector from the rating organization inspects the property to be insured and fills out an inspection schedule from which the rate is calculated. The rate is based on the application of many rules about discounts or charges for particular types of roofs, open or closed stairwells, sprinklers, guards who may or may not be required to clock in on their rounds, number of stories, type of business, occupancy of adjacent buildings, and so forth. Separate schedules are used for different types of commercial enterprises. After the introduction of schedule rating it was possible to offer incentives for the reduction of fire losses.

Schedule rating has its limitations, though. Since no one knew very clearly what caused decreases in fire losses, and since the experimentation and statistical studies necessary to learn this were beyond the capability of most of the fire insurance companies, the schedules that were developed tended to be analytically based rather than based on experience. The earliest fire rates were set by individual companies. When local rating boards were established a bit later, fire rates were based on collective judgments rather than on pooled information about loss experience (Parker 1965:172–73). The purpose of such rating pacts was not to make rates reflect loss experience but to restrain competition. Fire insurance did not have a strong empirical tradition. In addition, since no two companies used the same classification system, when people did get around to trying to make universal rating schemes in the late 1800s, what statistical evidence was available was essentially useless (Parker 1965:172, 178–81; Hardy 1926:111–267; Ketcham and Ketcham-Kirk 1922:276–379). By default the schemes had to be based on analysis.

The problem with basing the rates on "analysis" was that one might end up rewarding or punishing the wrong things. In the case of the territorial component of the rating schemes, for example, insurers rated various locales on the basis of water facilities, the efficiency of the local fire department, the appropriateness of the building codes, the enforcement of building codes, and so forth. Towns were rated from one to ten, and the idea was partly to provide an incentive to local public officials to improve conditions so that their constituents would have lower insurance premiums. But this rating of the protective system of towns turned out not to capture much of the geographical variation in fire losses. Fire insurers were rewarding and punishing the wrong thing, or at least they were placing too much emphasis on factors that did not account for that much variation.[2]

Current rating laws require that insurance companies file both fire insurance rates and statistical reports with state insurance departments. Despite the fact that insurance companies are required to participate in the collection of statistics for the annual reports and to provide support for the rate filings, fire insurance rates still are not based entirely on experience data. Judgment continues to play an important role. In New York, for example, state law does not exactly require statistical proof that a particular rate or classification scheme is justified. Instead, differences among risks have to be "demonstrated to have a probable effect upon losses or expenses" (section 183, subsection 1 of the Insurance Law). Magrath argues that this means that opinion supported with logic can be substituted when evidence is not available (1955a: 269–70). Greene (1973:660) goes further and argues that one *cannot* provide statistical support for fire insurance rates. Because fires are so rare and because so many factors are involved, by the time sufficient evidence has accumulated, building styles, management patterns, and fire protection technology will have changed sufficiently that the evidence does not apply to current conditions.

The problem described above occurs because of a shortage of information about what causes losses at the aggregate level. But this information shortage also creates problems at the individual level.

2. Some authors have argued that insurance redlining occurs because the territorial component of fire insurance rates does not adequately reflect geographical variations in fire losses. For a discussion of this issue, see Heimer (1982:44–46) and Syron (1972).

Many loss-prevention efforts require continued effort from the policy-holder. Fires will not be reduced by having metal barrels to store rags in unless the policyholders or their employees actually place the rags in the barrels. The usual way to encourage loss-prevention programs that require a sustained effort is to reward good loss experience. One may want to reward policyholders for implementing a particular loss-prevention program by including this feature in the schedule rate, but one would want to reserve the bulk of the reward for when policyholders prove that they actually have managed to make the innovation work and have reduced fire losses. But this is not feasible in fire insurance because fires are such rare events. One cannot tell for many years whether someone's loss-prevention efforts have had any effect. It is simply not possible to observe, within a single year for a single policyholder, the difference between one fire every ten years and one fire every twenty years or between complete ruin and trivial damage in that once-in-ten-years fire.

Obviously, this problem prevents the use of experience rating all by itself. When insurers cannot collect sufficient information on an individual policyholder's loss experience to make a useful supplement to a schedule rating scheme, they certainly cannot collect sufficient information to base the entire rate on the loss experiences of the individual. But when insurers do not have a very clear notion of how moral and morale hazard work, and when constant effort must be encouraged by making the rate vary with the outcome, the only hope for rewarding good risks is to use experience-based rates that capture variations due to vigilance, good habits, careful supervision of employees, and so on. Since fires are relatively rare events, one cannot collect this individual-level information, and that means that it simply is not possible to incorporate adequate incentives for loss prevention into a rating scheme.

In order to motivate an individual policyholder, an incentive has to be adjusted to individual efforts and choices. This requires measuring individual behavior well enough to indicate when efforts and choices deserve to be rewarded. Aggregate-level information can guide insurer decisions about what kinds of loss-prevention programs to require, but individual-level information is required to determine when loss-prevention programs have elicited policyholder effort.

Although the problem of controlling fire losses is serious in commercial fire insurance, it is even worse in personal fire insurance. Schedule rates at least permit many individual variations, including presence of loss-prevention equipment and programs, to be taken into account in rate setting. But since schedule rating depends on expensive inspections that are not cost effective in personal fire insurance, personal fire insurance premiums continue to be based on flat or "manual" rates. These rates have only a few categories and are based on construction, occupancy, and local protection codes. No incentives are provided for individual loss-prevention efforts.[3]

Providing Incentives
for Loss Prevention

Successful loss prevention depends on providing incentives to whatever actor can most effectively cut losses. In many cases this is not the policyholder but some other organization responsible for reducing the losses of many policyholders. Research on fire prevention and testing of fire safety equipment can be accomplished more efficiently by a central body than by individual policyholders. Similarly establishing standards for construction, fighting fires, and providing adequate supplies of water are services better provided by cities than by individual policyholders. In these instances, the problem is not how to motivate the policyholder to prevent losses, but how to arrange the provision of collective goods.

Loss-prevention strategies vary considerably in the permanence of their effect. Just as with contraceptives, some fire preventives are in the form of permanent structural features that function without human intervention (fire-resistive construction, segregation of hazardous manufacturing processes), while most require continued effort from those who would prevent losses. Sprinklers have to be maintained, fire brigades have to be drilled, trash must be disposed of. It is because so many loss-prevention programs require continual effort that reactivity is so intimately related to loss prevention.[4] Policy-

3. For useful discussions of rating and underwriting in fire insurance, see Adam (1965), Kelly (1965), Mountain (1965), Searl (1965), Sohmer (1955), and Longley-Cook (1970a and 1970b).
4. This is not to deny that reactivity is implicated in permanent structural features as well—one must, after all, be motivated to discover what kinds of walls or roofs will reduce fire losses and then to construct buildings using this knowledge.

holders must be induced to engage in loss prevention even though losses are collectivized, so that individual policyholders do not bear the full costs of their own losses, and even though individual policy-holders will often benefit more from investing their resources in other activities.

Before discussing these two problems in loss prevention, I will outline some of the basic physical features that help to determine which loss-prevention strategies will be most efficient in which situations.

Fire is a chemical reaction that requires three basic elements: a combustible fuel available to burn, oxygen to sustain the combus-tion, and a source of ignition to heat all or part of the fuel to the temperature at which the chemical reaction can be sustained. Those who work in fire insurance and fire safety fields emphasize that the removal of any one of these elements from the "fire triangle" will stop or prevent the fire. In addition, we now know that the spread of fire depends upon sustaining a complex chemical reaction in which intermediate reaction products are formed before final combustion products are formed. New fire-extinguishing agents prevent the for-mation of sufficient quantities of these intermediate products. For most practical purposes, though, fire prevention still involves control of fuel sources, oxygen, and sources of ignition.

The problem in loss prevention, then, is to interrupt this sequence or to prevent it from starting. Since we routinely use combustible materials and ignition sources, and since we are necessarily in en-vironments where oxygen is present, this is not so easy. No single solution will work in all cases. In a home it may make sense to worry about ignition sources (e.g., keeping matches away from children, being careful with smoking materials), but in a factory where a lot of welding is done it may make more sense to worry about keeping combustible materials away from the welding area. Loss-prevention strategies must be tailored to the use and occupancy of the building.

Both the amounts of combustible material and the sorts of ignition sources vary with the occupancy of a building. For example, accord-ing to one source, the combustible contents of different occupancies vary from about 9 pounds of combustible material per square foot of floor space in residential buildings to over 20 pounds per square foot for places classified as hazardous industrial occupancies (American Iron and Steel Institute 1971:27–45). Obviously a loss-prevention strategy that is appropriate for an occupancy with very little combustible material will not be equally effective for an occupancy with a great deal of it, especially if this material is being processed.

In designing loss-prevention programs, insurers must also consider the variations in the traits of the usual occupants of different kinds of buildings. Age, physical capacity, and alertness of those typically in a building vary with occupancy, and these variations will affect not only the danger to human life but also the likelihood that a fire will be discovered, reported, and put out. Institutional populations are often confined (e.g., in prison cells) or disabled (e.g., in nursing homes), while the occupants of residential buildings spend a good share of their time asleep, and the people in business and educational occupancies can be assumed to be alert (or at least alert enough to notice a fire).

A final constraint has to do with administrative costs and efficiencies of scale. Although it may be cost effective to segregate ignition sources from fuel sources in business occupancies, this probably does not make sense in homes. Similarly, the costs of fire inspections are high and usually have been judged to be prohibitive in the insurance of private homes. This means that many of the loss-prevention programs applicable to businesses are not used in private homes.

Loss prevention as a collective good

Loss prevention is often a public good. That is, if it is supplied for some policyholders, it can easily and cheaply be supplied for others. This possibility of getting the benefit free makes it difficult to motivate anyone to assume the costs of the first big investment in research, public waterworks, or a municipal fire department. Though all actors benefit from the provision of the good, each has an incentive to wait for someone else to make the initial investment. Insurance companies, especially mutuals, have organized incentive schemes so that public goods will be provided. As the theory of public goods predicts, insurers have had to provide some selective benefits, available only to members, to supplement the public goods available to all (see note 9 in chapter 1). But they have also had to offer *individual* benefits to induce members to keep losses low even when these losses would be borne by the insurance company (or other members of the mutual). In the case of insurance, then, we see that the problem of the provision of collective goods, which requires the provision of selective benefits of membership, is complicated by the problem of moral hazard, which requires individual-level benefits. Moral hazard is really a problem of the provision of a *public bad* (other instances of problems with the provision of public bads are discussed by other authors under the rubrics of externalities or the overgrazing of the commons).

Among the public goods important in fire loss prevention are the initial investment in knowledge, waterworks, fire departments, and building codes. As will be discussed below, these collective loss-prevention schemes have the advantage of being more immune to sabotage by policyholders whose incentives change once they are insured.[5]

One of the most important components of a loss-prevention program is knowledge. It is impossible to design a safer building unless one knows which materials are combustible and which are not. Someone has to figure out the safest way to wire a house for electricity. Without careful study it is not obvious how much fire losses can be cut by putting combustible items in noncombustible containers.[6] And experiments are required to determine whether one kind of wall finishing is considerably safer than another kind, whether fire retarding chemicals really work, whether a fire resistant wall will also withstand the impact and cooling effect of a high-pressure stream of water, and what time-temperature curve really describes an uncontrolled fire in a particular kind of structure.

But the acquisition of this sort of information is costly and time consuming, and given the information it is still difficult to know how to apply it. Practically speaking, this means that *individuals* do not generate or collect the information necessary for loss prevention, and also that they are not the ones who figure out how to use the information. Until some *group* is motivated to generate and apply such

5. In arranging for the provision of these public goods, insurers were probably as much motivated by a desire to avoid the huge and unpredictable losses from the rash of conflagrations in densely-settled cities with wooden buildings as by an awareness of the moral hazard problems that make collective loss-prevention so efficient. Because many fire insurers went out of business after each conflagration, the survivors were eager to make those first investments in collective loss prevention.

6. The American Iron and Steel Institute (1971:37) estimates that when more than three-fourths of the combustibles are enclosed in steel containers, such as filing cabinets, the "effective" hazard is only 10 percent of the original hazard.

information, then, many sorts of loss-prevention efforts are simply impossible.

This is a classic example of the problem of the provision of collective goods, in this case historically exacerbated by the fact that many of the actors believed that since fires are accidental there is no point in collecting information. Though everyone would have been better off if someone had investigated the causes of fires and used this information to prevent losses, policyholders were not urging insurers to provide this service, and insurers were not trying to induce policyholders to support such a venture.

The Factory Mutual organization, the first body in the U.S. to collect information about fire losses and to design loss-prevention plans, was formed in 1835. Zachariah Allen, the founder of the Factory Mutual system, constructed his mill to be less susceptible to fire and installed fire-prevention equipment. Despite this, his fire insurer refused to give him a lower rate. Although the insurers admitted that their position might be unjust, the directors decided that "a fire risk is a fire risk and we can make no reduction" (Factory Mutuals 1935:33). In exasperation Allen founded the Factory Mutuals specifically to encourage and reward loss prevention.

While the Factory Mutuals carried out extensive research, designed and tested fire-protection devices, and drafted construction rules, these activities were only possible because of innovations in organizational design. Prior to the formation of the Factory Mutual system, individual businesses were not encouraged to collect and use information about loss prevention, partly because many of the benefits of this knowledge were passed on to the insurer rather than retained by the innovating organization and partly because one could expect to use the information without having to pay to develop it if one just waited for someone else to make the investment. In theory a centralized system could carry out the research, design, and testing work more efficiently than could any single policyholder, but this was only possible if two conditions were met. Somehow policyholders had to be induced to support the centralized effort (see Olson 1971 for a discussion of this general problem). The Factory Mutuals got this support by agreeing to pass on to policyholders the savings from reduced fire losses. But this introduced the problem of how to motivate individual policyholders to keep their losses low, given that their savings were based on the pooled outcome rather than on their own outcomes alone. Somehow the Factory Mutuals had to tie policyholders' outcomes to their own behavior as well as to the behavior of the entire group. That is, the success of the mutual system depended on its ability to provide three classes of benefits: true public goods (such as general knowledge about the causation of fires) available to members and nonmembers alike, selective benefits available automatically to members (lower rates, information, blueprints), and individual benefits tied to a member's performance (the policyholder's own rate).

Some of the benefits of membership were automatically available to all participants in the Factory Mutual system. Information about how to reduce losses was disseminated to all members, who in many cases were also given advice on how to deal with individual situations. For example, the Factory Mutuals assisted applicants or members with building plans and made and kept blueprints of all the property they insured (Kelly 1957:252). While these services were intended to increase the likelihood that applicants could meet Factory Mutual standards without extensive changes after construction was completed (Factory Mutuals 1935:152), such assistance often served other purposes of the members as well. Files of blueprints were often used by companies planning changes in production processes as well as by Factory Mutual officials urging improvements in fire-fighting facilities.

In some cases the benefits of membership were not even controlled by the Factory Mutuals. Always sensitive to the problem of introducing incentives to cause loss, the Factory Mutuals were reluctant to offer business-interruption insurance and other sorts of consequential loss packages. In particular, they were opposed to offering insurance that would cover profits as well as fixed charges. Ironically enough, those stock companies that were selling business interruption insurance (Phelan 1965) were limiting this form of coverage to companies that carried their regular fire insurance with Factory Mutuals because these mills were "under the constant and minute supervision of the inspectors of the mutual insurance companies" (*Spectator* 24, no. 5 [May 1880]: 187; cited in Factory Mutuals 1935:310).

One of the main benefits of membership in the Factory Mutuals was the much lower cost of insurance coverage. But since rates were partly based on individual traits and outcomes, this reward was neither a public good available to both members and nonmembers, nor a selective benefit available automatically to members. Both rates and requirements took into consideration the special characteristics of individual policyholders (Kelly 1956:57; Factory Mutuals 1935:76, 85). By combining rigidity in some areas with flexibility in others, the Factory Mutuals were able to establish high standards for members while retaining the ability to offer *individual* rewards for individual behavior. By the 1880s, for example, all new policyholders were required to have complete sprinkler systems (Factory Mutuals 1935:97), and the centennial anniversary history listed ten strict requirements for membership, including an employee fire brigade and fireproof construction (Factory Mutuals 1935:191). But when standards were upgraded to take account of new knowledge, requirements were changed only gradually, first by giving discounts to those adopting the new standards and only later by making these features requirements for membership. And though much advice was only advice, policyholders might be required to pay higher premiums if they disregarded the advice and therefore increased risk. When the Factory Mutuals recommended placing shingles in mortar, one factory was reroofed without mortar, but the policyholder was penalized with a higher premium (Factory Mutuals 1935:48).

The inspection program is another component of this system of individual incentives and rewards. While continuous activity may not be required to get the fire-reduction benefits of fire-resistive construction, sprinklers have to be maintained, fire brigades have to practice, and night watchmen have to make their rounds. It is in motivating this sort of continuous fire-prevention activity that individualized benefits or costs, in this case based on the results of inspections, are especially important. Probably the most distinctive feature of the Factory Mutual program is the emphasis placed on inspection. An inspection is required to determine whether or not an applicant is eligible for membership. Then there are regularly scheduled inspections that include consultation with management and recommendations for modifications. Not all inspections are made by Factory Mutual inspectors, though; policyholders are required to make some inspections on a regular basis themselves and to fill out inspection blanks reporting the results. Finally the insurers do special investigations, especially to determine the causes of loss and to figure out how similar losses can be avoided in the future, and make surveys to assess the adequacy of particular features of loss-prevention programs.[7]

I have argued that the Factory Mutuals were instrumental in collecting and disseminating information about the causation of fire losses and in motivating loss prevention. Though the Factory Mutuals should not be taken to be average mutual insurance companies, mutuals have usually had more vigorous loss-prevention programs than have stock companies. Many of the class mutuals (for policyholders in a particular line of business, such as the Lumber Mutuals and the Grain Dealers Mutual) were formed specifically because policyholders were getting a raw deal from stock companies that did not distinguish finely enough between different kinds of enterprises and also did not reward loss-prevention efforts (see Bainbridge 1952; also Kelly 1957:251 briefly discusses the class mutuals). Other companies seem to have been emulating the Factory Mutuals (Cooper 1938:119–28).

Olson (1971) argued that public goods will not be provided without appropriate incentive systems. Mutuals seem to have been more effective than stock companies in constructing such incentive systems, particularly in the early phases of their history. Individual industrialists were sometimes large enough to make investment in research on fire prevention worthwhile, but stock companies discouraged this provision of public goods by appropriating too much of the saving from decreased fire losses. In this case, then, businesses did not find out how to prevent fires partly because they were waiting for someone else to pay for the research and partly because if they were insured they themselves got only part of the benefit if they did make the investment. Because the mutual passed savings on to policyholders, individual industrialists were motivated to figure out how to prevent fires and to share this information with others. Eventually the mutual organization itself took over the research. The problems of free riding are more easily overcome in small groups, and the Factory Mutuals were typically started by small groups of industrialists who knew each other and were able to motivate each other to invest

---

7. For discussions of inspections, see Factory Mutuals (1935:84, 93, 269–79, and 283–84), *Eastern Underwriter* (1950:30), and Kelly (1957:251). *National Underwriter* (n.d.) provides instruction in how to judge relative fire hazard.

in research. Because rates depended partly on individual behavior, even insured individuals were motivated to use the information once they got it.

Not everyone subscribes to the Factory Mutual view that "the primary function of a fire insurance company is to prevent losses, not merely to distribute them after the losses have occurred" (Factory Mutuals 1935:190). When stock insurers did become involved in individual loss prevention, they tended to stick to the more actuarial sides of it. Instead of designing new sprinkler systems, they would offer reduced rates to those who had safer factories, businesses, and stores; insurers were not supposed to help their policyholders figure out how to reduce losses or build safer buildings, but only to reward policyholders who happened to have safe buildings (see the Northwestern Insurance Company pamphlet cited in Hardy 1926:64).[8] In his discussion of loss prevention in fire insurance, Maatman notes that most insurance companies writing fire and allied lines coverages maintain some sort of fire engineering or inspection staff. But "the primary function of such staff is to evaluate mercantile, industrial, and public building risks on behalf of their underwriting departments prior to final selection" (Maatman 1965:163), though such personnel may also do inspections and provide consulting services for the larger policyholders (Maatman 1965:164). That is, the main function of this technical staff is not to reduce losses but simply to figure out who can be expected to have lower losses so that these policyholders can be offered lower rates.

We have shown that mutuals encouraged loss prevention. We must now ask why stock insurers have been so apathetic. Stock company profits do not depend on underwriting profit (the difference between premiums on the one hand and losses and expenses on the other hand) alone but on total profits. At least in recent years, total profits have depended considerably more on returns on investment than on underwriting profit (Squires and DeWolfe 1979). As long as a company can balance premiums and losses (and as long as competitors are not offering lower rates), insurers should actually be opposed to loss prevention since this cuts down the money available for investment. This will be especially true for individual-level loss-

---

8. This arrangement requires less expertise in both administration and contract writing.

prevention programs that would have to be motivated by decreases in premiums.

Mutuals are interested in investment income, too, of course, and the Factory Mutuals require an initial deposit, which is used for investing. The difference is that two interests (the policyholders' and the stockholders') are represented in the stock company, while only one is represented in the mutual. In the stock company, investment income is used to pay dividends to the stockholders; in the mutual, it is used to pay losses and to cut premiums. Because the interests of the mutual company are much more closely tied to those of its policyholders, it sometimes acts to benefit them even when this does not make economic sense (at least in the short run) for the mutual itself. If the mutual concerns itself with the welfare of its policyholders, it will be as interested in reducing their losses as in compensating for losses once they occur. Losses have many costs (loss of reputation, loss of steady customers, and so on) that are not compensated by insurance companies even when they give very broad coverage for loss of profits and other consequential losses as well as for direct losses due to fires. This suggests that it is not a historical accident that mutuals, rather than stock companies, first became interested in loss prevention; instead, the mutual principle was critical to the provision of the collective good.[9]

After it became clear that fire losses could be cut and that fire-prevention activities were effective, a market for fire-prevention research began to develop. Underwriters' Laboratories, the other leader in fire-prevention research, was originally formed when William H. Merrill was hired by several groups of underwriters to

9. North's (1953) discussion of the entrepreneurial policies of life insurers at the time of the Armstrong Investigation suggests that among life insurance companies mutuals differed little from stock companies. In both, the interests of policyholders were sacrificed to executives' attempts to increase the wealth of their families, expand the market shares of their companies, and influence legislation that might affect life insurers. We should keep in mind that policyholders in life insurance are individuals, not businesses as they often are in fire insurance (especially in the factory mutuals), so we should expect more inequality between the insurer and the policyholder in life insurance, and this should make a life insurance company more oblivious to policyholder interests. We might also expect the behavior of mutuals to be different when the company is just starting up than later on. Finally, we might expect smaller differences between mutuals and stock companies in life insurance than in fire insurance because there is less that an insurer can do to increase policyholder lifespans than to decrease policyholder fire losses.

curb the dangers of electrical fires at the Chicago Columbian Exposition of 1893. This was the first large fair to be lighted by electricity, and the insurers were understandably anxious—when electricity was first introduced to wealthy homes, these usually good insurance risks suddenly experienced a rash of fires. One important difference between the Factory Mutual Laboratories and the Underwriters' Laboratories is that the first does research that is then used by the Factory Mutual insurance companies in their loss-prevention programs, while the research of the second is mostly contract research for industrial producers who want Underwriters' Laboratories' certification that their product is safe and effective. In this case, then, consumers are paying for this research by preferring to purchase products certified as safe by Underwriters' Laboratories.

Since the formation of these two pioneer organizations, many other public and private fire testing and research organizations have grown up, though Underwriters' Laboratories and Factory Mutual Laboratories seem to have remained the leaders in the field.

Of course, information by itself is rarely enough, and while mutuals may be able to encourage the use of information in some restricted areas, and while individuals may be able to encourage fire safety by selective purchasing, other arrangements are often necessary. When consumers are purchasing especially expensive durable capital goods like houses, they may not be able to express preferences about individual traits like fire-resistive construction, especially when goods are being bought second-hand. Most people do not build their own homes, so they cannot usually select the materials from which they will be constructed. But even in the cases in which a consumer has a great deal of say, for example when a corporation is having new headquarters designed and built, it is impossible to pay attention to all the details that might affect fire safety. The corporation would have some difficulty in making certain that the electricians did all the wiring properly. The problem here is that the purchaser who is interested in preventing fires has very little control over those construction processes that will affect fire losses. This means that if fire prevention is going to be "built into" a home or a business, builders and designers have to be motivated to take fire prevention seriously.

Such mandatory use of knowledge about fire prevention is commonly arranged through building codes. Such organizations as the

American Iron and Steel Institute and the National Fire Protection Association compile model codes, though, of course, such codes must be adopted by the relevant local government bodies.[10]

Though businesses in general presumably have more say in the design and construction of the buildings they occupy than most private citizens have in the design and construction of their homes, most building codes apply to businesses rather than to homes. Though people spend at least a third of their time in their homes asleep and unlikely to detect fires, and though the vast majority of deaths due to fire occur in one- and two-family dwellings, there are very few safety codes that apply to these buildings (McKinnon and Tower 1976: sec. 8:12). For example, there are usually no regulations about fire-resistive or noncombustible construction, interior finishes, automatic fire-detection systems, numbers of exits, or other matters about which there are numerous regulations for public occupancies. This sort of neglect of safety issues in private homes is mirrored in other loss-prevention efforts as well, and I will argue later that this is partly because there is little profit for insurers in loss prevention in personal lines and partly because the problem of reactivity is larger there.

Insurers have not been neutral to the question of building codes, of course. Building codes are the functional equivalent of classification societies in marine insurance. If an insurer can get someone else to require that the policyholder meet a specified standard (and, even better, if the insurers can get this other organization to inspect to see that the policyholder in fact meets the standard), then the insurer gets some loss-prevention effort without having to negotiate with the policyholder about it. One important advantage of loss prevention through building codes or other uniform and independent requirements is that the insurer does not have to offer a lower premium as an incentive to meet the standard, and, if insurers can influence building codes, they may be able to raise the standard without giving a rate reduction, or they can seem to be giving the policyholder a gift in giving a reduction.

But it is not just the permanent sorts of loss prevention that re-

---

10. The reason that iron and steel manufacturers are interested in building codes is that for a while building codes specified that iron and steel structures were unsafe since they would melt at high temperatures and collapse.

quire collective effort. Other examples of collective loss prevention include the development of municipal fire-fighting organizations and the upgrading of municipal water supplies. Individuals can fight fires by themselves (and people were once encouraged to keep a couple of buckets of water already drawn in case of a fire during the night, or better yet to keep several buckets upstairs as well as several downstairs), but a collective effort is usually more effective. When people are trained to work together and roles are assigned in advance, when they know where the closest water source is and how to operate the necessary equipment, and when they do not have to be roused from their sleep and persuaded that they must come to help, they are more likely to be able to put the fire out quickly. But when such collective efforts depend completely on voluntary participation, they are unlikely to work. If there is ever a time when one will choose to be a free rider, it is surely when someone else's fire needs to be put out in the middle of the night.

Free riding does seem to have been an important problem in municipal fire fighting since there is evidence that citizens were *required* to participate in the provision of this collective good. Hardy discusses fire-prevention efforts in the American colonies and provides extracts from the records of New Amsterdam in the 1600s showing that the citizens were required to provide money for fire-fighting buckets, that fines were levied for defective chimneys and fireplaces, and that thatched roofs were forbidden (1926:21–23). A history of Kingston, New York, up to 1820 (cited in Hardy 1926:23) mentions that householders were required to provide leather buckets for fire fighting whenever an alarm was sounded.

Insurance companies organized some of the first fire-fighting brigades. Since insurers were not interested in providing a completely public good, fire fighters were instructed to limit themselves to assisting in putting out fires on policyholders' property. The insurance premium was the price charged for access to this collective good. To identify themselves as policyholders, property owners posted their company's fire mark, a metal sign with the policy number, above their doors. Later, when fire brigades became municipal efforts, insurers contributed funds and equipment and provided rewards for putting out fires (though presumably insurance companies only provided rewards for putting out their policyholders' fires; see, for example, Factory Mutuals 1935:49).

Another major difficulty in fire fighting was the inadequacy of water supplies and the problem of getting the water to the fire. Early fire engines had to be fed by hand, and the water often came from wells or cisterns. Providence, Rhode Island, for example, only got a modern waterworks in 1871, and then only with the assistance and sponsorship of Zachariah Allen, the founder of the Factory Mutuals (Factory Mutuals 1935:77). Even when there were public waterworks, volume and pressure were often inadequate for fire fighting, and Factory Mutual policyholders were required to have private fire hoses, fire hydrants, and private fire pumps to help make up for these deficiencies (Factory Mutuals 1935:191). Such problems are not entirely matters of the past, though. People located outside city limits often do not have good water supplies (for fire fighting, at least), and even within city limits, water supplies are not always adequate because the city may fail to inspect and maintain water-main valves, fire hydrants, and so on. These are all things that individuals really cannot do for themselves no matter how much they might wish to prevent fire losses.

Though individuals may not be able to do much about the condition of the city's water system or the quality of its fire department, fire-prevention organizations, representing individuals, fire insurance companies, and other interested bodies, can have an effect. One of the most important services provided by fire-prevention organizations is an independent inspection service that points out the deficiencies of a city or town's fire-prevention facilities.

What we see here is the effect of the consolidation of actors. While individuals would not be motivated to provide inspection services, insurance companies are. Since the formation of insurance companies, there are a few actors large enough to guarantee the provision of some of these collective goods. The National Board of Fire Underwriters surveys major cities and towns every five to ten years, or more often if requested or if there are special problems. These inspections include detailed investigations of construction practices (for example, the city building codes and the degree to which they are enforced), layout of the city, the water system of the city, and the fire department. Based on the *Standard Schedule for Grading Cities and Towns of the United States with Reference to Their Fire Defenses and Physical Conditions*, the inspection results in a written report describing the deficiencies in the city's fire-prevention system and as-

signs the city to one of ten classes according to its level of prepared-
ness. The city's grade is not made public, but it is supplied to the
state insurance department and to the rating bureau that has jurisdic-
tion in the area. The territorial component of fire insurance rates, in
turn, is based partly on the National Board of Fire Underwriters' rating of a city's fire-protection facilities. A city can upgrade its facilities in an attempt to get a better rating, and the National Board will
usually reinspect if this is requested.[11]

Once collective goods, like city waterworks, fire departments,
and research organizations, have first been provided, continued provision of their fire-prevention services is often not terribly problematic. An important advantage of such collective undertakings is that
incentives can be arranged in a relatively clean fashion. Since the fire
department is rewarded specifically for putting out fires, rather than
partly for putting out fires and mainly for performing other tasks as
are company fire brigades, we would expect more consistent performance from fire departments than from company fire brigades.
Because the motives of these collective bodies are less mixed,
we would expect less backsliding from them than from individual
policyholders.

Motivating continuous effort

Though many loss-prevention activities result in permanent
changes, or function without policyholder intervention because they
are collectively provided, it is surprising how many loss-prevention
activities require continual effort, though perhaps not continued financial investment. These are the sorts of loss-prevention activities
that constitute the greatest problem for insurance. The policyholder
must be continually motivated to engage in loss-prevention activity.
Since backsliding is always possible, the fact that a policyholder is
careful at one point in time does not necessarily mean that he or she

11. The inspection system is discussed in Todd (1966:118–39). These municipal
inspections grew out of the rash of big urban conflagrations in the early 1900s. One of
the ironies of this effort is that the relevant National Board committee had only made a
preliminary survey of San Francisco before its devastating fire in 1906. But the preliminary report recognized San Francisco's perilous situation, since "all the elements of
the conflagration hazard are present to a marked degree" (cited in Todd 1966:45). The
inspectors went on to add that "in fact, San Francisco has violated all underwriting
traditions and precedents by not burning up" (Todd 1966:45).

will be equally vigilant in the future. When another person or a sub-part of the organization shares responsibility for loss prevention (e.g., production workers, maintenance personnel, and guards might all have some responsibility for loss prevention), incentives are espe-cially problematic. In such cases, the insurer must motivate the policyholder to motivate someone else. Turnover and training of new personnel add further uncertainties. A new worker may not know the rules about storing combustible materials; housekeeping may deteriorate while one tries to convince the 12-year-old to share responsibility.

Edward Atkinson, an early leader in the Factory Mutual system, always insisted that "the only persons who can prevent loss by fire are the owners or occupants of the premises. . . . In nine cases out of ten [a heavy loss] is due to lack of care and order in the conduct of work" (cited in Factory Mutuals 1935:96). The evidence does tend to support Atkinson's view. Since Factory Mutual policyholders were required to have proper loss-prevention equipment, the cases cited in the history of this organization are particularly instructive. Very few of the semi-permanent, automatic loss-prevention systems are en-tirely immune to human error.

Most of the big losses experienced by the Factory Mutuals over the years were the result of several accidental events occurring at the same time, and quite often one or another of these accidental events was the result of carelessness (Factory Mutuals 1935:75, 162, 195, 279). For example, in 1865 a mill was destroyed in a fire that started when someone used an open light to investigate a leak in a barrel of gasoline. But the reason that the fire was so devastating was that the water-wheel was being repaired; therefore there was no power for the force pump, and the fire brigade had to rely on fire pails and a few streams from a small reservoir (Factory Mutuals 1935:75). In an-other case, an $853,000 loss (quite large for 1895) occurred because the night watchman closed a crucial valve, as he had been instructed to do, to save condensation. The engine room, where the fire started, had no sprinklers and contained the valve controlling the steam sup-ply to the fire pump. The insurer had recommended the installation of sprinklers in the engine room and the relocation of the valve, but these improvements had not been carried out. When the fire started, the closed valve could not be reached; no water could be supplied to the hoses, and it was not possible to put the fire out at the start (Factory Mutuals 1935:118–19). In a 1917 case, a $2,185,000 loss occurred primarily because sprinklers had been turned off to prevent them from freezing. The authors added a dismayed comment to their account of this last accident:

> This was a case of a modern mill, amply protected, and considered an excellent insurance risk, being completely destroyed by the failure of the human element. . . . If elementary precautions regarding the maintenance and operation of the fire protective equipment had been observed, the loss would have been nominal only.
>
> (Factory Mutuals 1935:152)

The view that human carelessness is responsible for many fire losses, suggested by these examples from the history of the Factory Mutual system, is supported by evidence cited by the National Fire Protection Association. According to their data on acts or omissions responsible for the start of the fire ignition sequence, accidents not involving human failure are relatively rare (McKinnon and Tower 1976: sec. 1: 30–33). Misuse of heat of ignition and misuse of ignited material, both of which fall under the category of human failure, account for a surprisingly high proportion of fires, just over 60 percent in one- and two-family dwellings and around 20 percent in industrial settings. About 56 percent of fatal residential fires are started by smoking materials (McKinnon and Tower 1976). It is hard to tell whether the comparative insignificance of human factors in industrial fires is due to successful loss-prevention programs that control human behavior or alternatively to the greater significance of mechanical failures (52 percent of fires in industrial settings are due to mechanical failures or malfunctions). People in industrial settings may be equally careless, but they may be careless in maintaining machines (or their carelessness may be dwarfed by the "carelessness" of the machines themselves).

Given that losses of insured owners are now borne by the insurance company, or shared among the policyholders, no single policyholder should be strongly motivated to avoid losses. Insurers, therefore, must devise some way either to keep policyholders motivated to prevent losses or to correct for human carelessness, error, or maliciousness. An important consideration here is that time and attention can be devoted to a limited number of things, and resources spent on loss prevention are resources lost to other activities. The opportunity costs of loss prevention are not trivial. Another problem has to do with economies of scale and other differences between commercial and private policyholders.

The usual solution to the problem of human error has been to install systems that compensate for the human failures or correct problems as quickly and as automatically as possible. If one cannot keep people from being careless with heat, fire, and flammable objects, then one can at least use fire-resistive construction and install systems to detect the fires automatically and put them out. Fire-resistive construction reduces losses to the building itself, while temperature-sensitive sprinklers reduce content losses (which can amount to 50 percent of the insurance value) and confine fires to their places of origin. Automatic fire alarms, sometimes hooked up to the fire department, have been an important way of getting the fire-fighting effort underway quickly.

But only fire-resistive construction is immune to human carelessness and can function without human intervention. Sprinkler systems, other fire-extinguishing devices, and fire alarms malfunction and need to be checked periodically to see that they are still in working order. And such systems do not function when they are turned off. Loss-prevention apparatuses are still a benefit even if they only work part of the time, but in order to get the full benefit, one has to have a program of inspections and testing, and this is more difficult to manage. Insurers cannot evade this problem of human responsibility.

But these systems are still designed to *correct* human failures rather than to *prevent* them. Presumably it is also possible to keep people from being careless with smoking materials, to clear away piles of rubbish, to store gasoline properly, and so on.[12] One obvious corrective for human failure is education. People may not know that

12. Trunkey (1983:31) provides evidence that collective loss prevention might be more effective here as well: "The average American cigarette contains additives in both the paper and the tobacco that cause the cigarette to burn for approximately 28 minutes. If these additives were omitted, the cigarette would burn out in less than four minutes. As it happens, most furniture, upholstery and mattresses made in the U.S. need more than four minutes' exposure to a burning cigarette for ignition. The problem and the solution are obvious. Omitting the incendiary additives from cigarettes would not change the taste of the cigarette smoke, but it would make smoking safer by reducing fire-related deaths, disabilities, and property losses.

"Of course, the cigarette manufacturers are not about to remove these additives voluntarily. That change undoubtedly calls for Federal legislation."

oily rags can ignite by spontaneous combustion or they may be unaware that oil fires can be spread by pouring water on them. Education is not enough, though; appropriate incentives are required
as well.

Because the odds of fires and fire deaths are still quite low and there
are few benefits and many costs attached to fire prevention, people
often do not engage in these sorts of loss prevention. It costs money
to install sprinklers or even smoke detectors. Carpets are nice; wood
paneling is considerably more attractive than fire-resistive paint
(though the wood can be impregnated with a fire retardant). And one
often has better things to do than clean the brush away from the
house, check the chimney, clean up spilled oil, or take the stack of
newspapers to the recycling center.

The costs and benefits apparently stack up somewhat differently
for businesses, though. A business may have enough trash to make
recycling economical and so may be more likely to clean up trash.
Money invested in sprinklers, water pumps, fire alarms, and steel filing cabinets is tax deductible, so these fire prevention systems are in
some senses subsidized. In addition, a business is often large enough
to see the results of its own fire-prevention activities. While fires may
be sufficiently rare events so that a homeowner may never have one,
they are not so rare that a business or factory will not. The problem
of alternative uses of resources is still far from trivial. Despite the
fact that loss prevention costs less and has more visible benefits for
businesses than for private individuals, businesses will still divert resources from fire prevention to production when there are shortages
(see Factory Mutuals 1935:151 for an example).

Businesses that engage in loss prevention are also offered discounted rates by insurance companies. But the reward of discounted
rates is contingent on passing inspections, keeping records, and
maintaining equipment, as well as keeping fire losses low. When
schedules and procedures for these sorts of activities are provided
and when a particular insurance rate is tied to observing them, then a
sort of predictable bureaucratic reward supplements the ultimate reward of reduced fire losses. What is important, though, is that the
reward given by the insurer is predictable, and this is presumably
what prevents backsliding. Of course, the reduction in fire losses is
also predictable, but this will be more noticeable to the insurer, who
normally experiences a large number of losses, than to any individual business, which would only experience a few.

There is no obvious reason why insurers could not offer incentives for loss prevention in homeowners' policies or other personal fire policies. Presumably, the reason they do not is that inspections are costly and it is not worth the money or the trouble to inspect private homes. Insurers do not give homeowners discounts for sprinklers, for fire-resistive construction and decoration, or for owning and maintaining fire extinguishers.[13] They have recently begun to offer a discount to those who have installed smoke detectors, and residential sprinkler systems are just beginning to be tested (*Weekly Underwriter* 1979a:21).[14] Insurers also have not figured out how to encourage greater care in the use of matches or gasoline, how to discourage smoking (and how to keep people from falling asleep smoking), and so on. That is, they have neither offered incentives for loss-prevention devices that compensate for human failure (which would be relatively easy to inspect for, since they are at least semi-permanent) nor for attempts to curb human failures.

Face Values, Loss-Adjusting Rules, and Indemnity

Insurance, including fire insurance, is based on an indemnity principle. Theoretically, a policyholder is not supposed to come out ahead when the insurance company compensates him or her for a loss. Otherwise there would be an incentive to cause losses, and insurers want their policyholders to be motivated to prevent losses or, at the very worst, to be neutral to losses. A central problem in insurance, then, has to do with the calculation of the value lost. Miscalculations of this value are costly not only because the insurance company may be paying out money that it does not owe, but, more important, because overpayment unbalances the delicate incentive system.

The main difficulty with this sort of ideal is that it is not very easy to determine exactly what the policyholder's loss is worth. In fire insurance, such determinations of value take place at two points, when

13. Insurers argue that household sprinkler systems are too rare for them to bother with, never noting that sprinklers might be more common if discounts on insurance premiums were offered.
14. Keeney (1979) and Kiorpes (1979) discuss other innovations in loss-reduction programs for residences.

the contract is negotiated and when a loss occurs. At the point when the insurance contract is first made, a maximum recovery for a total loss is often established. This is called the *face value* of the insurance policy and is one of the major determinants of the size of the premium. In some states (called valued-policy states), insurers are required to pay the full amount automatically when a total loss occurs; in other states, an evaluation is made to determine the current value of the building or goods.

But most losses are not total losses, so there must also be rules about how to establish the value of lesser losses. At the point when the contract is made, an explicit agreement is made about what rules will govern loss adjustment.[15] In some cases, the loss will be adjusted on a replacement-cost basis; in other cases, the insurer will agree to pay replacement cost less depreciation; in still other cases, current market value will determine compensation. Some of these rules represent departures from the idemnity principle. This section will be concerned with these various measures of the value of a loss, how they arose, and how they affect incentives for loss prevention in fire insurance. We will first discuss the problem of systematic overvaluation, then take up the problems of changes in value and discrepancies between measures of value.

The history of laws and customs about valuation and of policyholder reactions to various practices provides strong evidence that the incentive structure does function in the expected way. When property is overvalued, policyholders are more likely to experience fires.

Early mutual insurance companies seem not to have had much trouble with valuation, if we can take as evidence the fact that it does not figure prominently either in their company histories or in early treatises on insurance theory. During this period, it was certainly necessary to have some compensation value to which premiums could be pegged, but such a procedure would not have had the importance that it does now for three reasons. The first two reasons are technical ones. First, even though careful valuation procedures are necessary (partly because they provide a method for allocating the

---

15. This is the term used in insurance for the process of agreeing on the value of the loss that the insurance company is then obliged to pay. See Butler (1965) on loss adjustment in fire insurance.

costs of insurance), when the policyholders covered by an insurance company are fairly homogeneous, serious inequities are not introduced by failing to differentiate exactly by the value of their property. Early mutuals were small local organizations covering either dwellings or business buildings, but not both. This suggests that the values of the property covered by any given insurer were likely to be fairly homogeneous, and that crude valuation methods (based mainly on the square footage of floor space) were adequate. Second, in this early period, insurers may not have been aware that they could be nickel-and-dimed to death with claims on small fires and that it was therefore important to peg insurance rates both to the total value of the insured property, since this influences the magnitude of partial losses, and to the face value of the insurance policy, which determines both premium level and compensation for a total loss.[16] Insurance technology was just not that sophisticated at this time.

The third reason that valuation and loss adjustment procedures might have been less important is that they did not have to double duty as social control mechanisms and compensation procedures. Olson (1965) stresses that public goods are more likely to be provided in small groups than in large ones. Presumably it is also true that public *costs* (such as the costs of fire losses) are *less* likely to be imposed on the group by individuals in small groups than in large ones. When fire losses must be compensated by the policyholders themselves, a group of neighbors and friends, rather than by an impersonal insurance company, formal incentives to prevent losses are not as important. Besides experiencing the usual financial costs, people will also experience some extra nonfinancial costs if the neighbors believe their insurance rates have risen because one farmer wants a new barn.

Concern with face values seems to have developed first on the side of the policyholders. During the mid-1800s, fire insurance spread rapidly, largely because of the efforts of stock companies, and it was during this period that overinsurance became a problem. Overin-

16. There was a high mortality rate for insurance companies during this period, but it is difficult to know exactly what to attribute this to. State regulation of insurance surely accounts for some of the decline in insolvency. On the regulation of insurance, see Bickelhaupt (1961), Collins (1955), Hanson (1977), MacAvoy (1977), Magrath (1955a, 1955b, 1955c), Michelbacher and Roos (1970), State of New York Department of Insurance (1966), and Weese (1971).

surance can arise for two reasons—either because policyholders misrepresent the value of their property with the intention of burning it down to collect the insurance (or more innocently, with the idea that they just might come out ahead if there is a fire), or because of the "greed of agents and the rapacity of the company" (Mingenback and Mead 1906:214), who grow rich on the big commissions and extra premiums.

According to Mingenback and Mead (1906:214–15) and Dean (1925:115), both insurers and agents were responsible for the widespread overinsurance during the mid-1800s. Since they knew that only a small proportion of the policyholders would have losses, insurers had an incentive to ignore overinsurance; since commissions were based on premiums and premiums were based on the value of the property, agents had an incentive to encourage overvaluation. Other accounts suggest that if agents were not directly responsible for overvaluation, they were still responsible for encouraging the policyholder to misestimate the value. The agent would simply describe the relation between the face value of the policy and the amount recovered in the case of a total loss and let the policyholder do the overestimating.

What the agent often neglected to tell the applicant was that compensation, even in the case of a total loss, would not automatically be based on the estimated value of the property even though premiums had been based on this value. Instead, an independent assessment, made after the loss, would be the basis for compensation. Even worse, some policies contained stipulations that the companies were only liable for three-fourths of any loss that might occur, and the applications often contained warranties holding the policyholder responsible for any overvaluation of the property, making it possible to deny liability on the grounds of misrepresentation.

During this period, then, policyholders were reacting as if their insurance contracts were not indemnity contracts. But, since they were in fact indemnity contracts (at best), insurers and agents had little to worry about except that they had to carry out extra investigations for fraud and arson.

In this case, one evil followed another. In retaliation, some state legislatures passed valued-policy laws (Wisconsin passed such a law in 1874, Missouri and Ohio in 1879). According to these laws, once an insurance company had accepted an estimate of the value of the property, it had, in effect, agreed that this was the value of the property and could not pay less compensation when a total loss occurred. The intent of the laws was to force insurance companies to accept responsibility for the actions of their agents. If the agents either misestimated the value of the property themselves or accepted someone else's misestimation, then it was surely not obvious that the policyholder should be the one to suffer when the mistake was detected. Whatever the intent of the laws, most insurers agreed that the effect of the valued-policy laws was mostly negative (see Mingenback and Mead 1906:219–20; Dean 1925:124). While making insurers more cautious, the valued-policy laws left the incentives of the agents as they were before, and strengthened the incentive of the policyholders to overvalue their property. The valued-policy laws guaranteed that once overvaluation had occurred, the insurance contract would be what it seemed to be and not a contract of indemnity. One insurance commissioner described the valued-policy law as "an act to encourage incendiarism and facilitate the business of selling out to insurance companies at inflated prices" (Dean 1925:164).

But we need not rely on the opinion of insurers in this matter. In 1900, Leslie Shaw, governor of Iowa, vetoed a valued-policy law that had passed the state legislature. In explaining his veto, Shaw cited a good deal of evidence, collected from neighboring states, about the effects of valued-policy laws (see Dean 1925). Though insurance rates had remained relatively stable in states without valued-policy laws in the late 1880s (Indiana and Illinois), in states that had passed valued-policy laws (Wisconsin, Ohio, and Missouri), fire insurance rates rose 100 percent during the same period (Dean 1925: 121). The evidence indicates that the number of fires per insurance policy had risen, and this strongly suggests arson. Dean (1925:124) concludes his discussion by asking, "Has this law made an incendiary of one out of every two hundred policyholders in the states where it has had time to develop its full educational effect?" This interpretation is consistent with the observed increase in rates. Interestingly enough, none of these discussions is directly concerned with the effects of changes in values. Insurers were aware that misestimation of value introduced an incentive for arson but conceived of this as a problem that could be solved once and for all by making an accurate estimate when the insurance contract was signed. But making a correct estimate once is hardly an adequate or permanent solution to the problem. Property values change, and whenever they drop an incentive for arson is introduced, just as it would be if property values had been misestimated to begin' with. Arson rates tend to rise whenever property values drop, and this problem can be expected to be worse in valued-policy states.

The basic problem has to do with a discrepancy between insured value and other measures of the value of the property. Whenever insured value exceeds other measures of value, there will be some incentive for arson. Overvaluation is only the most obvious way such a discrepancy can arise. Discrepancies can also arise from depreciation of property or changes in the market for real estate, particularly when they are not accompanied by corresponding changes in the costs of maintaining property. These problems are often exacerbated by conventions in insurance about how premiums should be pegged to property values and how compensation payments should be calculated.

One of the most important conventions in fire insurance is the requirement of 80 percent coinsurance. Only about 2 percent of all fires result in a total loss (Whitford 1965:52). Knowing this, policyholders might decide that it does not make sense to carry insurance equal to the full value of their property since a smaller insurance policy would cover the likely loss from a fire. Since most fire losses are partial losses, people hardly ever collect insurance compensation equal to the full value of their property. If insurers charged a rate based on face value alone, they would, in effect, be charging a lower rate to policyholders who carried smaller insurance policies.

There are two ways to rectify such an inequity: insurers could vary the rate according to the ratio of insurance to value, or they could vary compensation according to the same ratio. The first alternative is sometimes used in mercantile fire insurance, and coinsurance discounts are given for higher rates of insurance to value. The second alternative, the 80 percent coinsurance rule, is considerably more common. The coinsurance clause is a device through which an insurance company limits its liability for a loss to no greater a proportion of the loss than the proportion of the insurance recommended by the company that the policyholder has elected to carry. Insurance companies usually require that if policyholders are to receive the usual rate and to be compensated fully for partial losses, they must carry insurance to cover 80 percent of the value of the property.

But what is most important about the coinsurance clause for our purposes is that it decides the question of which estimate of the value of the property will be used by fire insurers. Since insurers were anxious about the possibility of the premium being eaten up by small claims, they were naturally concerned with replacement costs. It was logical, then, to peg insurance rates to the replacement cost of the building or goods. The 80 percent coinsurance rule therefore requires that the policyholder carry insurance to cover 80 percent of the replacement cost. But replacement cost (or even replacement cost less depreciation) often diverges considerably from market value, and when this occurs, there is an incentive for arson.

Insurers have argued that the appropriate measure of the value of the property was its actual cash value. But actual cash value can be estimated either by replacement cost minus depreciation or by market value. Problems have been created when these two estimates diverge and when policyholders have been using one measure of value and insurers another. Gradually, insurers have come to calculate actual cash value in a different way for partial losses (replacement cost less depreciation) than for total losses (market value). This division is appropriate, since what is relevant for policyholders is the estimated cash value of the partial loss in the *market for repairs* and the estimated cash value of the completely destroyed building in the *real estate market*. Insurers have adopted a bifurcated compensation scheme to correspond to the bifurcated incentives that characterize policyholders.

Some of the problems created by changes in values in combination with these insurance conventions are fairly straightforward because the changes in value are ones that can be anticipated. One of the most common of these is due to depreciation. If a piece of property has been in use for 20 years, the materials out of which it is constructed are no longer as good as new. Owners of old houses have to repair the roofs, for example. When a fire occurs, the insurance company can adopt several different policies. Insurers can argue that they should restore the house to usable condition by paying the cost of repairing the damage. But, in such a case, homeowners are not just restored to their previous condition—they are better off. The new roof is less likely than the old one to need extensive repairs. If a major repair has been made, the market value of the home may have risen; so, if the homeowner decided to sell, he or she would make a profit. All this may provide some incentive for the policyholder to burn the roof whenever it needs to be replaced. There are plenty of instances of just this sort of thing happening (see Mingenback and Mead 1906:193–95, or issues of the Insurance Crime Prevention Institute *Report* for examples). It is for this reason that insurers often use replacement cost *less depreciation* as their measure of actual cash value.

The obvious disadvantage of this arrangement is that quite often the policyholder will not have wanted a new roof and would not have chosen to purchase it (even with the insurance "discount" or "trade-in"), even if it did raise the market value of the house. This is particularly true for people on fixed incomes. Because of these sorts of considerations, insurers are sometimes willing to violate the indemnity principle and give insurance on a replacement-cost basis, or, when the loss is trivial, the insurance coverage is large, and the replacement or repair does not substantially enhance the value of the property, to pay replacement cost even when actual cash value is specified in the contract.

More serious problems arise when changes in value are unpredictable and when such changes have little or nothing to do with changes in the usability (or use value) of the property. Housing values drop during depressions; so, if homeowners are paid the current market value when their house burns down at a time when its value is low, they often will not be able to replace the home. In valued-policy states, a different problem occurs. The insured value of the property is now considerably above the market value of the property. In such cases, policyholders may be tempted to burn their property, collect the insurance money, and purchase something fancier. Arson was a big problem during the Great Depression, and many insurers have argued that the high incidence of arson in the late 1970s and early 1980s was due to economic instability.

Localized changes can create even more havoc than widespread economic changes, perhaps because insurers are less inclined to retool to cope with the new situation and have difficulty pinpointing the areas where new techniques must be used. In ghetto neighborhoods, housing values and property values drop dramatically and then may remain low. In such cases, it is unclear how insurers should gauge the value of the property. It is clear that the market value is low, but it is equally clear that there is a huge discrepancy between market value and replacement value. If insurance coverage is based on market value, and if the property burns, then the owner will be unable to afford to repair or rebuild the property. Alternatively, if the owner is compensated for replacement value less depreciation, then there is a strong incentive to buy up slum property, burn it down, and then reinvest the money elsewhere. Slum property ownership patterns provide evidence of this dilemma. On the one hand, dilapidated, partly burned buildings attest to the difficulty of repairing when insurance is based on market value (unless a shortage of housing drives prices up). On the other hand, vacant lots suggest that many people have found it expedient to buy cheap and sell dear (to the insurance company).

This dilemma about the appropriate basis for estimation of slum property values (and for compensation) has been central in the debate about redlining and how to structure the F.A.I.R. Plans (Fair Access to Insurance Requirements).[17] Describing a typical situation in which an underwriter has to decide whether or not to approve an application for insurance coverage for a well-maintained slum dwelling whose replacement cost is about $40,000 and whose market value is only $25,000, Howland (1979: 109) notes that if the underwriter approves the application for a $20,000 policy (80 percent of the $25,000 market value), he will be ''violating his company's requirement of 80 percent or more insurance to replacement cost.'' And no one will be surprised to learn that such policyholders have an especially high loss-to-premium ratio—how could it be otherwise when the discrepancy between replacement value and market value is so large? Small losses are bound to consume the entire premium or more, just as they would in any other circumstance in which a piece of property was ''underinsured'' in the sense that the ratio of insurance to replacement cost was low for the established rate.[18] The alternative, of course, is to require a considerably larger insurance policy, which may provide an incentive for arson for the policyholder who does not object to carrying such a large policy.

17. For discussions of the redlining problem, see Aetna (1979), Donahue (1979), Fritzel (1979), Heimer (1982), *Insurance Advocate* (1979), *Insurance Marketing* (1978), Melewski and Lampi (1978), Ross (1969), Rosser (1979), Squires and De-Wolfe (1979), Syron (1972), *Weekly Underwriter* (1979b, 1979c, 1979d, and 1980).
18. Note that this is an alternative explanation of the exceptionally high losses experienced by slum property holders.

Faced with this choice of providing incentives for arson or having their insurance premiums eaten up by small losses (and, just incidentally, encouraging further deterioration of inner-city property, since, in the case of a total loss, the building cannot be replaced with the insurance payment), and given a little arm-twisting by the government and civil rights groups, insurers have come up with some experimental programs to meet the needs of inner-city policyholders.

The basic idea of these new packages is to encourage repair and rebuilding. One package, in which premiums are based on replacement cost, provides that the property must be rebuilt at the same site before the difference between replacement cost value and market value will be paid. Another package is written on the market value of the property and provides for replacement cost up to the policy limit. But the amount of insurance may vary up to 20 percent from the market value of the property. This latter provision is important because it limits the size of the discrepancy between the insurance policy and the market value (so that the incentive for arson is not too great) while easing the difficulties of those who must try to repair or replace when the insurance compensation is inadequate. A third alternative is a "variable percentage replacement less settlement endorsement," which allows policyholders to insure at less than 80 percent of replacement value but still get full coverage (up to the policy limit) for partial losses (see Vanderbeek 1979; also Bazaire 1979). In those cases in which a policyholder is offered the choice of market value (if he or she does not repair or replace) or repair or replacement cost (if repairs are actually made), the insurance company may stipulate which materials will be used for the repairs, substituting cheaper materials of comparable quality where possible (S.V.d'A. in *Independent Agent* 1978:50; Masimore 1978:266). In short, the logic of these programs is that insurers should take responsibility for encouraging property holders to maintain their property by offering full replacement cost coverage to those who will repair and rebuild, but, if the property owner chooses not to rebuild, then he or she is paid market value, since, in effect, the owner is selling the property to the insurance company, and there is no reason that insurance companies should have to pay higher prices than other purchasers.

Modes of evaluating the worth of property became increasingly complex as insurers became more aware that the evaluation scheme introduces incentives for loss prevention, for maintaining property,

or for arson. At the beginning, insurers did not think of the evaluation scheme as a problem of incentives, but simply as "settling up."
Later insurers did begin to see that property evaluation was a matter
of incentives (especially under valued-policy laws), but they did not
see that values were not fixed and that several distinct and perhaps
incomparable values were being juggled in their calculations and in
their policyholders' heads. During this period, insurers were concerned with indemnity and tried to make sure that their policyholders
did not come out ahead financially when they had fire losses.

But some of these evaluation schemes were too restrictive. Policyholders were not really interested in the small increments to property
values that resulted from repairs with new materials; instead, they
were irate at having to pay for part of the repairs (the amount due to
depreciation) themselves. As they learned how policyholders were
affected by these evaluation schemes, insurers tried to adjust the
evaluation procedures to maintain neutrality in policyholder motivation. If paying replacement cost, rather than replacement cost less
depreciation, did not motivate the policyholders to burn down their
buildings, then there was no real reason not to pay replacement cost.

These innovations allowed insurers to adjust for small predictable
changes in value. Perhaps one reason that insurers were willing to
review their evaluation procedures in these cases was that they themselves had to face problems associated with small, predictable economic fluctuations. If policyholders had trouble making up for depreciation, insurers had similar problems coping with inflation and
appreciation. Such changes are annoying in many cases, serious in
others (e.g., when an insurance company has to pay repair costs for
thousands of policyholders at inflated prices), but still they usually
do not distort the incentive structure. They are a different sort of
problem than the purposive misestimation of property values that
had occurred earlier. If that was fraud, these were closer to accounting problems.

But learning to cope with the incentive-neutral "accounting problems" introduced by small, predictable economic changes did not
prepare insurers to cope with the problems introduced by large and
unpredictable changes in value. As it turned out, these were often
quite important to policyholder motivation. Insurers adjusted to this
by introducing changes that they believed to be inconsistent with the
indemnity principle. But if indemnity concerns both financial value

and use value, these changes were *consistent* with the indemnity principle. By paying market value when the policyholder does not choose to replace or repair after a fire, the insurer is making certain that the policyholder remains in the same financial position; by paying compensation or replacement costs when the policyholder repairs the damage, the insurer is making certain that the policyholder's property has the same use value as it did before the loss occurred. This adaptation, then, can be seen as a bifurcation of the basis of the indemnity principle to correspond to the bifurcated incentive system that presumably characterizes policyholders. As argued earlier, insurers have finally realized that the market for repairs is different than the market for real estate.

Insurers have still not gone so far as to try to quantify noneconomic values (such as attachment to a particular house or a strong desire to move) to come up with some estimate of the sum of financial and other losses. This is what would be necessary to develop a truly incentive-neutral scheme for estimating the value of property and for deciding on appropriate levels of compensation for losses. Instead of attempting to do this, insurers have usually left the question of total value and total loss or gain to be considered in investigations by underwriters or loss adjustors. When noneconomic values are sufficient to change the balance of the incentives, then the underwriter should refuse coverage or write it in a different way or else the loss adjustor should begin a fraud or arson investigation, depending on when this imbalance is discovered. But some of these considerations have worked their way into the policy conditions and the procedures for estimating values. At least, insurers now recognize that use value is sometimes different than market value and that both affect policyholder motivation; both should therefore be considered in fixing compensation levels and in establishing appropriate rules for estimating property values.

Though we have been concerned almost exclusively with the principles and rules theoretically used in loss adjustment, it is wise to remember that loss adjustment does not always proceed according to the theory and that many policyholders are aware of this. According to Laurence Ross in his book *Settled Out of Court* (1970), insurance adjustors are very much interested in getting cases off the books, and therefore they often sacrifice the indemnity principle to expedience. Lawsuits are far more costly than most compensation payments, and "nuisance payments" do reduce administrative costs by getting rid of troublesome policyholders. Since policyholders' incentives are influenced not just by the theory but also by the practice of loss adjustment, we must ask whether the difference between theory and practice is sufficient to transform the insurance relation into one that rewards dishonesty. Conservative estimates of losses and refusals to consider nonfinancial losses may represent an attempt to make certain that there will still be no reward for fraud even when the effects of lenient loss-adjustment practices are taken into account.

Conclusion

That human behavior contributes to the overall likelihood of fire losses is indisputable. What is less obvious is how to manage such reactivity in fire insurance. Because fire losses are relatively infrequent, because loss prevention is expensive compared to the cost of fire insurance, because loss prevention requires continuous effort, and because property values fluctuate a good deal, it is difficult to construct an incentive system to reduce fire losses. But unless insurers can design such incentive systems, they will be unable to calculate very accurately about the likelihood of loss since policyholder behavior will change once the insurance contract is signed.

In order to show how insurers develop appropriate incentive systems, I have analyzed two problems faced by insurers and have provided evidence about how each of these problems has been solved in specific historical situations.

The first problem is that of morale hazard and loss prevention. In general, once an insurance agreement is made, policyholders lose one of their incentives to prevent losses. Unless policyholders are offered some sort of reward to engage in loss-prevention efforts, losses may rise. This problem has been particularly sticky in fire insurance for several different reasons.

At first, insurers were skeptical that policyholders really could do much to decrease fire losses. The mutual structure facilitated the provision of crucial public goods, such as knowledge about how to prevent fire losses. The difference in fire losses between mutuals, particularly the Factory Mutuals, and stock companies served to convince people that a great deal could be done to prevent fires. Since fire losses are relatively infrequent, it is hard to see the results of a loss-prevention program. Therefore, one cannot arrange to reward policyholders for good loss records but, instead, must reward them for installing sprinklers and water pumps, for training company firemen, for rearranging factory layouts so that flammable products are isolated from sparks, and whatnot. But, since policyholders can be careless about their participation in such programs, the problem of morale hazard is not really eliminated by this reward system. Partly for this reason, it is sometimes necessary to make someone besides the policyholder (e.g., the municipal fire department rather than the company fire brigade) responsible for loss prevention. Since fire premiums for private homes are insufficient to cover the costs of inspections, and since fire insurers cannot really afford to offer meaningful reductions to those who install smoke alarms and other fire-prevention equipment, most loss-prevention programs can only be used in commercial lines and not in personal lines of fire insurance.

Insurance compensation for a loss can be thought of as a trade of cash for a piece of property. Because property values change in response to market fluctuations, with age and use, and with changes in the utilities and preferences of the owner, how such values are represented in the insurance contract is very important. If the insurance value is smaller than the actual value of the property, policyholders who suffer losses will not be able to rebuild or replace their businesses or homes. But if insurance values are larger than actual values, then insurers will be offering policyholders an incentive to destroy their property in order to collect the insurance money. The second problem faced by insurers, then, is how valuation practices affect incentives to preserve or to destroy property. I have discussed this problem in the light of the controversy about valued-policy laws, which require insurers to pay policyholders the full face value of the insurance policy when there is a total loss, and in the light of innovations introduced to solve the current insurance redlining and arson problems.

The history of fire insurance provides ample evidence that calculation of appropriate rates has been a serious problem. In some cases, the difficulty was due to competition and continual adjustment of rates by agents trying to sell insurance policies. In other cases, the problems were technical in nature—insurers had not collected the data necessary to base their rates on experience, had developed formulas that did not really reflect reality, or had failed to keep the formulas current. But many of the problems in calculation seem to be directly related to the reactivity of risk. Complaints about instability in rates and increases in the cost of insurance in valued-policy states tell us that insurers could not predict from precontractual conditions what their losses would be when insurance contracts provided an incentive for arson. They would have to wait for new experience to accumulate under the valued-policy conditions, and even these predictions might prove unreliable if economic conditions changed. The existence of a redlining problem tells us that insurers (partly for bureaucratic reasons) have not designed contracts to curb the reactivity of risk in cases where market value and replacement value do not coincide. And, though the Factory Mutuals were able to solve many of these problems, the disastrous fires that did occur, because sprinkler systems had been turned off or because company fire brigades had chosen to save their homes and families rather than the factory, tell us that calculation about expected losses will be difficult unless contracts provide incentives for continual vigilance by the right people.

This chapter has shown how fire insurers have used contractual arrangements to fix otherwise reactive risks, and how the details of such arrangements have been influenced by the nature of fires, by bureaucratic requirements, by the peculiar incentive problems associated with collective goods, and by historical circumstances, as well as by the contributory role of human behavior in the causation of fire losses.

4

Marine Insurance Contracts and the Control of Risks at Sea

Because of the formidable challenge of the sea itself, the difficulties of supervising a captain and a crew while they are at sea, and the possibility of assistance being rendered in the case of a disaster, the problems of reactive risk are magnified in marine insurance.[1] Because the amount of damage that will result from any given marine accident depends on whether the ship has been kept in good shape, whether the captain and crew are on their toes during the crisis, and whether others who happen to be in the vicinity offer assistance, insurers cannot calculate the likelihood of loss from natural events alone. Rather, they must think about the combined effects of physical forces and the human reactions to them. Insurers face several problems: (1) to make human behavior somewhat predictable, so that the losses from the combined effects of accidents and human reactions to them can be predicted, (2) to control human behavior so that people do not deliberately cause losses, and (3) to motivate people to keep the losses as low as possible despite the fact that

1. Readers interested in good introductions to marine insurance should look at Winter (1952), Dwelly (1965), Marshall (1965), and Oxford (1965). Information on the history of marine insurance can be found in McDowell (1965), Trennery (1926), and De Roover (1945), as well as in histories of Lloyds (Martin 1876) and other insurers. Knauth and Knauth (1969), McGuffie (1958), and Gilmore and Black (1957) provide information on salvage and admiralty law. United Nations Conference on Trade and Development (1978) gives some idea of how marine insurance law can be expected to change in the future.

losses are being paid for by the insurer. Insurers have to take the relevant people into account, but they also have to figure out how to keep these people from taking them into account in turn.

Given the importance of reactive risk in marine insurance, marine insurers have four general problems in calculating the likelihood of loss. The first is to standardize the situation so that insurers will know what risks they are covering, and will be able to keep policyholders from changing their behavior once they have insurance. Implied and express warranties and franchise agreements solve this problem by specifying the conditions of coverage. A second problem is to decide what kinds of losses will be insurable. Here insurers must decide which sorts of losses are most subject to policyholder control. When the policyholder can control or influence losses, the probability of loss is more likely to change with insurance coverage. This means that when the person controlling the loss is a hierarchical subordinate to the policyholder (e.g., as in the relation between ship captain and shipowner), insurance coverage will be more problematic than if they are only related through a market (e.g., as in the relation between ship captain and cargo owner). A third problem has to do with supplying incentives to appropriate people. When a ship has an accident at sea it does not matter much whether the owner of the ship or cargo wants to reduce losses. What matters is whether the captain and crew and especially other potential rescuers are motivated to do their part. Insurers have tried to arrange incentives to make these people's efforts predictable. Finally, the way insurers calculate the value of property may sometimes provide incentives for owners to destroy property so they can collect insurance payments. If insured value is above real value, losses will be above what insurers have predicted. When an insurance policy covers several items (the value of the hull and expected profits) or when the value of the property fluctuates (as is often true for cargo), insurers must design valuation procedures carefully if their estimates of losses are to be valid. In the rest of this introduction I will show in more detail what role each of the problems plays in marine insurance.

A fundamental problem in marine insurance is ensuring that the vessels are capable of carrying the cargos they have contracted to carry on the voyages they have agreed to take. A ship must be designed and built to do a specific kind of work in a particular body of water. A barge to carry goods on the Mississippi will not be fit to cross the ocean with the same cargo. In addition to being designed and built for a particular trade, the vessel must be kept in shape for that trade. An oil tanker should not embark on a long trip without having had the engine repaired, or without having stocked enough fuel or food. The problems of routine maintenance are probably more serious in marine insurance than in other lines of insurance because vessels are away from port for long periods of time. In addition, if the vessel should have an accident, a higher proportion of the total value is likely to be lost than in other lines of insurance, since it is hard to save the cargo of a sinking ship.

In order to make sure that the policyholder pays attention to problems of ships' capabilities, insurers make the validity of the insurance policy contingent on the policyholder meeting requirements specified in express and implied warranties. In order for the insurance contract to be valid, the ship must, first of all, be certified by a specified classification society. The classification society sees to it that the ship is designed, built, and maintained appropriately for its trade, and it can require the shipowner to make necessary repairs. (By placing the responsibility for inspection in the hands of someone other than the policyholder, insurers decrease the chance that this important function will be sacrificed to more pressing activities.) Though this is probably the most important express warranty, other express warranties have to do with the flag of registration, trading routes and seasons, and so on. The point of such warranties is partly to force the policyholder to meet certain minimum conditions, and partly to exclude certain dangerous practices or conditions. Calculation of expected losses is facilitated when the conditions of the contract are fixed in this way.

Implied warranties, such as the implied warranty of seaworthiness and the implied warranty of prompt attachment, are similar in effect to express warranties. The difference is mainly that the standard involved is a variable one. Seaworthiness, for example, depends on the time of year, the type of vessel, the route being taken, the cargo being carried, the usual standards applied in such conditions, and so on. Under the implied warranty of prompt attachment a delay in the start of a voyage cannot be so long that the risk is no longer the same as the risk that the insurer agreed to cover. Implied warranties are rather like the arguments made about the "reasonable man" in other areas of law. They are variable standards that provide a way for community customs and norms to be taken into account. They provide a legal requirement that the policyholder abide by the spirit as well as the letter of the agreement. They render policyholder behavior more predictable by making explicit the insurer's assumption that the policyholder will follow standard practices.

A third loss-prevention provision is the deductible or franchise agreement. Such agreements require the policyholder to bear small losses, and, in the case of deductibles, to participate in larger losses. In this way, the interests of the policyholder are made more congruent with those of the insurer. Franchise agreements also make it possible for the insurer to vary the coverage with the type of cargo, for example, so that policyholders have an incentive to adjust their packaging to the perishability of the cargo. Franchises and deductibles facilitate insurers' calculations by making it less likely that policyholders' behavior will change with insurance coverage.

When insurers are trying to control reactive risks, they have to vary their strategies with the controllability of the behavior in question. Some events are accidental, some are directed entirely by the policyholder, many are in between. Some acts are difficult to control because someone else has responsibility for them, and the policyholder cannot completely regulate this other person's behavior. This is true, for example, of the policyholder's ability to control the acts of the captain and the crew. In general, one cannot completely control an act when one has delegated responsibility for that act to someone else; in addition, one has even less control when physically separated from the person to whom one has delegated responsibility. The common problem of the accountability of superiors for their subordinates' actions is exacerbated by the subordinates being located out at sea. The reactivity of risk varies with both social and physical distance. Even so, policyholders have to be made to take some responsibility for the actions of their employees. The question, then, is whether it is wise (from a motivational point of view) for the insurer to cover losses due, for example, to mutiny, pilferage, or negligence.

But not all acts are deliberate, and this second sort of lack of control presents another problem for the insurer. In many cases, policyholders or their agents will have caused losses unintentionally. Obviously, one will not want to encourage such carelessness by covering all unintentional acts, but there are limits to the policyholders' ability to pay attention to all of the details, or to motivate their subordinates to attend to them.

Insurers have dealt with this problem of control by defining some acts as covered perils while excluding coverage of others. When the loss can be attributed directly to one of these excluded acts, the policyholder cannot recover. In general, the more direct the policyholder's control over the act and the more deliberate the act, the less likely it is that a loss caused by such an act will be compensated by the insurer.

If the problem is sometimes to make policyholders behave responsibly, to exercise due diligence or to motivate their agents to do so, at other times the problem is to get people to try to reduce the loss while an accident is occurring. In some cases, the people who must be motivated to act are people not associated with the venture at all. The problem of keeping losses down during an accident, then, can be broken into three parts: (1) how to motivate policyholders and their agents to behave like "prudent uninsured owners" and to try to keep the losses as low as possible, (2) how to make the captain and crew take into consideration the interests of the cargo owners as well as the interests of the shipowner, and (3) how to motivate others who happen to be at the scene of the disaster to do whatever they can to rescue lives and cargo or to save the ship.

In a sense, these three are variants of a single problem. In each case, insurers must get a person to act in the interest of another person (or other people); the differences between the three cases have to do with the amount of overlap between the interests of the person with control and those of the person on whose behalf he or she is acting.

Loss reduction during an accident is similar to other sorts of loss prevention in that the insurer must motivate people to exercise whatever control they have. But the insurer motivates this loss-reducing activity in a slightly different way. Though most of the law on loss prevention is concerned with whether a loss is truly accidental, the law on loss reduction during an accident *assumes* that the loss is accidental and is instead concerned with getting the policyholder and others to do whatever possible to reduce losses. There is no question of whether the policyholders are to blame, of whether they *deserve* to recover.

Finally, reactive risk is an important consideration in rules about how to evaluate the worth of a ship or cargo. The problem here is to set values that will discourage policyholders from destroying their property. In deciding how to settle questions about the amount of compensation, insurers and shipowners decided early on that the best procedure was to agree beforehand what a ship or cargo was worth. Then, when a loss occurred, they would be able to avoid lengthy and troublesome disputes about value. The difficulty is that if one fixes the value of the cargo or vessel in an insurance contract, this does not mean that it will remain fixed in real life. If the value rises, then getting only the agreed value will be a hardship for the policyholder, who will not be able to replace the ship or cargo. If the value has dropped, the cargo owner or shipowner may be tempted to exchange the ship or cargo for the insurance money by deliberately causing a loss.

While one might argue that this problem could be solved by renegotiating the insured value whenever the market for ships or for a particular cargo altered substantially, this is not a satisfactory solution because the policyholder may have agreements (such as loans or mortgages) that are pegged to the (high) insured value. In addition, the reason for having a fixed value to begin with is to avoid having to negotiate about value when a loss occurs.

As a result of these difficulties, provisions have been made to adjust the value upward but usually not to adjust it downward. This creates an incentive for fraud whenever the shipping or cargo market is bad. In addition, a policyholder usually carries several different kinds of insurance, so overvaluation may be substantial and the incentive to cast away the vessel or destroy the cargo may be even larger than one might initially suspect. One of the main reasons why this problem is not more serious is that policyholders have so little control over their property. For a change, this lack of control works to the advantage of the insurer.

Still, there is substantial insurance fraud, and this is partly because of the ambiguous connection between repairs necessitated by wear and tear and repairs necessitated by small accidents. Much insurance fraud in marine insurance takes the form of padding claims and making illegitimate claims. Clauses about depreciation are intended to reduce the incentive for this sort of fraud.

Finally, marine insurers, unlike fire insurers, do base their rates on the experience of the policyholder.[2] Because marine losses are

2. One of the chief differences between marine insurance and other lines is that the rates are set by the underwriters rather than by rating organizations. Though they may follow guidelines issued by underwriting associations, underwriters have a great

relatively frequent occurrences, policyholders can be rewarded or punished for their outcomes.

Insurers are particularly likely to consider the partial loss experience of a policyholder, since this is more controllable than the total loss experience. A high rate of small accidents indicates that the management is not really exercising due diligence. In addition, many partial losses fall into a "twilight zone," as Oxford (1965) calls it. These losses are primarily expenses due to routine maintenance or to minor accidents due to the wear and tear of the sea. If policyholders routinely charge such losses to the insurance company, this means that they are not doing maintenance work until it is absolutely necessary. It also means that the insurer cannot expect these policyholders to act as prudent uninsured owners would in the case of accidents, trying to keep the losses as low as possible. Policyholders with lots of partial losses are morale hazard risks; their behavior has changed as a result of being insured. Though insurers do not know exactly what causes the losses and do not peg the rates to specific good or bad characteristics, they can reward good management, vigilance, and competent work by giving low rates to those who manage, by whatever method, to keep their losses down.

Insurers do take into consideration factors other than loss experience, though, and some of these are related to reactive risk. For example, they consider the reputation of both the owner and the captain, but, in considering these factors, they again use experience-based information. Organizations like Lloyds keep careful records about the work biographies of captains, owners, and ships, and underwriters have access to these. How all of this information is juggled is not

---

deal of latitude in deciding what rate is appropriate for a particular client. And, partly because marine insurance is so international that it would be ludicrous for any single government to try to regulate it, there is little interference in the form of rate regulation. This means that rates can be used to motivate and reward policyholders more easily in marine insurance than in other lines.

Marine insurance rating tends to be based considerably more on judgment than on formulas, though formulas are used to make the first estimates of what a rate should be, and rates are usually set individually rather than being set for large categories of policyholders. For discussions of rating, see Winter (1952:98-109, 227-42) and Oxford (1965:285-301).

As a general rule marine underwriters consider policyholders' loss records for the past five years when they are setting their rates. Though they compare a ship or a fleet to other ships or fleets with similar characteristics, they usually try to make each policyholder pay for his or her own losses over the long run (Oxford 1965:289).

very clear, though, and this lack of clarity may make it difficult for policyholders to fake good intentions. They cannot get reductions simply by installing more safety equipment or even by hiring good captains; instead, they must use these assets to produce good loss records.

This emphasis on experience rating suggests that moral hazard, morale hazard, and reactivity in general are more likely to be taken into account in marine underwriting and ratemaking than in other lines of insurance. When a rate is so heavily based on experience, policyholders are rewarded or punished for the entirety of their experience—including machinery, captains, crew members, management systems, and the owners' diligence. Whatever produces a good loss record is rewarded.

In this chapter, I will discuss the issues outlined above, stressing the way in which insurance practices are designed to shape policyholder behavior and to make it easier for insurers to estimate expected losses.

Warranties, Implied Warranties, Franchises, and Moral Hazard

One is rarely as motivated to protect someone else's property as to protect one's own. When the insurer has agreed to bear the cost of accidents, then in a sense the property belongs to the insurer, and we might expect policyholders to be less concerned about avoiding accidents once an insurance agreement has been signed. We might especially expect changes in how a policyholder balanced chances of gain against chances of loss. If the policyholder reaps the gains and the insurer takes the losses, we might expect the policyholder to take chances to increase profits even if the likelihood of (insured) losses would rise. For example, as insured ships age and deteriorate and as repairs are needed, shipowners may decide that it is simply not worth their time to keep things in order and may fail to train or supervise new crew members. Often owners will not actually *decide* not to maintain their ships, but instead they will become a little more lax, a little bit less attentive because they are instead investing their resources in other projects. Or, for example, the owner of an oil tanker might decide that on net balance it is worthwhile to save the pilotage fee and negotiate a treacherous passage without assistance, despite the fact that this would increase the chance of an accident and an oil spill.[3]

This change in incentives is a serious problem for insurers because when the behavior of the policyholder changes after the insurance is arranged, the likelihood of loss will be different and the insurer will be unable to anticipate the level of losses and to set premiums appropriately. *The insurer's calculations have to be about some particular set of conditions.* In order to predict a shipowner's losses, the insurer must know what route the ship will follow, what kind of cargo it will carry, what condition it will be in, and so forth. Expected losses are different for winter voyages than for summer voyages, for trips around the Cape of Good Hope than for trips through the Suez Canal. The insurer needs to make certain that the policyholder's decisions about routes, cargos, timing of voyages, and so forth do not change once an insurance agreement is made.

Marine insurers typically use three techniques to keep their policyholders from altering their behavior, and therefore increasing the likelihood of loss. First, when insurers believe that the likelihood of loss depends on some condition, they can specify that the insurance agreement will be valid only if the policyholder meets that condition. Such express warranties are written into the contract and become conditions of coverage.

Implied warranties, the second technique, though not explicitly written into the contract, are important conditions of coverage that are part of the contract by custom (or by law) and often have to do with the standard practices of shippers. Implied warranties, in a sense, put a lower limit on laxness since they require that an insured shipper maintain the standards and customs of the shipping community. In effect, they *require* policyholders to behave as the insurers' knowledge about marine traditions would lead them to expect. Failure to follow these standard practices invalidates the insurance contract and will often keep the policyholder from receiving compensation for losses.

The third technique is not intended to mandate specific actions or to force policyholders to follow standard procedures, but instead is supposed to motivate policyholders to behave as they did before they

---

3. Mostert (1974:236) argues that this sort of calculation may ultimately lead to compulsory pilotage or convoys.

had insurance coverage. By making the policyholder bear a portion of each loss, franchise or deductible agreements require policyholders to assume some of the consequences of their own failure to prevent the loss. When policyholders lose too, the reasoning goes, they will be more inclined to try to prevent losses and, equally important, they will continue to behave in predictable ways.

Express warranties

An express warranty is in effect a guarantee given by the policyholder; it works to prevent policyholders from altering their behavior for their own advantage in ways that will increase the likelihood of loss. Express warranties are written agreements included in the basic policy itself, included by endorsement to the policy, or incorporated into the policy by specific reference to some other document. As defined in the Marine Insurance Act (1906) of Great Britain, a warranty is a statement

> by which the assured undertakes that some particular thing shall or shall not be done, or that some condition shall be fulfilled, or whereby he affirms or negatives the existence of a particular state of facts.
> (section 33 [1])

Such phrases as "American Ship Atlas," "packed in wooden crates," "to sail on or before 2/1/83," or "subject to survey and approval by United States Salvage Association" are express warranties because they contain allegations of facts relating to the risk. Other express warranties include trading warranties, loading warranties, warranties about war, and warranties about classification.[4]

The purpose of trading warranties is to prohibit vessels from sailing in dangerous waters during the most hazardous periods and to confine ships to the sorts of waters that they were designed and built to navigate. They therefore specify geographical limits and seasons within which the ship can operate. Sometimes such warranties are tailored to particular vessels, for example restricting an old vessel to a coastal trade, but many times insurance policies instead use Institute Warranties, sets of standardized trading warranties put out by organizations like the Institute of London Underwriters and the American Marine Underwriters.

---

4. On express warranties, see Winter (1952:222), Dwelly (1965:258), Wilmot (1975:8/33), and, for a slightly different view, Greene (1973:284).

Loading warranties, which may be tailored to individual vessels or may follow the rules of a particular underwriters' board, prohibit a vessel from loading more than its registered under-deck capacity on any given passage, or from loading more than a certain percentage of the cargo on deck, or from carrying a particular kind of cargo. Many vessels have load-line markings (Plimsoll marks) painted on their hulls so that it is easy to tell whether they are conforming to the rules for that particular season and sea (Winter 1952:75-78).[5]

Many express warranties have to do with war insurance. During World War II, for example, ships were required to carry prescribed documents to prove their nationality. Without such documents a vessel might be held in port or prevented from entering a port. This in turn might lead to the vessel being unable to restock supplies, refuel, or get repairs, therefore eventually leading the vessel to become unseaworthy and to suffer some sort of loss. If the vessel did not carry the required documents, the hull policy was null and void (Winter 1952:343).

Warranties about classification are also commonly included in hull policies. Such warranties provide that the vessel will be classed by a particular classification society; if such class cannot be obtained for one reason or another, then the insurance agreement will not be binding.

Classification and classification societies have played a very important role in marine insurance. The classification society is an independent organization that sets standards for how ships should be built and maintained and then provides inspectors to see that individual ships do in fact meet these standards. Insurers require that ships be classed with particular societies (such as Lloyds, American Bureau of Shipping, Det norske Veritas, or Bureau Veritas), and that they be inspected on a regular basis (often annually). The shipowner pays for the inspection and must make repairs as required by the classification society. The standards of the classification societies change as advances are made, so the shipowner is not simply being required

5. See Mostert (1974:194-96) for a history of the development of the Plimsoll lines and a discussion of the disastrous effects of changing loading limits for oil tankers. Because oil tankers pass through both the Northern and Southern Hemispheres on their trips to and from the Middle East, there is some question about whether they should use summer or winter loading limits. When they load for Northern Hemisphere summers but round the Cape of Good Hope during its stormy winter weather, losses are high. Tankers often dump oil to avoid accidents.

to maintain standards but in addition may be required to improve the condition of the vessel.

The separation of the classification and inspection service from the insurance service seems to have been quite important in shipping history. This division of responsibility has had two main effects: it has enabled the insurers to insist that high standards be met without having to engage in negotiations with shippers about exactly what these standards should be and whether exceptions could be made in particular cases; it has also made possible a continual evolution of regulations so that the standards have changed both as the ships themselves have changed and as safer methods were developed.

Classification society standards are not absolutely rigid, though, since the competition between the various classification societies for the business of shipowners means that if a society's standards are too high, its customers will turn to other societies. The complete erosion of standards is prevented by the fact that the classification society has two customers, the policyholder and the insurer, and the latter has an interest in maintaining high standards.[6] Certain societies (such as Lloyds) are believed to have higher standards than other societies, but in addition they are rumored to favor domestically constructed vessels (Huebner 1914:26).[7]

The teeth of warranties are not in the specific requirements but instead in the effect on the insurance contract of violating a warranty. In the case of a breach of warranty, the insurance contract is void from that point on. That is, the insurance contract is *void whether or not any loss that might occur is related to or traceable to the breach of warranty* and whether or not the breach of warranty is only a temporary state of affairs. While insurers do have to prove breach of warranty, once this point is established, they do not have to prove that the policyholders were at fault or that the breach of warranty either caused or contributed to loss. In addition, a warranty must be

6. According to Mostert (1974:247), when aging supertankers can no longer pass classification surveys without extensive repairs, respectable companies sell them to shipping lines that register their ships under flags of convenience. Thus are standards maintained, at least by some. Flag-of-convenience ships must get insurance from someone, though. The chief disadvantage of such registry seems to be that flag-of-convenience ships are prohibited from entering certain ports (Mostert 1974:247), not that they cannot get insurance.

7. Further information about classification and classification societies can be found in Winter (1952:98–109, 125) and in Barlaup (1976).

literally complied with, whether or not this exact compliance has any influence on the risk. Though these rules are indeed harsh, policyholders can often arrange continuity in coverage with "Breach of Warranty," "Deviation," or "Held Covered" clauses and by paying some additional premium.

Implied warranties

A marine insurance contract is still subject to a number of implied warranties that are part of the insurance contract as a matter of custom, court decision, and statute, even though they are not written into the contract. The principal implied warranties include the implied warranties of legality (the only warranty that cannot be waived by mutual agreement), prompt attachment of risk, no deviation, and seaworthiness.

The implied warranties of no deviation and prompt attachment are really just specific forms of the general legal principle that a formal contract cannot be varied without the mutual consent of the parties to the contract. Changing either the route to be traveled or the time during which a voyage is to be made may substantially alter the likelihood that losses will occur and is therefore not permitted without some special arrangement between the policyholder and the insurer.

Though franchise agreements, express warranties, and other implied warranties are all important in controlling risk and in keeping losses in bounds, the implied warranty of seaworthiness is probably the single most important attempt on the insurers' part to motivate loss-prevention activities. Originally, the seaworthiness of the insured vessel was a condition for the liability of the insurer. If the vessel could be shown to have been unseaworthy, the insurer did not have to pay for any losses. Now this holds only for voyage policies, while for time policies, which are more common, the shipowner is only required to exercise due diligence, and the loss will be covered unless it is *directly* caused by unseaworthiness.

According to the 1906 Marine Insurance Act of Great Britain, "A ship is deemed to be seaworthy when she is reasonably fit to encounter the ordinary perils of the seas of the adventure insured" (section 39 [4]). Under a voyage policy, the ship was supposed to be seaworthy at the beginning of the voyage, and if the voyage had several stages that required different kinds of preparation or equipment, there was also an implied warranty that "at the commencement of each stage the ship is seaworthy in respect of such preparation or equipment for the purposes of that stage" (section 39 [3]).

Since the standard involved is both comprehensive and variable, compliance with this implied warranty is no mean feat. In order to be seaworthy, a vessel must be "suitably constructed and equipped, properly officered and manned, and sufficiently fueled and provisioned to carry the specific cargo insured on the particular voyage described" (Winter 1952:216). Court decisions have even extended seaworthiness to include fitness for loading and unloading so that defective containers or improperly packaged cargo may constitute unseaworthiness (Johnson 1963:1). In addition, shipowners cannot meet their obligation simply by exercising due diligence (Mullins 1951:228), or by having the vessel inspected by the classification society. Any undiscovered defect that made the vessel unseaworthy would still constitute a breach of warranty. What it means to be seaworthy also depends on the kind of voyage that is being undertaken, the kind of cargo that is being transported, the stage of the voyage, the season of the year, and the ocean or river to be sailed (Winter 1952:216–19). Given the inclusiveness and the variable nature of the standard, the question of seaworthiness must be decided on an individual basis and, in the final analysis, is a question of fact that can be determined only in a court of law.

In theory, breach of the implied warranty of seaworthiness automatically voids a voyage contract. If the vessel is not seaworthy when it sails or if the vessel is not adequately prepared for a later stage of the voyage, the contract is void. If, however, some accident damages the ship and it becomes unseaworthy as a result of this, this unseaworthiness does not void the contract unless there is an opportunity to repair the vessel and this opportunity is not taken.

The burden of proof of unseaworthiness is on the insurer, though, and unseaworthiness is very difficult to prove since one must usually show that the loss was not due solely to catastrophic action of the forces of nature on a seaworthy vessel (Winter 1952:219). Since it is so difficult to prove breach of warranty in this case, Winter counsels against insuring vessels about which one is unsure. He also points out that an underwriter can get into a good bit of trouble by charging that a vessel is unseaworthy. Since shipowners will lose business if it gets out that their vessels are not seaworthy, they might well sue an insurer who publishes such views (Winter 1952:219–20).

Though the situation was relatively clear when most insurance policies were voyage policies, most policies are now time policies, and the law for time policies is quite different. Later rules have modified the situation even further. To begin with, the obligation to send the ship to sea in a seaworthy state is no longer an implied warranty (Marine Insurance Act [1906], section 39 [5]). This means that if the ship proves to be unseaworthy, the policyholder will not be guilty of breach of warranty, and the policy cannot be voided. Instead, one must apply the ordinary rules about losses caused by the policyholder (Wilmot 1975:11/8). Second, unseaworthiness is a defense only if the policyholder was privy to and should have been able to prevent it. This is a much more limited requirement since, for example, the policyholder can usually not be expected to know of defects in the materials from which the ship is built. Finally, the insurer will be exempted from liability only if the loss was directly caused by unseaworthiness. In short, recovery will be denied only if unseaworthiness caused the loss and then only if the policyholder could have prevented or corrected it.[8]

Franchises and deductibles

Insurers in general mold their insurance coverage to trade practices and base their estimates of expected losses on the assumption that policyholders will follow standard practices. This is particularly important in cargo insurance since standard practices and aver-

---

8. The original reason for the distinction between time and voyage policies had to do with the fact that a ship is often not in port when a time policy first takes effect or is renewed. This means that the policyholder has no way of determining whether the vessel is seaworthy at that point and that the insurer has no way to prove that it was not. American and British legal traditions differ on the implications of this argument. The British position is outlined above. According to American custom, *if the vessel is in port* at the time the policy attaches, there is an implied warranty of seaworthiness and a continuing obligation on the part of the policyholder to use due diligence to maintain her in seaworthy condition during the term of the insurance. Breach of the implied warranty of seaworthiness will void the contract, but breach of the continuing obligation to maintain the ship will merely prevent recovery in the case of a loss due to unseaworthiness. This seems also to be in line with the Hague rules on such questions, under which policyholders must exercise due diligence and are responsible for seeing that their agents and servants do so as well. Though there is a substantial difference between exercising due diligence and providing a seaworthy vessel, just as there is between being prevented from recovering if the loss is due to unseaworthiness and having the entire contract voided, the general effect on policyholder behavior should be the same.

age losses vary from one commodity to another, and losses depend on how the cargo is packaged and transported.

One might expect that insurers would give different rates depending on what the cargo is and how carefully it is packed. Though there may be some tendency to do this, insurers more commonly charge a basic *rate* but alter the *conditions* of the insurance according to the nature of the cargo and the practices of a particular cargo owner. The usual way one does this is with a franchise clause, a form of deductible agreement that says that the policyholder does not get to claim against the insurer unless the loss exceeds a specific proportion of the value of the goods. If the loss is below this percentage, the insurer is not liable; if the loss is greater than this amount, the policyholder recovers in full. For example, the policyholder may not be able to recover anything from the insurer if less than ten percent of the cargo is lost.

Franchise agreements vary considerably, depending on what exactly is being insured. Apparently one of the original purposes of the franchise was to make it possible to insure everything at the same rate. Since some goods, like fruits and cheeses, are much more perishable than other goods, like coffee beans or pepper, one would want to have different franchises for these different types of goods. These franchises were listed in a memorandum clause. A typical American one lists about fifty different commodities. On some commodities policyholders will be able to recover nothing except general average losses; on others they can recover nothing unless the loss exceeds 20 percent, and so forth (Winter 1952:210–13). Insurers commonly insert clauses modifying the provisions made in the memorandum clause to take account of policyholder practices, or to fix the franchise on goods not listed in the clause.

Though modern underwriters are not so concerned about having a uniform rate for all insured goods, they still use franchise clauses. When goods are extremely perishable, it makes little sense for this risk to be borne by the underwriter rather than by the owner. Risks that are small or easily anticipated should instead be made part of the owner's regular budget. But in addition, underwriters do not want to encourage shoddy packaging or the shipping of defective goods. It is quite common, then, for an underwriter to refuse to give any particular average coverage or to insist on a large franchise when he or she knows that skins have not been properly cured, that cotton is not properly baled, that sugar or cement is not packed in plastic-lined sacks, or whatever. If policyholders are unsatisfied with this arrangement, then they can make sure that goods are properly packaged and in good condition.

We must still explain why insurers would choose to use franchise clauses, which are relatively clumsy, rather than just alter rates. Perhaps policyholders are more sensitive to having to bear part of the loss than to having to pay a higher rate. It is easier to pass a higher rate on to a consumer, and easier to calculate with this sort of constant than to know what to do about the remaining uncertainty introduced by the franchise clauses. The extra trouble may provide a better incentive than the higher rate.

Though franchises are used in both hull and cargo insurance, deductibles are used only in hull policies. A deductible clause provides that in the case of a partial loss due to a covered peril, the policyholder can only make a claim if the loss exceeds a specified amount and then can claim only the *excess* over the specified amount. The policyholder participates in all losses.

Once the voyage is underway, cargo owners have no control over their goods, although the shipowner still retains some indirect control. This suggests that there might be some point in forcing a shipowner to participate in the losses (even when they are greater than the franchise), although there would be little point in forcing the cargo owner to participate in losses. Losses that are larger than the franchise amount are presumably not matters that a cargo owner can control by packaging or processing of goods; instead, they are accidents. Such accidents may be under the control of the captain and crew, if anyone, but certainly they are not under the control of the cargo owner. This difference in arrangement for the cargo owner and the shipowner suggests that the main point of the deductible is to provide an additional incentive for loss prevention.

Though these rules about express warranties, implied warranties, and franchises are all intended to make policyholder behavior more predictable and to reduce marine losses, they have slightly different functions and should be seen as a sort of three-pronged attack on morale hazard. Express warranties are conditions of the contract, some of which are significantly related to the amount of risk, others of which probably are not. The chief advantage of such warranties is that they fix the conditions so that all parties will know exactly what the rules are.[9] If one knows for sure that the vessel will not be sailing in the Arctic during the winter, one can design the other rules with this limitation in mind. This is presumably especially important to the classification societies, which set many of the standards policyholders are required to meet.

If express warranties are intended to standardize the risks as much as possible, implied warranties are intended to recognize the variability of marine situations and to force policyholders and their agents to adjust their behavior accordingly. While there is some consensus about minimum standards of seaworthiness, insurers and shipowners also agree that most of the standards cannot be made specific but must be modified with the characteristics of the vessel and of the venture, and with changes in the standard practices of the seafaring trade. This means that insurers can expect shipowners to adjust their standards upward as new techniques are developed, and up-to-date loss-prevention activity is thus a prerequisite for the validity of marine insurance contracts. Because insurers know what standard practices are at any given time, the requirement that a ship be seaworthy makes it easier for the insurer to predict losses.

Finally, franchises and deductibles force the policyholders to share the burden of the accidents. When it is not possible to list all of the actions that must be avoided because they will lead to losses, or alternatively to specify the procedures that will eliminate accidents, then one must motivate policyholders and their agents to use good judgment. Forcing them to share losses is one way to do that. This practice also makes losses more predictable since the incentives of policyholders do not change with insurance coverage.

Such an explanation of the ways that marine insurers encourage loss-prevention activities is somewhat unsatisfying, though, given that we know that different techniques are used in other lines of insurance. For example, in fire insurance, policyholders are given discounts for installing sprinklers or for constructing their buildings in particular ways. Why do fire insurers use a system of discounts while marine insurers use express and implied warranties and franchises and deductibles? In the first place, fire insurers do use the equivalent

---

9. A second advantage of express warranties is that they tend to limit the disputes about violations. Since policyholders are required to follow the letter rather than just the spirit of the agreement, there is little point in arguing about whether the violation actually increased risk.

of express and implied warranties. But instead of the insurer requiring that the policyholder meet a particular set of standards, the city makes this requirement. Buildings are required to conform to the city construction and fire codes, and this is a condition for the validity of the contract. In the second place, deductibles are commonly used in fire insurance as well as in marine insurance. It is true, though, that little use is made of franchises in fire insurance. Presumably, this is partly because one does not need to provide the sort of differentiated incentive that is necessary when someone else has partial control over the goods.

But the big difference between marine and fire insurance has to do with giving deductions for installing loss-prevention equipment or developing special procedures to prevent or reduce losses. Marine insurers do not usually give such deductions. In fact, marine insurers have rejected classification society suggestions that incentives be offered to encourage policyholders to meet higher standards. When Det norske Veritas, the Norwegian classification society, developed the special F-class, a set of standards designed to decrease fire losses on ships, it tried to convince the insurers to cut premiums of policyholders who met this new, higher standard. The insurers refused. In refusing to offer such a discount, insurers argued that if these innovations really did decrease fire losses, then the improved loss experiences of those who adopted the innovations would result in decreases in their premiums in the long run.[10]

Experience with supertankers tends to vindicate insurers' conservatism. Designed with all the newest safety equipment, they have nevertheless experienced high losses. Sometimes the causes have been obvious. Because the bridge is so far from the water, supertankers sometimes run down trawlers without ever realizing what has happened (Mostert 1974: 32). Because there are only two good training centers, it is difficult to get competent captains (Mostert 1974: 28). Because of the automated equipment, crews are less vigilant and less adept at predicting and diagnosing difficulties (Mostert 1974: 171). But in many cases the causes of problems have been less clear. Some tankers are designed with only one boiler. When this boiler breaks down the ship cannot be steered since all the equipment is electronic and auxiliary generating systems do not provide suffi-

10. This case is discussed in Barlaup (1976: 121–28) and Heimer (1980: 62–68).

cient power (Mostert 1974:166). Despite extensive tests during de-
velopmental and pre-launch phases, no one anticipated that supertankers would sometimes crack or that they would have explosions in
their tanks during cleaning operations (Mostert 1974:78–82, 130–
35). Only after several years of trial-and-error adjustments and heavy
investment in research did people figure out how to avoid tank
explosions.

These experiences suggest that insurers have a right to be suspicious when owners assert that losses will be lower because of innovation. Innovations may have unanticipated side effects, and it is difficult to predict the net effect of changes in the behavior of the
captain and crew adjusting to new equipment. Insurance losses are
difficult to predict in such circumstances.

The most obvious explanation for this difference between fire and
marine insurance is the difference in their rating methods. While fire
insurers use schedule rates that look at the different characteristics of
potential policyholders, marine insurers base their rates on the overall experience of the policyholders. This is because although fires
occur quite infrequently, marine losses occur relatively often. This
means that successful loss prevention, the real goal, can be rewarded
in marine insurance, while in fire insurance it cannot.

Attenuation of Control and
the Insurability of Reactive Risks

Only losses from accidental events are insurable. One cannot buy insurance to cover losses that one can prevent. Though insurers are backing off from this stance somewhat, it is this argument
that has inhibited the development of divorce insurance and other
forms of coverage that would compensate for losses over which the
policyholders or their beneficiaries have control. It is also for this
reason that life insurance companies do not cover policyholder suicides, or cover only suicides that occur two or more years after the
insurance policy was purchased, and will not pay benefits to beneficiaries who murder the policyholders.

But although it is clear that insurers will want to ban insurance of
losses due to events over which the policyholder (or the beneficiary
when they are different) has direct and complete control, and that
they will be happy to provide coverage for losses over which the

policyholder (or beneficiary) has no control whatsoever, many events do not fall into either of these categories. No single rule will cover all of the cases in this gray area between perfect control and no control. The policyholder may lack control for a variety of reasons, and the reason for lack of control has important implications for insurability. In deciding whether policyholders should be able to recover losses that result from actions that fall in this gray area, insurers will want to give coverage without decreasing the incentive for the policy-holder to keep losses low by exerting as much control as possible.

In marine insurance, such questions of control are raised in discussions about whether it is appropriate to give insurance coverage for barratry (in which the captain intentionally commits an act that causes a loss), negligence, theft and pilferage, and so on, and whether the rules about such coverage should be the same in cargo policies and hull policies. In this section, I will outline the rules about insurance coverage of these cases and will try to show how these various rules are consistent with the principle that only truly accidental losses are insurable. We will see, for example, that insurers recognize Williamson's (1975) principle that control is greater in organizational than market relations, and vary coverage appropriately.

One of the chief distinctions between marine insurance and other sorts of insurance is that marine property owners have very little opportunity to keep watch over their property. But while property owners who are physically separated from their property have less ability to protect their interests than those who are physically near to their property, they are not entirely helpless. After all, the shipowners appoint the ship captains and have the power to prosecute or fire them. And, even if owners do not appoint the rest of the crew, they still exercise indirect control over their activities since it is possible to instruct the captain to dismiss a particularly bad crew member or to give the captain very specific instructions about criteria to be used in the selection of crew members.

In these cases, then, it is clear both that shipowners have less control over the actions of the captain and crew than over their own acts, and that owners still have considerable, though indirect, control. This means that it would be unfair to deny insurance coverage completely when acts of the captain and crew either cause or contribute to losses, but also that it would probably not be wise to give complete coverage since this would discourage owners from carefully supervising and selecting the captain and crew. We might, therefore, predict that insurers would adopt a sort of intermediate strategy of being more willing to give insurance coverage as the owners' control decreased by becoming more indirect. This would not necessarily mean that insurance to cover the acts of the captain would be prohibited, but instead that shipowners would have to make special arrangements to purchase such coverage, while coverage of the actions of the crew might be provided more or less automatically.

Cargo owners are in the same situation as shipowners, except that another step is added to the chain of control (when the cargo owner and the shipowner are different), and this extra step is across an organizational boundary. While cargo owners may be able to exert considerable pressure on shipowners, they cannot order shipowners to do anything, and they also cannot assume that shipowners will automatically transmit their wishes on down the line to the captain and crew. Insurers should adjust their rules on insurance coverage to take account of the facts that cargo owners' control is even more indirect than shipowners' and that the extra step is a qualitatively different one, since it is across an organizational boundary. We might predict, then, that cargo policies would automatically cover some sorts of events that hull policies would not, since such coverage would have little effect on the cargo owner's attempts to control the behavior of the shipowner, captain, and crew.

Not all actions are deliberate; some are unintentional. This is a second way that the policyholder's control can be attenuated. In this case it is less clear that one can motivate people to prevent losses by prohibiting insurance coverage. There is a sense in which unintentional acts are accidents. While it is certainly true that people have some control over their unintentional actions, insurers have usually been willing to provide insurance coverage for unintentional actions, in some cases even the inadvertent actions of the policyholder.

Another way to say this is that the problem of moral hazard (in agents or employees of the policyholder) is treated differently than the problem of morale hazard. Presumably this is partly because insurers believe that morale hazard can be controlled in other ways. One can safely give coverage for carelessness if one eliminates major opportunities for careless acts by requiring regular inspections by a classification society and by requiring the crew to follow specified procedures and to obey the instructions of the master. Perhaps this is one reason why the organizational system of the ship is so hierarchical.

When marine insurers prohibit·insurance coverage for willful acts, though, they have in mind a very strict interpretation of this phrase. The person must have intended not only the act but also its consequences (Wilmot 1975:8/11). The problem is that an action does not always lead to a particular kind of loss but often only increases its likelihood. The person has not exactly intended a particular consequence to occur, but is aware that the likelihood of the consequence is increased. In such cases, we would neither describe the person as having willfully caused the loss, nor would we say that the person had simply been negligent; instead we would describe the action as reckless or grossly negligent. It is hard to discriminate between such cases empirically, of course, since we are mainly talking about states of mind. Wilmot argues that "since the person's state of mind is difficult to establish, the degree of likelihood of a loss following from a particular act will often be used as an indication of the degree of intention to cause loss on the part of the person acting" (1975:8/12).

But neither recklessness nor gross negligence is a category in English (and therefore international) marine law. This problem is to some degree taken care of by rules about the burden of proof. While in English cases insurers are sometimes required to prove willful misconduct in order to avoid paying compensation, it is up to the policyholder to demonstrate that the loss could very likely have been due to an accidental event. The worst cases of recklessness or gross negligence will then end up being treated as cases of willful misconduct since the policyholder will be unable to prove that no one actually intended the consequences that flowed from the intentional act.[11]

Thus far I have argued that when considering the question of the degree to which a policyholder controls an event that causes a loss, and therefore whether the policyholder should be able to get insurance coverage for it, insurers take into account two different ways in which control can be attenuated. If the policyholder only indirectly controls an event, either because he or she has delegated responsibility to someone else or because the person who controls the event is in

11. The question of burden of proof in cases of willful misconduct is discussed in Wilmot (1975:8/13).

a different organization, then a loss caused by such an event may be insurable. The less direct the policyholder's control, the more likely that insurers will agree to permit insurance coverage. The second limit on control has to do with the deliberateness of the action itself. Although insurance coverage of losses due to the willful misconduct of the policyholder will always be prohibited, many insurers are willing to provide insurance coverage for some kinds of negligent acts even when committed by the policyholder.

But obviously any loss-causing event can, and must, be described in terms of both of these dimensions. The policyholder's control over an event will be more or less direct at the same time that the person directly responsible for the event will have acted more or less deliberately or inadvertently. The accompanying table shows how we might classify various marine perils as being more or less directly controllable by the policyholder and more or less deliberate. In the remainder of this section each of these cases, and the arguments that insurers advance about whether insurance coverage of losses stemming from such events should be permitted, will be discussed. I will discuss first deliberate and then unintentional acts, showing how insurance coverage of these acts varies with the directness of the policyholder's control over the action.

The rule that policyholders should not be able to recover from losses caused by their own willful acts is quite well established (see Marine Insurance Act [1906], section 55 [2][a]), though justified willful misconduct (for example, sinking a ship to prevent capture by an enemy) would not prevent recovery from the insurance company.

In cases of willful misconduct, the person causing the loss is acting contrary to the wishes of the policyholder. In the case of barratry, the captain, whose actions the owner can only indirectly control, intentionally causes a loss to the owner or intentionally commits an illegal act that causes a loss (Winter 1952:183).

Though barratry is usually listed among the perils covered in both hull and cargo policies, Winter, at least, does not really agree with this practice:

> As the master is the agent of the owner in the management of the vessel, it is quite proper to exclude the risk of barratry of the master in an insurance on the hull. It is rather illogical to insure the owner of the vessel against the wrongful acts of one whom he himself has entrusted with the care of the ship.

(1952:183)

Variations in Control of Loss-Causing Acts

Control by Policyholder	Extent of Direct Control	
	Deliberate (Willful misconduct)	*Unintentional*
Direct a) shipowner b) cargo owner	insurance fraud	failure to exercise due diligence (recovery permitted only if negligence is not proximate cause)
Indirect, one step shipowner/captain	barratry by captain (hull insurance)	ordinary negligence (recovery permitted unless owner has failed to exercise due diligence)
Indirect, two steps a) shipowner/captain/crew b) cargo owner/shipowner/captain*	a) barratry by crew (hull insurance), pilferage (hull insurance) b) barratry (cargo insurance)	ordinary negligence (recovery permitted unless owner has failed to exercise due diligence)
Indirect, three steps cargo owner/shipowner/captain/crew*	pilferage (cargo insurance)	ordinary negligence (recovery permitted unless owner has failed to exercise due diligence)
No control	pirates, rovers, thieves, belligerent acts of hostile governments	accidents

*Note that one of these steps is across an organizational boundary.

The strength of Winter's conviction on this matter is evidenced by the fact that he gives two lengthy discussions of barratry (1952:177, 183–84); in each instance he implies that insurance coverage of barratry is exceptional, before he finally confesses that "as a matter of practice it is usual to insure the hull owner against the risk of barratry" (1952:184). Though one could argue that there is little to be accomplished by providing an incentive for owners to do what they have already done (giving the captain a different set of instructions), and though one would expect a shipowner to fire a barratrous captain whether or not the insurer covered the loss, presumably a shipowner would choose and supervise the captain more carefully if barratry were not covered.

That Winter is specifically concerned with the directness of the policyholder's control over the person committing the barratrous act is clear from the fact that he endorses insurance coverage of the barratrous acts of the rest of the crew: "With respect to the mariners, the case is different in that these men are not directly chosen by the owner but rather by the master" (1952:183–84). Similarly, Winter considers it perfectly sensible to insure the cargo owner against the risk of barratry since one "who has no voice in the selection of the master or crew should have protection against their wrongful acts" (1952:184).

Rules about pilferage, theft, and similar acts provide another illustration of the principle that the insurability of an act varies with the directness of the policyholder's control over it. Insurance policies have always included coverage for losses due to thieves, pirates, rovers, or the hostile actions of other governments. Such acts, though deliberate, are clearly not under the control of the policyholder. Pilferage, in contrast, is more susceptible to control by the policyholder and is therefore not included in the original list of covered perils.[12]

In marine insurance, the peril of "thieves" (sometimes referred to as "assailing thieves") means the taking of property by force, while "pilferage" means the taking of property by stealth. Pilferage was not commonly insurable because the loss was the result of the criminal actions of regular crew members, passengers, or stevedores who had a right to be with the property. Insurers were worried that if they

12. Winter (1952:175) and Wilmot (1975:6/39) reproduce the list of perils popularized by Lloyds in the 1700s and still in use today.

permitted shipowners to purchase insurance protection against pilferage, they would be encouraging greater laxity in the selection and supervision of employees and would discourage the shipowner from ferreting out the culprits and punishing them.

Although the cargo owner has considerably less control over the actions of pilferers, much petty theft can be avoided if the merchant packs the goods properly when preparing them for shipment. One would expect containerized shipping to decrease the theft rate. And of course the cargo owners do have some indirect control because they can threaten to stop shipping goods with a particular shipping line if the shipowner does not do something about pilferage problems.

Despite the arguments against such coverage, pilferage is now commonly included in the list of perils covered by marine policies. Apparently coverage of pilferage was granted largely because of economic pressures. Merchants were eager to have this coverage, partly because suits against the shipowners were rarely resolved quickly, and once one insurer provided such insurance the others could hardly refuse.

Winter claims that the results of giving this coverage have been disastrous. Insurers have had little success in recovering from shipowners who, in theory at least, are responsible for the losses. And when pilferage insurance can be bought cheaply, merchants need not spend so much on packaging and are inclined to ship their goods in inferior packages.[13] Winter (1952) makes it sound as if commercial relations will deteriorate seriously because of this decline in standards, but no doubt he exaggerates a bit. Though the incentive to control loss may decrease with insurance coverage, one would expect that pressure from customers and rising insurance costs would check the merchant's tendency toward shoddy packaging.

When negligence contributes to a loss, negligence or some other peril might be the proximate cause. Under the Marine Insurance Act of 1906, the insurer was liable "for any loss proximately caused by a peril insured against, even though the loss would not have happened but for the misconduct and negligence of the master or crew" (section 55 [2][a]). If, for example, a ship was stranded and this stranding was the result of negligent navigation by the master, the shipowner could still recover the damages because the last peril before

13. Pilferage is discussed in Winter (1952:87, 123, 184-85).

the loss was the stranding, a covered peril, not the negligence of the master.

But there are many cases in which the negligence itself is the proximate cause of the loss. If, for example, the captain miscalculated the damage to a vessel and decided to abandon ship and also decided to set fire to the ship so that it would not become a danger to other ships, the captain's actions would be the proximate cause of loss.[14] Up until 1887, the owner would not have been able to recover for this sort of loss. The reason for prohibiting recovery was simply that negligence was not one of the perils insured against, and the insurance policies were not all-risk policies.

In 1887 the House of Lords decided in the Inchamaree case that negligence was not covered if it did not operate through the agency of another insured peril. Once this question was settled, insurers drafted the Inchamaree clause to extend coverage to include loss or damage directly caused by the negligence of the master, officers, crew, or pilots.[15] But there is a catch here. Such negligence is covered provided that it has not resulted from lack of due diligence by the policyholder, the owner, or the manager of the ship. Their negligence is *not* a peril covered by the insurer. In addition, the insurer will not compensate losses caused indirectly by the negligence of the policyholder if the only peril through which this negligence operates is the negligence of the captain or the crew.

Thus, insurers' policies on recovery for losses depend on whether the policyholder had any control over the loss, whether it was truly accidental from the point of view of the policyholder. When policyholders directly and intentionally cause losses, they are not permitted to recover. But there are many losses over which policyholders have some, though not complete, control. We have argued that in deciding whether to permit recovery in such cases, the insurers will try to motivate the policyholders to exercise whatever control they do have. This means that they will tend to permit recovery when there is evidence that policyholders have done whatever they could have done and will deny compensation in the other cases.

In those ambiguous cases in which the losses are not entirely acci-

14. This is the case of Lind v. Mitchell (1928) 32 *Lloyds Legal Reporter* 70 (C.A.).
15. A brief account of the history of the Inchamaree clause can be found in Winter (1952:271–72).

dental, policyholder control depends on two things: the directness of the contact between the policyholder and the person responsible for the loss-causing event, and the intentional or unintentional nature of this event. The more indirect the control of the policyholder over the potential loss-causer, the more likely it is that the policyholder will be able to recover for the loss. There is little point in trying to encourage policyholders to control the actions of those very distant from them. In marine insurance this problem of indirect control is exacerbated by the fact that the vessel and cargo are often physically separated from their owners. Not only is there social distance (levels of hierarchy and organizational boundaries) between owners and those working with the property, but there is also physical distance (miles of sea). In addition, the more unintentional an act, the more likely it is that the policyholder will be able to recover for the loss. Policyholders can never recover for losses that they themselves have deliberately caused, but since insurers distinguish between negligence that works through other perils and negligence that directly causes losses, policyholders are sometimes permitted to recover when they themselves have been negligent. And while insurers sometimes distinguish between captain and crew when discussing intentional acts, they do not make such distinctions when discussing unintentional acts. That is, more levels of indirectness are relevant for deliberate acts than for unintentional acts.

But while we can give a good account of why insurers would deny coverage in some of these cases but permit recovery in others, and while we can use the principles outlined above to predict when coverage will be permitted and when it will be denied, this should not lead us to believe that there is no other way to accomplish the same result. If the point is to motivate policyholders to do whatever they can to keep losses down, then one can do this either by denying coverage in certain situations or by asking policyholders to prove that they really did all that was possible. That is, if one wishes to encourage policyholders to control pilferage by employees, one might deny insurance coverage for pilferage, or, alternatively, one might compensate policyholders only if they could prove that they had done whatever was possible. One might, for example, investigate to see that the policyholder really was ignorant of the existence of a ring of thieves among the crew, or one might grant insurance coverage if the policyholder had designed appropriate systems of procedures to guard against dishonest or careless acts of employees.[16] If the ship-owner conducted detailed interviews with the captain, required personnel reports about other crew members, had strict rules about firing careless or dishonest crew members, had rules specifying safety procedures, and so on, the insurer might be quite happy to grant pilferage coverage without any additional fee. The point is that one really has three options: (1) to encourage policyholders to do whatever possible to prevent losses by excluding coverage of losses that are partly controllable; (2) to check to see that particular losses really were accidental (in the sense of not being controllable by the policyholder); or (3) to check to see that in general such losses could be assumed to be accidental since the policyholder had followed appropriate procedures. Marine insurers use the first two of these methods, using the third only in inverted form (the contract is void if the policyholder violates express or implied warranties). In addition, marine insurers are often willing to cast some of their principles aside and give insurance coverage even when the policyholder has some control over the loss if the policyholder will pay some extra premium.

Reducing Losses at Sea:
The Sue-and-Labor Clause,
General Average, and Marine Salvage

Because policyholders are often separated from their property and are therefore unable to destroy the property even when it would be advantageous to do so, incentives to cause loss are less important in marine insurance than in other lines of property insurance. But this lack of control has negative implications as well as the positive ones to be discussed in the section on valuation later in this chapter. In particular, a policyholder who is unable to cause losses will also lack the resources to prevent or reduce them.

Because of this combination of lack of control by those motivated to reduce losses (the owner or the insurer) and lack of motivation to reduce loss by those who have some control over the ship and cargo (the captain, the crew, and whoever else might be on the scene when the

16. In fidelity bonding, compensation is denied if the insurer can show that the policyholder was aware of previous indiscretions of the perpetrator.

vessel is in distress), special rules have been developed in marine insurance and in maritime law to encourage loss-prevention efforts. Those who physically control the property must be motivated to reduce losses, and maritime law arranges incentives to reduce losses by specifying the rights and duties of the various parties. In general, owners have a duty to try to reduce losses and a right to be repaid for loss-prevention efforts. Insurers have an obligation to compensate policyholders for loss-prevention efforts and also to repay the policyholder's share of rewards given to people who salve property. Salvors have a right to a generous reward. In marine insurance these various rules are discussed under the headings of sue-and-labor clauses, general average agreements, and marine salvage.

The sue-and-labor clause

The sue-and-labor clause is intended to make sure that policyholders will do whatever is in their power to reduce losses. The idea is that though the insurance company has agreed to compensate losses, policyholders should not simply abandon the ship whenever there is a slight danger but instead should behave as if they would lose something if the ship were destroyed.

Because the insurer usually cannot communicate with policyholders or captains to give instructions at the time of an accident, the insurer must specifically charge policyholders and their agents with the duty of protecting the property.

The sue-and-labor clause, then, specifies the obligation of property owners to behave as they would if uninsured and of the insurer to repay property holders for the expenditures entailed in protecting the property. Note, though, that this agreement is not simply a restatement of the common law duty of a policyholder to exercise due diligence. Instead it is an affirmative agreement that the policyholder will do whatever possible to save imperiled property. Through this clause the duty implied by the law is converted into an express obligation.

Included in most insurance policies just after the listing of the covered perils, the sue-and-labor clause reads as follows:

And in case of any Loss or Misfortune, it shall be lawful and necessary for the Assured, their Factors, Servants and Assigns, to sue, labor and travel for, in, and about the Defense, Safeguard and Recovery of the said Vessel, &c., or any part thereof, without prejudice to this Insurance, to the Charges whereof the Underwriters will contribute their proportion as provided below.[17]

The recovery permissible under the sue-and-labor clause is over and above recovery for the damages actually sustained to the goods or hull (Maritime Insurance Act, 78 [I]). Even if the property is a total loss and the policyholder claims for the entire face value of the policy, the extra expenses of trying to prevent the loss can still be recovered. There is no requirement that the saving acts be successful in this case. Note the difference between salvage awards and sue-and-labor clauses here. Since salvage awards are theoretically paid out of the value of the salved goods, salvors do not get an award unless they are successful in salving part of the property.

According to Marshall (1965:276), one of the main purposes of the sue-and-labor clause these days has to do with the subrogation of the insurer to the rights of policyholders. Quite often when losses occur policyholders will be able to sue other parties to recover some or all of the loss (this is especially true, for example, in cases where cargo losses are partly due to the actions of shipowners or their agents). But in marine law, the policyholder is the one who must bring the suit. The insurer cannot bring the suit unless it is initiated by the policyholder. For this reason insurers often require that policyholders agree to initiate the relevant suits if they are to recover from the insurer.

Despite the clear wording of the sue-and-labor clause, there is some dispute about the obligation of the captain and the crew, as agents of the insured, to prevent losses. According to an earlier section of the Marine Insurance Act, the insurer should repay the policyholder even if a loss would not have occurred but for the negligence of captain and crew. The Inchamaree clause further strengthens this position, stating that the policyholder may even recover for willful acts of the captain and crew. But the Marine Insurance Act section on suing and laboring states that policyholders and their agents have the duty to minimize loss. The question, then, is whether the insurer can

17. There are slight variations in wording depending on what sort of policy it is. This particular version is in the December 1951 Syndicate Hull Form, which is reprinted in Winter (1952:455–62).

deny coverage when the captain and crew have not done everything possible to reduce losses. Though Wilmot (1975: 12/2–12/6) discusses this question in great detail, the English cases on the subject (for example, British and Foreign Marine Ins. Co. v. Gaunt [1921] 2 A.C. 41, and "Gold Sky" [1972] 2 *Lloyd's Reporter* 187) suggest that there is no consensus on this at present.

The sue-and-labor clause is intended to encourage the policyholder to prevent or minimize losses even though these losses will ultimately be borne by the insurer. Such clauses contain both a carrot and a stick. The carrot in this case is the promise to compensate the policyholder not only for losses to property but also for the expenses of trying to reduce damage even if these efforts are unsuccessful. The stick is the threat that if the policyholders do not try to minimize losses, and do not encourage their agents to do so too, they will be denied compensation for the losses that are sustained. By making the insurance coverage contingent on policyholders continuing to behave as if they had something to lose, the sue-and-labor clause helps curb the reactivity of risk in marine insurance.

General average

When in order to save the venture as a whole, a portion of either the ship or the cargo must be sacrificed, these losses are called general average losses, and, in marine law, all parties are required to pay their shares of such losses. The general idea is that "that which has been destroyed for all shall be replaced by the contributions of all" (Winter 1952: 205).

The idea of the general average rule is to get the captain and crew to engage in a loss-reduction program that will minimize the losses of the group as a whole rather than sacrifice the interests of some to those of others. It forces the captain and crew to consider the interests of cargo owners as well as the interests of the shipowner. Presumably, without this sort of rule, the captain and crew would jettison more cargo than they would with the general average rule, since it would be in the short-run interest of the shipowner (whose agents they are) to save the hull at the expense of the cargo. If the sue-and-labor clause is intended to force the policyholder to act in the interest of the insurer, the general average rules are designed to force the shipowner, the captain, and the crew to consider the interests of the cargo owners who have entrusted their goods to them. Obviously it is in the long-run interest of the shipowner to deal fairly with cargo owners, to protect their cargo even when the ship is in danger. But what the general average clause does is to make sure that shipowners pay for each instance in which they must sacrifice cargo in order to save the venture. At the same time, the agreement that the loss will be borne by all parties allows the captain and crew to act quickly without wasting time debating about who will suffer if some particular item is jettisoned.

The general average rule certainly does not replace the other methods of controlling the behavior of a shipowner and the captain and crew. Shipowners will continue to be motivated by the prospect of losing their regular customers if they acquire a reputation for ignoring their interests. One could argue that the general average rule encourages the spread of information about accidents and the jettisoning of cargo. By making cargo owners share the losses, the general average rule encourages the dissemination of information and motivates cargo owners to band together to look for reliable carriers of their goods.

When general average losses are paid by insurers rather than policyholders, another step is added between the people who actually jettison the cargo to save the ship and the people who suffer the financial loss. Presumably adding this step does decrease the effectiveness of such a system of social control. Now the effectiveness of the rule depends on insurers punishing shipowners whose crew jettison more cargo than necessary, and on insurers punishing cargo owners who continue to make contracts with such shippers. Winter (1952:95–96), at least, believes that general average rules continue to be effective despite this change.

Probably the main reason that the general average rules continue to be used is not that they have such an important impact on the incentives of the policyholders (in particular, the shipowners) but instead that they are woven into the fabric of marine insurance law, since general average rules existed long before the laws themselves were codified. One would have to substantially rework both the law and the basic concepts in order to eliminate all uses of the concept of general average.

Though sue-and-labor clauses and general average rules are both intended to encourage loss-reduction efforts, sue-and-labor clauses encourage policyholders to protect their own property while general average rules are intended to encourage actors to be concerned with common rather than individual welfare.

Marine salvage

Marine salvage is the saving of ships or cargo from the perils of the sea. Both the act of saving (or "salving") the ship and goods and the reward paid to those who have done the saving are called salvage. The salvage award is paid as a general average expense—that is, all parties involved in the venture are required to contribute and are able to recover their contributions from their insurers—since salvors are supposed to try to save the entire venture rather than try to save only the hull or to recover only the cargo of a single owner.

The point of the salvage rules is to encourage people to assist vessels in distress (Sutton 1949:4). The specific arrangements about how large the award should be, how it should be divided among the salvors, and so forth, all reflect this interest in encouraging assistance from whoever might be in the vicinity when a vessel is having trouble. In this case the problem is not to motivate policyholders or their agents—they are already obligated to try to save the vessel and cargo and are, therefore, not eligible for salvage awards—but instead to force policyholders and insurers to act in concert to motivate third parties.

The first requirement is that the salvage award must be substantial. If the idea is to encourage the undertaking of dangerous rescue operations, the award should provide an incentive to potential salvors rather than remunerate them exactly for services rendered. Traditionally, salvors received half of the salved value. Now, however, since the value of ships has increased so much, salvage awards are rarely more than 20 percent of the salved value.

If the purpose of the salvage award is to provide an incentive to rescue ships and cargo in danger, then presumably in dividing the awards among the various salvors one will want to give the largest rewards to those who have the most control over salvage operations. Awards used to be given only to the captain and crew of the salving vessel on the grounds that if one wanted to encourage the giving of assistance, one had to offer incentives to those who were actually out there. More recently, the trend has been to give a greater proportion of the award to the owner of the saving ship, since the success of the rescue operation is increasingly (since the invention of the steam-powered ship) due to the power of the ship rather than to the skill or bravery of the captain and crew.

Awards to the captain and crew are generally based on rank, with higher ranking personnel receiving larger awards. There are two reasons that awards should be related to rank. The first is a straightforward economic one—if one wants to offer an incentive, the size of the award must vary with the salary of the person receiving it. In addition, though, one might want to give larger awards to higher ranking personnel because they control the activities of those of lower rank. If the captain cannot be convinced to engage in salvage operations, then it will do little good to have a crew ready and willing to rescue a sinking ship.

But there must also be incentives for a captain to *accept* assistance when it is needed. Mostert (1974:154) notes that captains of supertankers sometimes turn away salvage tugs who offer assistance in the early stages of a crisis. Because the services of salvors are expensive and must be borne entirely by the shipping company (rather than by the insurer) if an accident is averted, captains will be inclined to refuse assistance until an accident is inevitable.

Once the ship or cargo has been saved, it is no longer in the interest of the parties involved to offer general incentives for salvors. A general willingness to go to the rescue of ships in trouble is a public good (Olson 1971), and it is always difficult to get people to contribute their share of the expenses of such a good. Recognizing this conflict of interest between those whose property has just been salved and the shipping community as a whole, marine law provides that the amount of salvage award will be determined by the courts or arbitrators rather than by those who must pay. In this way, the owners of the salved property are required to provide the public good, the incentive, whether they wish to or not.

Because insurers cover many different ships and are therefore likely to need the services of salvors more than once, their interests should be somewhat closer to those of the shipping community as a whole, and they should therefore be quite willing to provide this public good. This situation is somewhat similar to the role of fire insurance companies in subsidizing early fire fighting groups and their current offers of rewards to those who can provide information about arsons. In other lines of insurance, loss-prevention efforts are often encouraged by giving discounts to those who install appropriate equipment, devise training programs for their employees, and so forth. But in marine insurance such incentive systems are not likely to be very effective since policyholders have little direct control over the property. This means that incentives have to be offered to those who are with the property at the time of a disaster. One way to do that is to offer to reward these people if they save the ship and cargo—this is the purpose of salvage awards. Alternatively, one can refuse coverage to shipowners who fail to motivate their captains and crews to try to reduce losses—this is the purpose of the sue-and-labor clause—and make all parties share sacrifices necessary to save the bulk of the ship and cargo—this is the intent of the general average rule. In any case, the insurer must encourage those who have control to "take the role of the other" (in this case, the insurer), and the most effective incentive seems to be to make their outcomes contingent on their actions. We saw a similar tailoring of incentives to control in the distinction between franchises and deductibles. Franchises are intended to motivate care during the packing phase when *cargo owners* have control, while deductibles are intended to motivate care during the shipping phase.

Indemnity Contracts
and the Problem of Valuation

The purpose of an insurance contract is to indemnify policyholders for a loss of the kind covered by the policy. Ideally, this should be an exact compensation so that policyholders receive neither more nor less than they have lost. Insurers are especially concerned that policyholders not receive *more* than they have lost since this would introduce an incentive to destroy property. And as Wilmot (1975:14/1) comments, "This sounds splendid until one starts to think about it."

Both the ideal and the method for achieving it are unclear. If the purpose of the insurance contract is to restore policyholders to their position before the loss occurred, insurers could take this to mean that policyholders should be in the same position as if the fateful voyage had never commenced or, alternatively, that they should be in the same position as if the trip had been completed successfully. A second ambiguity is whether compensation should be based on the objective value of the lost property or whether subjective value should be considered as well. Compensation based on subjective value would presumably include not just the market value of the ship (or what the owner originally paid for it plus improvements less depreciation), but also some additional compensation for less tangible losses. Shipowners have presumably also invested the time and expense necessary to select and purchase ships, to outfit them for their special purposes, to build up business connections, and so on.

But even when everyone agrees about exactly what theoretical value is supposed to be compensated, there is still likely to be disagreement about whether a given method is the best way to calculate this value. Rather than resolving the question of how to give "perfect indemnity" (which is what insurers call the theoretically appropriate amount of compensation), insurers have accepted that this is an unattainable ideal and have, instead, devoted themselves to devising practical methods for computing approximate measures of indemnity.[18] The rules of marine insurance thus specify a series of conventional measures of indemnity that are substituted for the theoretically perfect value.

In setting the measure of indemnity, two methods are commonly used. One method involves establishing the value of the property beforehand, at the time the contract is made. The policy is then for a specified amount, which is written into the contract, and this sort of policy is called a "valued policy." The second method involves leaving the calculation of the compensation until after a loss has occurred. What is agreed beforehand in this case is the "basis of valuation," the method for calculating the amount of the loss, including what items will be included in the calculations, what measures of value will be used, and so on. While it is usual to specify a particular sum in policies covering hulls or single shipments of cargo, in open cargo policies covering many shipments it is more common to specify a basis of valuation. In either case the value is *fixed*; the difference is only that in some policies this fixed value has not yet been calculated.

18. When insurers discuss the actual compensation rather than the theoretically appropriate compensation, they refer to this as the "measure of indemnity." See chapter 2, pp. 45–46, for a discussion of the measure of recovery, a related concept.

In "unvalued" or "nonvalued" policies, which are relatively rare
in marine insurance (except in carriers' liability insurance), the value
of the insured property is left to be determined when a loss occurs. In
such cases, the insured value is neither frozen in an amount written
into the policy nor fixed in a calculating formula, but instead is permitted to fluctuate with market conditions and with changes in the
condition of the property itself.

In most forms of property insurance, the amount for which a policy is written (the "value" of the policy) is the limit for which the
insurer will be liable in the case of a loss. But while the upper limit is
fixed, the amount for which the insurer will actually be liable in the
case of a total loss is determined only at the time the loss occurs, and
is based on the value of the property at that time and place.[19] In marine insurance, in contrast, the rule has always been that the value
paid in cases of total loss is fixed at the inception of the policy. Presumably this is partly because of the difficulties entailed in estimating the value of the cargo after it has sunk in the middle of the ocean
or of the ship after it has been wrecked off the coast of Tasmania. It is
simply impractical to calculate the value of the property at the time it
is lost. Shipowners and merchants also need to have fixed values for
their property in order to make decisions and engage in normal business activities. If one has taken a business loan to purchase cotton
cloth, the banker will not be especially pleased with the story that not
only has the ship sunk but in addition that the insurer is only willing
to pay a small compensation since the bottom fell out of the market
just before the boat sank. For partial losses the measure of indemnity
must be determined at the time the loss occurs, because that value
can be calculated by agreed methods after the fact.

Valuation is an important issue in the study of reactive risk because this is a point at which incentives either to protect or to destroy
the property are introduced into the contract. In theory, the marine
policy is an indemnity contract and will therefore have no effect
whatsoever on the incentives of the beneficiaries. But since the attempt to provide perfect indemnity has been sacrificed to the practical problems of settling compensation claims speedily and econom-

19. There are exceptions to this rule. In "valued-policy" states in the U.S., a fire
insurer is required by law to pay the policyholder the value stated in the insurance
contract when a piece of property is entirely destroyed by fire. See the section on face
values in chapter 3.

ically, it is no longer obvious that the measure of indemnity and the actual value of the property will match sufficiently well so as to encourage policyholders to protect their property.

In the following three subsections, then, I will try to point out the characteristic failings of the systems of valuation used in marine insurance and to assess their combined effect on the motivational system of the policyholder. The question really is whether the general policy that policyholders should never recover more than they have lost is negated by the concrete methods used in calculating losses.

Since the method for valuation and the effects of incorrect valuation are different for cargo, hull, and freight insurance, I will discuss the three separately. It should be kept in mind, though, that the person who owns the hull may well have a freight or cargo interest as well, and that the effects of over- or undervaluation of each separate interest may have to be added together. In addition, sympathetic insurers have devised several kinds of excess policies that make up for deficits in primary insurance coverage. Such policies sometimes provide redundant coverage. While each insurer covering a different sort of interest may be sensitive to the problem of moral hazard and the incentive to destroy property introduced by overvaluation, the combined effect of these various policies may nevertheless be to encourage the destruction of the insured property.

Valuation in cargo insurance

Cargo policies are almost invariably valued policies.[20] But the policies do not always name a specific monetary value, instead stating a *basis* of valuation, such as "valued at invoice cost plus 10 percent plus prepaid or guaranteed freight." The reason for stating a basis for valuation rather than a specific sum is that cargo policies are often "open" or "floating policies" (as opposed to "single-risk policies") covering many different shipments over a long period of time. It would be extremely inconvenient to write a new insuring agreement stating the insured value for each shipment as it is scheduled, and when the basis of valuation is clearly described this serves just as well to fix the insured value and to curtail endless disputes when losses occur.

---

20. This is not the case in Norway, though, as will be discussed below. See Wilmot (1975 : 14/4–14/9).

Two bases of valuation are commonly used, and in each there is some potential for insured value to vary from actual value. The first method sets the value of the cargo at the invoice price plus other specified expenses plus some margin for profit (Marine Insurance Act, section 16[3]; Marshall 1965:273).[21] The disadvantage of this method is that the value of the cargo often increases substantially during a long sea voyage so that merchants are not actually indemnified for their losses. Of course the policyholder can arrange to get excess insurance coverage when (or after) an increase in value occurs. These excess insurance policies also are valued policies and are sometimes, but not always, carried by the original insurer.

If changes in price are common, this procedure is both cumbersome and unnecessary. When there is a well-established market (with published prices) in the commodity in question, a second method of valuation is often used. In such cases the value of the cargo is set at the highest market value that the cargo attains during the voyage or at invoice cost plus expenses plus profit, whichever is higher. Merchants usually prefer to use this method of valuation because the full value of the cargo will automatically be protected and also because the insurer, rather than the merchant, absorbs the effects of market fluctuations. This method of valuation is common in the insurance of coffee, cotton, rubber, sugar, and similar cargos.

The main difficulty, in terms of increasing incentives to destroy cargo, is that insured value will fairly often exceed the actual cash value of the cargo. While insured value is adjusted upward with increases in actual cash value, there is no provision for a decrease in insured value with decreases in actual cash value. The rationale for such an arrangement is that since policyholders will always have invested invoice cost and expenses, there is a sense in which the property will always be worth that much to them regardless of how much the market value of the goods declines.

While this argument has some merit, we must not neglect the effect of the discrepancy between insured value and market value on the policyholder's motivations. As long as actual cash value is greater than or equal to the insured value things are fine. But if market value has been rising but then begins to drop precipitously, and if the poli-

---

21. The invoice is the seller's bill for the goods and also sets forth the terms of the sale.

cyholder receives as compensation the highest market value achieved during the voyage, then it is clear that the policyholder would be better off with the insurance money than with the cargo. Similarly, if policyholders not only will not realize any gains but also stand to lose because the market value has fallen below cost, they might conclude that it would be economically rational to trade the cargo for the insurance money.

But not all discrepancies between insured value and actual cash value arise because of changes in market value. In particular, when insured value is based on some combination of invoice cost, other expenses, and a margin of profit, the insured value may be higher than actual cash value from the very beginning. This could happen either if the insured profit margin were larger than the profit the beneficiary would be likely to make by selling the goods, or, alternatively, if the expenses or profits had already been included in the invoice cost but were covered a second time in the insurance contract.

Presumably the insurability of expenses and of profits should depend on who is the beneficiary of the insurance policy. If the seller of the goods is the beneficiary, then some profit and many of the costs will already be reflected in the invoice cost. An insurer who wishes to avoid overvaluation would then include in the valuation formula only invoice cost and other costs not already incorporated in the invoice. In the case of the buyer, the insurance might cover the invoice cost, nonrecoverable freight paid by the buyer, insurance premiums paid by the buyer, and also a profit margin, since the buyer's profits have not yet been earned. The same effect can be achieved by limiting compensation for extra expenses and giving a generous allowance for profits, or by limiting the profit margin and being generous with extra expenses.

In practice, though, insurers do not seem to worry much about overvaluation of cargos, and little attention is given to the problem by marine insurance writers (see Oxford 1965; Marshall 1965; Dwelly 1965; and Winter 1952). Marine insurance codes do not prohibit overvaluation but only the failure to reveal it (Wilmot 1975:14/18), and no particular bases of valuation are specified in marine insurance laws.[22] The laws do make it clear that the insurer is bound by whatever value (or basis of valuation) is stated in the policy.

---

22. Section 16 of the Marine Insurance Act specifies how to ascertain insurance value, but these guidelines apply only "subject to any express provision or valuation in the policy."

While it is true that such valuation practices will often introduce an incentive for fraud (either through market fluctuations or through inclusion of illegitimate items in the basis of valuation), in fact there is little danger because cargo owners only rarely have control over the vessels carrying their goods and "cannot compass the destruction of (their) property without collusion on the part of those in custody of the property" (Winter 1952:171). Obviously when the shipowner or the charterer of the ship also owns the cargo, and especially when there are substantial variations in the market value of the goods being transported, the insurers should worry considerably more about the incentives introduced by valued policies and should be more cautious about the bases of valuation written into the contracts. Both of these conditions are more common with bulk cargos such as petroleum, oil, grain, and so on.

Valuation in hull insurance

In cargo insurance, the differences in valuation stem from two sources: the problem of adding together without duplication the various values embodied in the cargo, and the problem of finding suitable indicators of these values. Because a current estimate of market value is almost always available and because the time periods over which expenses will be incurred or profits earned are relatively brief, the problems of estimating the values embodied in the cargo are not terribly serious.

The valuation of the hull is considerably more complex than the valuation of cargo because it is not obvious which indicators of value should be used and how to combine the various measures, because the problem of accurately summing current capital value, future income, and extra expenses is more difficult when several parties (such as the mortgagee or the charterer as well as the shipowner) may have insurable interests in the hull, and because expenses and benefits are spread over long periods of time.

As usual, though, the ideal is clear: "The amount should be fixed at the point where the owner will be fully reimbursed in the event of a total loss but will have no inducement to compass the destruction of his vessel in order to procure the insured value" (Winter 1952:265). Winter (1952:265) goes on to suggest that the value can be thought of as the present value of all the net freight (profit) that the vessel would earn during its productive lifetime plus the scrap value at the end. This suggests that in estimating the value of a ship one would want to consider current freight rates, increases or decreases in freight rates with changes in the demand for and supply of tonnage, the age and condition of the vessel, and so on. These factors should be reflected in the market value of the ship; so the current purchase price of similar vessels will ordinarily provide a reasonable estimate of the value of a ship.

But it is easy to see that market value will often not adequately reflect the value of the vessel to the owner. Special features, such as modifications to facilitate loading and unloading from particular docks, which would not be useful to other potential owners, might not show up in estimates of its market value. And compensation based on the market value of the ship would not cover the disruption of the business or the inconvenience of replacing the ship if it were lost. In order to cover these sorts of values, shipowners usually carry "disbursements" or "increased value insurance" in addition to their ordinary hull policies.

Despite the fact that net freight is theoretically included in the valuation of the hull, shipowners are usually permitted to carry freight insurance as well. This is partly because freights include income to cover expenses as well as the profit supposedly reflected in the valuation of the hull itself. There is also a sense in which already existing freight contracts represent an additional value, since as Wilmot (1975:14/3) argues, "It seems clear that one must imagine a sale of the ship free of any existing freight contracts."

In marine insurance, then, separate policies cover the capital value of the ship, some of the future income of the ship, and other special values and expenses. These three types of insurances on the hull must be coordinated so that the policyholder does not make a profit in the event of a loss. The main way this is done is to have a valued policy on the hull and to place strict limits on the amounts of freight insurance and disbursements insurance that the shipowner can carry. In the remainder of this subsection, I will discuss first the valuation of the hull itself, then disbursements insurance. Freight insurance, which may be carried by the shipowner, the charterer, and/ or the owner of the cargo, will be taken up in the next subsection.

In practice, it is not at all clear how vessels are valued. Though the discussions emphasize that insured value should closely approximate market value, there seem to be no special rules for actually determining the value. In negotiating the policy, the shipowner simply states the value of the ship and the insurer customarily accepts this assessment.

While insurers need to worry about unscrupulous shipowners overvaluing their vessels, they must also be wary of discrepancies between insured value and market value that arise through economic fluctuations, and they must watch out for shipowners who are eager to take advantage of these. Winter (1952:265–66) stresses that such changes in the market may occur in relatively short periods of time, with the result that an initially fair value ends up providing a serious temptation. He goes on to argue that underwriters must have up-to-date knowledge of the value of ocean tonnage.

"In a time of commercial stagnation, when there are more ships than there is employment for them, the valued policy, especially the high-valued policy, is a real menace to the underwriters," Winter (1952:171) warns. There is plenty of evidence to justify his conclusion. In the late 1860s, a depression coupled with an archaic evaluation system provided strong motives for Norwegian shipowners to cast away their vessels. Because wooden sailing ships were not classified separately from metal steamships and because values were based on seaworthiness and size, rather than market value, wooden ships were insured for sums far above their market value. When the depression hit, and ships could not find employment, many sailing ships mysteriously disappeared (Færden 1967:143–44).

Similarly, at the end of World War I, when "ocean tonnage values disappeared like mist before the rising sun" (Winter 1952:179), many vessels were cast away. Because there was suddenly excess tonnage, market values dropped dramatically, and the owners of unemployed vessels sank them to collect the insurance, which was based on inflated wartime valuations. Wooden sailing ships, which had been brought back into service during the war, were especially likely to disappear under suspicious circumstances (Winter 1952:293). At the end of World War II, a similar deflation of hull values occurred, but the temptation to cast away vessels was somewhat curbed by the introduction of dual-valuation clauses (discussed below; Winter 1952:266–68).

Though this practice of giving valued policies sometimes creates an incentive for the shipowner to cast away the vessel, several other practices of marine insurers lessen the danger. One of these is the

practice of having relatively short policy periods. Hulls are customarily insured for only a year at a time. If during the course of the year
the insurer uncovers evidence suggesting that the shipowner is the
sort of person who might cast away the vessel if there was a substantial difference between the insured and market values, then the insurer can refuse to renew the policy. The annual renewal date is also
a time when insured values can be adjusted to compensate for changes
in market values that have occurred during the intervening year, so
large discrepancies will only develop when market fluctuations are
occurring very rapidly.

A second protection measure applies only in a few countries. In
most countries (including Britain and the U.S.) an insurer cannot
challenge the value stated in the policy after the agreement has been
signed. To challenge the value is tantamount to challenging the validity of the policy. The insurer either pays the stated value or nothing, since a successful challenge results in the voiding of the policy.
In the absence of fraud or material misrepresentation the question of
value cannot be reopened and policyholders are freed from any need
to prove the extent of their economic loss when covered accidents
occur. Statements of this point are unambiguous (Dwelly 1965:266;
Winter 1952:378).

According to Norwegian law, though, an insurer can sometimes
disregard the value stated in the policy (Wilmot 1975:14/13–14/19).
Under Norwegian law, an insurer can disregard the value stated in
the policy when it is so different from the true insurable value as to
be unreasonable. If this happens because the policyholder has supplied incorrect information (with which the insurer could estimate
the value of the vessel), then the policy in effect becomes an unvalued
policy. Only in cases where there is evidence of fraud is the policy
voided. The Norwegian system is thus more similar to practices in
other lines of property insurance.

In British and American law, though overvaluation itself is not
grounds for suspension of the agreement, a failure to reveal the overvaluation might be. If the failure to reveal overvaluation is held to be
a material misrepresentation or if the policyholder is held to be guilty
of fraud in some matter related to valuation, the policy is voided and
the insurer is absolved of any obligation.[23] In no case does the policy
simply become an unvalued one.

23. The relevant cases on these points include the following: Ionides v. Pender
(1874) *Lloyds Reporter* 9 Q.B. 531; Slattery v. Mance (1962) I *Lloyds Reporter* 60;

Overvaluation of the hull itself is not the only problem. To make matters worse, insurers also permit policyholders to purchase disbursements or increased value insurance to cover the costs of the hull owner above the market value of the ship in the case of a total or constructive total loss.[24] Usually the intangible portion of this kind of coverage is limited to 25 percent of the initial hull insurance; insurance on tangible interests (such as the insurance premiums and some freights) is also carefully controlled.[25] But though only the intangible portion of the increased value insurance is really a valued policy and must be paid with no evidence about the amount actually lost, this requirement will make little difference if the interests represented here have already been covered in the hull policy itself and perhaps also in the freight insurance.

Insurers' discussions of disbursements or increased value insurance do not concentrate on this sort of problem, though. Apparently the problem instead is that policyholders wish to *substitute* increased value insurance for regular hull insurance. The rates for increased value insurance are considerably lower than the rates for full-form hull insurance (which covers partial losses, total losses, general average, and salvage expenses) because no partial losses are paid out of disbursements insurance. Carrying an excessively large portion of the insurance as disbursements insurance then has the same effect as underinsuring the vessel, in the sense that partial losses will be unusually high for a vessel of that stated value and the regular premium will not be adequate to cover them. Apparently increased value insurance is not so much used to jack up the amount that one can collect in the case of a total loss as it is used to cut the premiums that one has to pay for a fixed amount of coverage for total losses (Winter 1952:286; Heimer 1981:310–11).

The importance of valuation of the hull should not be overestimated, though, since only compensation for total loss or constructive total loss is based on the value stated in the policy. For other pur-

"Medina Princess" (1965) I *Lloyds Reporter* 361 at page 386; and Thames and Mersey Mar. Ins. Co. v. Gunford Ship Co. (1911) A.C.H.L.

24. Constructive total loss is defined in section 60 of the Marine Insurance Act of 1906 as a loss "where the subject-matter insured is reasonably abandoned on account of its actual total loss appearing to be unavoidable, or because it could not be preserved from actual total loss without an expenditure which would exceed its value when the expenditure had been incurred."

25. See Winter (1952:278–79, 285–89) and Marshall (1965:280) for discussions of disbursements insurance.

poses, the policy is in effect an unvalued policy; the amount of compensation depends on the actual cash value of the loss. This is not to say that the stated value of the hull is irrelevant to the compensation of partial losses. In marine insurance the liability of insurers for partial losses is fixed by the percentage of the total value of the hull that they insure (Winter 1952:385). If only half of the stated value of the hull is insured with a particular insurance company, then this company will only be liable for half of any partial loss. Policyholders might insure only part of the value of the vessel, and in such cases they will bear a portion of each partial loss themselves.

Since in most cases the loss will be partial rather than total, this suggests that when we are concerned with incentives to cause losses we must ask about the shipowners' interest in getting a new piece of equipment "for free," rather than about their interest in casting away the entire vessel. And we must ask how this opportunity to get "free" repairs or replacements is affected by valuation.

In marine insurance, as in other lines of property insurance, the insurer is reluctant to buy owners a new piece of property whenever they experience a loss. Insurers do not want to replace old property with new, since this will create some incentive for the policyholders to try to trade in old property for newer models with up-to-date materials and modern gadgets. In order to avoid offering this incentive, property insurers typically pay replacement cost less depreciation, in this way forcing the policyholder to pay for the increased value of the property that may result from repairs with new materials.

But there are always difficulties about how to calculate depreciation so as not to unfairly penalize policyholders with new property or with old but well-maintained property. In marine insurance, the rule (called "thirds-off") used to be that the insurance company would pay only two-thirds of the repair or replacement costs, since it was assumed that on the average new materials and equipment would cost about a third more than the old property was worth. But since this rule was unfair to the owners of new ships and since metal did not deteriorate as quickly as wood, many times the thirds-off clause was replaced with another clause specifying that repairs and replacements would be paid for "without deduction of thirds, new for old." Current rules specify that certain types of property are to be replaced with new for old without the owner having to contribute, with the proportion to be paid by the insurer decreasing as the ship ages until, when the ship is over fifteen years old, the rule of thirds-off applies for most items. Provisions depend on the age of the vessel and on the durability of the particular item. One such sliding scale can be found in the York-Antwerp Rules of 1950.[26]

The connection between valuation and compensation is important to the overall incentive system for another reason. Underwriters are often concerned that too many of their premium dollars will be spent compensating partial losses and that nothing will be left to pay for the occasional total loss or constructive total loss. Because of this, underwriters sometimes encourage policyholders to overvalue their ships, and in this way they end up introducing an incentive for the shipowner to cast away the vessel.

This dilemma is most acute in the insurance of older vessels, during depressions in shipping, or during periods in which there is excess tonnage for other reasons. In these cases the market value of ships declines, but repair and replacement costs remain high. Insured value can be set equal to either market value or replacement value. If insured value is set equal to market value and premiums are pegged to this, then there will not be enough premium money to cover both partial and total losses, and, if a large partial loss occurs, the shipowner will be unable to cover the cost of the repairs with the insurance compensation. But if underwriters urge owners to set insured value equal to replacement value, in effect to overvalue the vessels, then they are providing a significant incentive for owners to cast away vessels. If the discrepancy between market and replacement value is due to a depression in the shipping market or to excess tonnage the ship will be earning very little, and the opportunity costs of casting away the vessel will be trivial.

Adjusting the rate to take account of the discrepancy between replacement value and market value, as an old underwriting axiom suggests (Oxford 1965:286), will not solve the problem that a single partial loss may exceed insured value. Instead one must provide for two distinct estimates of value, one of which will be the basis of compensation in case of total or constructive total loss and the other of which will be the basis of compensation for partial losses (see Winter 1952:266–68 and Wilmot 1975:16/2). With this sort of dual

26. For a discussion of the new-for-old clauses, see Winter (1952:270–71, 383–84, 417). The York-Antwerp Rules are reprinted as appendix P in Winter (1952).

valuation, the premium volume would be high enough to cover both partial and total losses, and the ceiling on compensation payments would be high enough to cover repairs on a seriously damaged vessel. At the same time there would be no incentive for owners to destroy their vessels since in the case of a total loss the owner would be compensated only for the relatively low market value. The dual valuation clause was widely used in the U.S. just after World War II when warships were being sold at very low prices and repair costs were out of line with purchase prices.[27]

Since partial losses are evaluated at the time they occur, there is a sense in which the portion of the policy that has to do with partial losses is an *unvalued* component. The dual valuation scheme can be seen as a way of changing the weights of the valued and unvalued portions of the insurance policy. Instead of having the same limit apply to both, the dual valuation scheme places a lower limit on the valued portions and a higher limit on the unvalued portions, making it possible for policyholders to collect only relatively small amounts without providing proof of value (in the case of a total or constructive total loss), but allowing them to collect larger amounts when submitting documentary evidence about the cost of repairs.

Valuation in the insurance of freights

Freight refers to the price that the owner of the cargo pays the shipper for transporting the goods. Freight is not a tangible good; one is not insuring an object that can be destroyed but instead is insuring payment for a service. And because there is some question about whether the service will be rendered satisfactorily or whether the voyage will be interrupted by an accident, no *single* person owns this payment for the entire period covered by the insurance. If the voyage is successfully completed and the goods delivered "in specie," then the shipowner owns the freight, but at intermediate points the money involved may be owned either by the cargo owner, or by the person who has the charter. This means that at least two, and sometimes three, persons have an insurable interest in the freights. These ambiguities make it possible for policyholders to use freight insurance to overvalue their businesses, decreasing the motivation to avoid losses.

---

27. Note that this sort of dual valuation has only very recently been developed in fire insurance, in response to the insurance redlining crisis.

Some portion of the shipowner's interest in the freight is already covered in the hull insurance (Winter 1952:311; Wilmot 1975:14/4). But even if the hull policy covers net freight, the owner of the ship still has an insurable interest in the freight since the hull insurance does not cover the expenses of the shipowner in earning those profits. The shipowner's insurable interest in the freights, then, should in theory be limited to the amount of the gross freight that has already been invested in hiring and feeding the crew, loading the cargo, and so on (Winter 1952:312).

The insurable interest of the cargo owner is in some sense the inverse of that of the shipowner. The cargo owner's interest includes that portion of the freight that is *profit* to the shipowner as well as that portion that covers the shipowner's expenses, but only insofar as these are earned prior to delivery. When a portion of the freight is paid and earned before the end of the voyage, this also changes the ownership of the insurable interest in the freight. Winter (1952:314) argues that prepaid, nonreturnable freight is a bad idea since it "removes the chief incentive to the diligent prosecution of the voyage and makes the shipowner less likely in the event of disaster, to use all possible efforts to carry the cargo forward to destination."

The shipowner's insurable interest in the freight is also decreased when the ship is rented to another person who then contracts with cargo owners to transport their goods. In this case, the charterer takes over some of the owner's insurable interest in the freight.

Even though the owner's interest in the net freight is covered in the hull insurance, a hull with a particular expected earning over its lifetime may or may not earn that freight. When a vessel is being repaired, for example, the owner may have to forfeit freights. Because of this, many insurers believe that the owner does have some insurable interest in the net freights as well as in that portion of the freights that covers expenditures to earn the freights. One can think of this as the difference between expected and actual freight earnings.

Marine insurers, weighing these various arguments, usually permit insurance of existing freight contracts but claim that they will not allow policyholders to insure future freight contracts that do not already exist (Winter 1952:320–21). This limitation is enforced in a more lenient form: insurers also cover what they call "anticipated" freights. In order for shipowners to have an insurable interest in anticipated freights, there has to be some reasonable chance that they will in fact get particular freight contracts. Although an insurer would not grant coverage for freights on a return voyage if the policy-holder were sailing for one country with a load of cargo and then intending to arrange for return shipments after arriving there, the insurer might be willing to grant coverage if the policyholder had entered into negotiations with cargo owners about transporting their goods on the return voyage but had not yet signed a contract.

Presumably the reasoning here is the same as that of fire insurers who are reluctant to give business interruption insurance to cover profits as well as expenses. If one covers profits as well as routine expenses that cannot be avoided, one removes a powerful incentive for the policyholder to get the business back on its feet. The difficulty, of course, is that the shipowner must be willing to make expenditures and investments in the hope of getting freight contracts.

Because the freight is not a tangible property, it is somewhat difficult to prove that one has an insurable interest. In the case of an anticipated freight contract that does not materialize, for example, it is nearly impossible to tell whether this is because the anticipation was only hope (or outright fraud) or whether the arrangement was really an insurable one but simply fell through. Because of these difficulties, insurers must be quite careful about giving insurance to cover freights. Typically these sorts of contracts are made on a P.P.I./F.I.A. basis.[28] That is, the policyholder is freed from the necessity of proving that he or she had an insurable interest, and the fact that the insurer has agreed to give coverage is taken as an admission that the insurer conceded that an insurable interest existed. When a loss occurs, then, the insurer cannot get out of compensating the policyholder by arguing that no insurable interest existed. This is a very tight contract indeed, probably as restrictive (to the insurer) as valued-policy provisions.

The main dangers in freight insurance arise, then, because of the duplication of interests already covered in the hull policy and because of the speculative problem that insurers are often willing to insure anticipated freights when no contracts yet exist. Winter (1952: 320) argues that the insurance of anticipated freights is "open to gross abuses and may in fact be used as a cloak for a mere gamble." Because this problem is so serious, most hull policies contain a warranty that the amount of freight insurance that can be placed on a

28. The acronyms mean "policy proof of interest, full interest admitted."

P.P.I./F.I.A. basis (that is, without a contract to prove that there is an insurable interest) shall be limited to a particular percentage of the insured value of the vessel. In effect, then, the policyholder is permitted to cover the value of the hull, freights that are already contracted, and some extra anticipated freights. Though any one of these items alone might not create much incentive to cast away a vessel, when the three are combined, and when market conditions are not ideal, there may be substantial incentive to scuttle the vessel, especially if the policyholder has managed to overvalue the vessel to begin with.

Incentives and counterincentives

This section on valuation has been concerned with the provisions about compensation to be paid in the case of a loss and with the question of the effect these agreements have on the motivations of the policyholder. If policyholders will usually receive an insurance payment that covers their losses but no more, then presumably they will not be much inclined to scuttle their ships or destroy their cargos since these are parts of ongoing business enterprises that are worth considerably more than the insurance. But if the compensation is considerably larger than the current value of the ship or cargo, the policyholder may be motivated to trade. In trying to determine whether insurers will very often be paying more than indemnity, we have had to look not just at the way that the value of the cargo, hull, or freight is set to begin with, but also at the way that hull, cargo, and freight insurance fit together so that, for example, a small overvaluation on the hull policy added to a larger overvaluation on the freight policy may end up yielding a substantial incentive to cast away the vessel, which neither policy alone would provide. In this final subsection, we will examine some of the factors that lessen the importance of the incentives introduced by overvaluation of marine property.

To begin with, the problem of incentives to destroy property are considerably smaller in cargo insurance than in hull insurance. First, the valuation of the cargo tends to be based on some more or less objective standard such as the invoice price or current market price when an independent international market exists. This means the base value is usually fairly well established. Second, there is not much added on to this initial valuation. Often a fixed percentage for profit is added, and sometimes provision is made for the payment of freights. But the limits are fairly strict here, and in general what is added on is an estimate of additional expenditures rather than additional insurance for anticipated or hoped-for income. Though there is some redundancy, then, insured value cannot rise very much.

But the main reason that insurers do not worry too much about cargo owners destroying their cargo when the value is fixed in their policy is that cargo owners usually do not have much control over their property. If cargo owners wished to destroy cargo, they would have to enlist the assistance of a captain and crew or dock workers who are not even their own employees.

In hull insurance the situation is somewhat different. First, the valuation of the hull is not based on anything so concrete as an invoice, and the market price of a vessel is hard to establish because vessels are not usually interchangeable. Second, one must consider the effects of hull, freight, and disbursements insurance together. These three coverages may involve substantial redundancy.

While in practice it may almost always be true that the use value of the ship will be greater than its insured value even when one adds together the hull, freight, and disbursements insurance, it is still clear that there is substantial potential for abuse in the rules about valued policies and permissible combinations of insurance. The rules do not *guarantee* that use value will always exceed insured value. This means that small changes in the market may shift the balance so that insured value comes to exceed use value and that valuation practices will often provide an incentive to cast away vessels.

Though insurers are sometimes quite worried about this problem, they are not nearly as worried as we might expect. Presumably this is either because the insurance agreement contains counterincentives or because other shipping practices contain them. One obvious counterincentive, of course, is the illegality of the act of casting away a vessel to collect insurance money. In the rest of this subsection I will discuss other sorts of counterincentives.

The first reason that insurers do not worry as much as we might expect about shipowners casting away their vessels is that shipowners are not usually in possession of their property. The ship is usually out to sea or docked in some foreign port while the owner is at the home office. In such cases it is clear that someone else will have to do the work of sinking the ship and, as argued in the section on the attenuation of control, it is rather different to do something oneself than to try to motivate someone else to do it. A ship cannot be scuttled without the assistance of the captain and crew.

A second reason that underwriters might not worry is that casting away a vessel is no simple task. The problem of attenuation of control works in the insurers' favor here: even the worst-intentioned owner may not be able to get a ship destroyed, and not all captains succeed in scuttling vessels even when they are instructed to do so. Martin (1876: 263–70) relates a rather amusing tale of a captain who failed abysmally in his attempt to cast away the vessel—he made his attempt in calm waters too close to shore. People on the shore could see that the vessel had run aground and kept coming out to offer their assistance. The captain, stupidly enough, refused their assistance, and all of these salvors then provided evidence to the court that the captain had been trying to sink the ship. The captain was hanged, and though the captain was following the owner's orders, the owner was not hanged.

This incident illustrates some of the difficulties typically encountered in casting away a vessel. In order to succeed, one needs the cooperation of the captain and the crew. The ideal circumstances for casting away a vessel include rough seas, dangerous and remote locations, and so on. But while these circumstances may be ideal for destroying ships, they are far from ideal for getting the cooperation of the crew and captain in destroying the ship since conditions dangerous for ships are also dangerous for them, especially when they must abandon a sinking ship.

An additional problem, of course, is that when there is a large conspiracy like this, as there must be if the ship is to be successfully scuttled, one has difficulty in maintaining the conspiracy. Some members of the group may suffer from feelings of guilt at their dishonesty; some may want to blackmail the owner; some may worry that others will tell the tale first and wonder if they should not protect themselves from long prison terms by talking first (a classic instance of the prisoner's dilemma). And finally, the tale of being shipwrecked is always an exciting one and it is difficult not to discuss the experience with one's spouse and buddies. Conflicting stories may emerge, or some drunken sailor, caught up in the storyteller role, may realize that the adventure is even more exciting when the audience discovers that this was no ordinary shipwreck but instead a planned accident.

A third reason that overvaluation is not such a serious problem is that unless the owner is planning to stage an accident (and is successful), he or she will be rather unlikely to benefit from the overvaluation. Most losses are partial losses, and overvaluation does the owner no good in this case unless the loss is very large. When partial losses occur, the value stated in the policy establishes a maximum recovery and determines whether or not the owner recovers fully (except for deductibles and such like) or is a coinsurer. But the insurance compensation depends on the costs of repairs or replacements rather than on the value stated in the policy. These costs are established at the time the loss occurs by loss adjustors and salvage organizations. So except in the relatively rare case of a total loss, the owner does not benefit by overvaluation.

This is not to say that there is no insurance fraud in marine insurance—only that most of it does not involve total loss. A far more significant sort of marine insurance fraud is the practice of claiming that all of the routine repairs should be paid for by the insurance company because they are due to covered accidents rather than to normal wear and tear or perils not covered by the insurance policy. Overvaluation of the vessel is probably irrelevant to this sort of fraud, although overvaluation of freights may encourage fraud about partial losses since one can collect insurance to cover lost freights if the ship is temporarily out of service because of a covered accident. Restrictive rules about when one has a freight interest may lessen this problem.

What this suggests is that when one is worried about the incentives to destroy vessels or to stage smaller accidents, one should not be so much concerned about the overvaluation of the hull since it is rather difficult to destroy a ship completely. Instead one should worry about overvaluation of the freight interest, since this sort of fraud is much easier to manage.

During periods of economic prosperity, overvaluation may introduce few incentives to destroy cargo or ships to collect insurance money. Though the individual insurances may overvalue the hull, freight, or cargo, and though when these insurances are added together there may be substantial overvaluation, the use value of the ship, cargo, and commercial contracts will very likely outweigh the total insured value. And when the illegality of insurance fraud and the difficulties of destroying property that is physically controlled by others are added to this, the incentives to destroy property should be trivial.

But the outcome may be radically different when the shipping markets are depressed. Ships and cargo may be worth substantially less than their insured value; shipping contracts may be scarce, and those that exist will be in danger of cancelation. This means that the owners will find that the use value of the property has dropped substantially below the insured value. And though cargo owners and shipowners must still persuade captains, crews, or dock workers to do the destroying, such persuasion might well be easier when these employees are facing the prospect of unemployment due to the depressed market. This suggests that insurers will want to take seriously the problem of valuation and will want to make certain that use value is larger than insured value and remains so even when economic conditions change.

Conclusion

In marine insurance, as in other lines of insurance, one cannot really estimate the likelihood of losses from particular perils without making some assumptions about human behavior and its relation to these perils. In particular, one cannot really talk about the expected losses without considering the problem of equipping and maintaining the vessel; of motivating the captain, crew, and other agents of the policyholder to exercise due diligence and act in the interests of the policyholder; of offering incentives to reduce losses when an accident does happen; and of preventing the policyholders from deliberately destroying their property when the insurance money is worth more to them. The problem of managing reactive risk, then, is one of making certain that the behavior of the policyholders and their agents is not so outrageous as to increase the losses beyond what insurers have calculated, beyond what can be covered by the premiums.

Since human behavior is so important in determining what the loss experience will actually be, insurers have to figure out some way to make sure that the people involved behave more or less *as expected*. In a sense, then, these attempts to manage reactive risks are not really attempts to reduce losses so much as attempts to make sure that human behavior does not cause the losses to be larger than expected. The behavior need not be exemplary, but it must be *no worse than expected*. This is why marine insurers tend to insist that everyone meet minimum standards rather than reward those who meet high standards. Predictability about loss is more important than the lack of loss. High but predictable losses are paid for by the policyholder; unexpected losses must be covered by the insurer.

Human behavior can have three very different effects on loss experience: (1) by deliberately causing losses, people can raise the losses above the expected levels; (2) by exercising due diligence and by engaging in the usual loss-prevention activities, people can hold losses to the expected or normal level; and (3) by engaging in loss-reduction activities at the time an accident occurs, people can cut losses substantially below what they would otherwise be.

Notice, though, that in the cases of preventing and reducing losses, standards for normal behavior are assumed to exist. Policyholders and their agents are expected to behave as well as or better than the standard. In the case of loss-prevention efforts, the relevant standards are due diligence and seaworthiness—standards defined by the community. In the case of loss-reduction efforts, the standard is the behavior of the prudent uninsured owner. The existence of such standards means that the insurer recognizes that the relevant question has to do with the *level* of effort required, not with whether *any* effort is required or not. An agreement to make *some* effort is implicit in the undertaking of a marine venture, so the question of complete passivity by either policyholders or their agents is excluded.

The management of reactive risk in marine insurance is primarily a problem of seeing that the relevant actors adhere to these standards rather than slip below them. Most of the insurer's efforts are concerned with making certain that having insurance does not alter policyholders' incentive structures (and thereby indirectly alter the motivations of their agents). The only incentive to rise above such standards is the promise of a decrease in premium through experience rating if one's losses are exceptionally low. By increasing the predictability of policyholder behavior, marine insurance institutions make it possible for insurers to calculate appropriate rates, and this in turn makes market transactions possible.

5

Insurance Against Dishonesty and Nonperformance

Fidelity bonds in general guarantee that an employee will not do anything dishonest.[1] Surety bonds are broader in scope and guarantee a specific performance. A fidelity bond might be a contract to repay an employer if an employee embezzles, while a surety bond might be a contract to compensate the owner of a building if a contractor failed to do repairs in a specific time period or did them in a shoddy fashion. Traditionally the bond was a contract between the person who would be compensated in the event of a failure of one sort or another (called the obligee), the person whose performance was being guaranteed (called the principal), and the person who agreed to give the guarantee (called the surety). The person whose performance was being guaranteed was the one who applied for the bond and paid the premium (or provided collateral, or whatever). The bond was usually a precondition for being hired to do a job, although there are other sorts of bonds, such as court and judicial bonds, not related to occupations. While surety bonds are still arranged this way, fidelity bonds are now usually two-party contracts with the bond arranged for and purchased by the beneficiary (the obligee) rather than by the person whose honesty is being guaranteed.

In general, insurance covers losses that the policyholder can do little to prevent. What distinguishes fidelity and surety bonding from

1. While this field of insurance is called surety bonding, it is subdivided into fidelity bonding and surety bonding. Further subdivision is discussed in a later section, "Organizational Correlates of Surety and Fidelity Losses." For a general introduction to bonding see Denenberg (1965) and Porter (1966).

other lines of insurance is that the person who has bought the bond usually has some, often substantial, control over whether a loss occurs. According to insurers this is a very dangerous situation. In other lines, insurers worry that policyholders will cease to exercise due diligence and that, as a result of their carelessness, losses will rise. When losses are ultimately borne by the insurer, the policyholder has less motivation to be careful. Marine insurance contracts specify that policyholders will be unable to recover unless they have acted as "prudent uninsured owners" and have done whatever was possible to minimize losses.

Obviously this sort of problem is considerably more serious in fidelity and surety bonding where losses are not really accidental; the loss to be covered is directly due to the actions or failures of the bonded party. While it is true that the person who is compensated is not the person causing the loss, the loss-causer is to some degree relieved of the responsibility of repaying the loss when covered by a bond.[2] And the beneficiary of the bond does not need to worry so much about checking to see that the bonded person is behaving properly, has the competence or financial strength claimed, and so on.

Thus, two sorts of checks on the behavior of the bonded person are removed by having a bond. First, the beneficiary will have less need to check to see that things are in order. This is essentially the same as the problem of morale hazard in other lines of insurance except that presumably such indirect control over the behavior of another person is more effective than attempts to control sparks or ocean waves. In addition, the bond removes a second check, in that people covered by bonds will have less fear of damaging the beneficiary and less fear of having to repay the loss.

Fidelity and surety bonding are interesting, then, because they provide examples in which control over losses is considerably greater than in other lines of insurance. This difference will enable us to study the problem of controlling reactive risk in a relatively pure form.

If we wished to study a pure case of the difficulties introduced by insuring losses due to the controllable actions of a person, fidelity and surety bonding each have their own peculiar advantages and disadvantages. The advantage of fidelity bonding is that the loss-causing

---

2. In theory, however, the bonding company collects from those responsible for losses.

action, a dishonest act, is completely controllable. There is not much accidental about stealing from one's employer. In surety bonding, in contrast, the loss is only partly controllable by the person covered by the bond. Contractors may not be able to fulfill contracts for reasons beyond their control. Increases in the prices of raw materials, defaults by subcontractors, or bad weather may make it impossible to meet contract deadlines no matter how much the contractor wishes to. Faithful performance, unlike honesty, depends partly on the performances of other people and also on conditions over which no one has any control. That is, in some cases nonperformance may be partly accidental. In this sense, then, fidelity bonding provides the purest case of insurance of a reactive risk. Dishonesty is not at all accidental; nonperformance may be partly accidental.

But we are also interested in *who* controls the loss-causing event, and for this reason fidelity bonding is no longer such a pure case for the study of reactive risk as it used to be. Since the person who buys the bond is now quite often the person who receives the benefit from the bonding company rather than the person who causes the loss, fidelity bonding has come to resemble the crime insurance included in a homeowner's package or insurance against barratry in marine insurance. When the bond is bought by the beneficiary rather than by the person who actually controls the loss-causing event, one set of controls is removed. The insurance company no longer checks up on the credentials or behavior of the bonded person. The responsibility for this sort of checking is left with the employer, the beneficiary of the fidelity bond. That is, the responsibility for controlling the person who can cause the loss is left entirely in the hands of someone who will not lose as a result of this person's actions. The problem of morale hazard is thus exaggerated in the case of modern fidelity bonding, but modern fidelity bonding, when arranged in this way (the bond purchased by the beneficiary rather than the potential loss-causer), will provide less evidence about *insurers'* techniques for controlling the actions of bonded people.[3] Surety bonds, in contrast, are still bought by those who control the losses.

---

3. Not all fidelity bonding is arranged in this fashion, though. While fidelity bonds in large commercial enterprises are usually taken out by the employer, rather than by those covered, this is not true of court bonds, public official bonds covering high-level employees, or fidelity bonds covering executives of large companies.

Since we are interested in two variables, how controllable losses are and who controls them, we need to examine both fidelity and surety bonding. Fidelity bonding will give us information about how insurers manage reactive risks when losses are *entirely under human control*. Surety bonding will give us information about how insurers manage reactive risks when it is the *policyholder who can control losses* (to the extent that they are under volitional control). This chapter will then be concerned with the methods by which bonding companies attempt to manage reactive risks.

Because the losses in fidelity and surety bonding are largely controllable, many insurers have argued that the rating procedures for them should be fundamentally different than those used in other lines of insurance. In particular, they have argued that the premium should be simply a service charge since sureties are merely providing a service of guaranteeing performances and stand to lose no money since losses will be repaid. Further, if bonding companies assume that losses will occur and peg their rates to expected losses, then underwriters will relax their standards and give bonds when they should not, and losses will rise. Though in fact surety and fidelity insurers only recover about a third of their losses through "salvage," this fiction was important because it influenced the policies of surety and fidelity companies. (The threat of collecting salvage also reminds policyholders that they had better act as "prudent uninsured owners" because in some senses they are.) Because they believed that they were merely providing a sort of credit service, bonding companies for a long time resisted doing any actual rating. What they did do was really a categorical version of insurance rating. That is, they checked to see whether the person seeking the bond was an honest person and had a good reputation and then decided whether to give the bond. But since the premium was viewed as a service fee, it did not vary very much with the likelihood of loss. Companies either gave bonds or denied them, but they did not classify applicants as somewhat honest or somewhat competent and charge them a slightly higher premium than they would charge applicants with spotless records. This question of whether bonding companies should try to set rates that reflect the likelihood of loss is discussed in the second section of this chapter.

But bonding companies do set rates that vary with the likelihood of loss, and the structure of these rates is the subject of the third section. The rating scheme is more complex in fidelity bonding than in surety bonding. Because the party buying the bond does not really have any direct control over whether a loss occurs, the fidelity contract is closer to a standard insurance contract. (The employer can engage in loss-prevention efforts, but these are, in principle, no different than loss-prevention efforts in fire and marine insurance.) Both the insurer and the policyholder can admit that losses are likely to occur without feeling as if they are saying that it is *acceptable* (no one is to blame) if there are losses. The admission that a loss may occur is not being made to the person who directly controls whether the loss occurs. The complexity of the rating system varies with the reactivity of the risk, and this varies with the distance between the policyholder and the potential loss-causer (just as in fire and marine insurance).

Because no one has figured out how to predict individual honesty or performance, bonding rates vary with features of organizations. Most of these variables are measures of organizational control over individuals, such as closeness of supervision and the like, but a factor adjusting for the "type of business" captures residual variations in the honesty or competence of the average employee in that kind of enterprise.

In a fourth section I discuss how bonding underwriters choose policyholders and how they adjust rates to fit these policyholders, given that variations in honesty and competence are not directly taken into account in ratemaking. Experience rating allows bonding companies to incorporate information about honesty and competence as it accumulates and also makes policyholder outcomes (premiums in this case) depend on good behavior. Insurers are also interested in any new evidence about the dishonesty of subordinates (and require policyholders to submit this) or any indication that the financial circumstances (and therefore incentives for theft) of policyholders or their agents have changed. Such new information allows for the renegotiation of contracts as conditions change.

Bonding companies also stress that since losses in fidelity and surety bonding are not accidental, loss-prevention activities are particularly important. In the fifth section of the chapter, I will examine the sorts of loss-prevention techniques used in fidelity and surety bonding and the situations in which they are most likely to be used. Besides requiring collateral and arranging to have joint control, bonding companies also offer advice about how to arrange supervisory systems and how to set up systems of internal and external control (such as multiple signing of checks and audits, respectively). They also warn principals of their legal obligations to repay the bonding company should a loss occur.

Loss prevention in bonding focuses on information asymmetries. When they have only imperfect information about policyholders, bonding companies will usually try to make such information irrelevant. This can be accomplished by requiring the deposit of collateral that can function as partial prepayment for the loss. Alternatively, by arranging for close supervision, the bonding company can make some loss-causing acts impossible. Such arrangements have much the same function as locating loss-prevention activities in the hands of disinterested third parties in fire and marine insurance. In a few cases, bonding companies have agreed to provide probationary bonds while collecting information about the policyholder. Other organizations supervise the activities of the policyholder during the reputation-building phase.

This interventionist approach distinguishes loss prevention in bonding from loss prevention in other lines of insurance. In other lines one does not find nearly so much interference in the affairs of a client. What this suggests, in part, is that when information asymmetries are really serious, insurers must arrange special institutions for collecting this information and must arrange to incorporate it into their calculations as soon as it is available. The likelihood of loss can be reduced if the exchange is cut into smaller pieces. One has less to lose in each part of the interaction and therefore can make continuation contingent on performance, curtailing the relationship if negative information starts to accumulate. This is essentially what fidelity and surety bonders do when they arrange for joint control, have banks act as co-fiduciaries, or make periodic checks of organizations to whom they have given bonds. These arrangements both alter the incentives of those who might cause losses and provide current information about how these individuals are behaving. Both the incentives and the information make calculations about reactive risk more reliable. Insurance companies can always adjust premium levels to cover losses they anticipate. What they cannot manage is losses whose magnitude they cannot estimate. Incentives are crucial not because they reduce losses but because they keep them from growing.

Surety Ratemaking and
the Expectation of Loss

In the previous chapter on marine insurance, I argued that how much control a policyholder has over a loss is a central determinant of whether insurers will be willing to cover that sort of loss. The less controllable a loss, whether because the event is not under *anyone's* volitional control or because someone other than the policyholder controls the loss-causing event, the less likely that losses will increase with coverage and the more willing insurers will be to grant it.

In fidelity and surety bonding we see this same principle at work, but in exaggerated form. Since almost all fidelity and surety losses are under volitional control, the principle that only uncontrollable losses should be insurable suggests that insurance of fidelity and surety losses should not be possible. That this question is a central one in bonding is clear. Insurance writers stress that bonds are not really insurance but guarantees; surety and fidelity writers debate about how to set rates given that no losses are anticipated. Just as losses may rise if insurance coverage is granted for controllable losses, so they may rise if insurers start to admit that they expect losses and charge rates intended to cover compensation for them rather than just the service of providing guarantees.

Given later discussions about how suretyship differs from insurance, it is somewhat surprising that the first bonding company wrote bonds according to insurance principles. The people responsible for forming the first fidelity company in England in 1840 apparently believed that the rates for fidelity bonds should be set in the same manner as rates were set in other lines of insurance. During 1839 and 1840 two articles by a Professor DeMorgan appeared (one in the October 1839 issue of the *Quarterly Review*, discussed in Insurance Institute of London n.d.:6; and one in the August 1840 issue of the *Dublin Review*, discussed in Morgan 1927:164–66) arguing that the principles of insurance could just as well be applied to dishonesty as to fire, life, health, or anything else. DeMorgan (1840:61, cited in Morgan 1927:164) suggested that "the number of persons out of a thousand taken at hazard, who cannot resist a given temptation, should be found to be nearly the same as those out of another thousand who cannot resist it." Following this logic, he argued that if one can determine, from past experience, the instances of dishonesty in the relevant population, then one can require premiums sufficient to cover losses and offer insurance against dishonesty.

The Guarantee Society of London, formed according to this plan (apparently with DeMorgan's participation), commenced business on June 24, 1840. It began by doing only a fidelity business (the company is still in existence) and insured the honesty of clerks, secretaries, and so on. Since this company wrote fidelity bonds on an insurance basis (that is, it expected losses and set premiums accordingly), numerous business houses were circularized to find out what average fidelity losses actually were. This information was supposed to provide the basis for rate setting. Despite this, the company only accepted selected risks: "None but those who could bring satisfactory testimony to their previous good conduct" (DeMorgan 1840:62, cited in Morgan 1927:164) were to be allowed to join.

By 1843, though, the Guarantee Society had changed its emphasis slightly. Though there is no indication that the company had abandoned its earlier "insurance principles" (the assumptions that losses would occur and that premiums should be scaled accordingly), the later literature put out by the company stressed that premiums are not directly related (except dichotomously) to the reputed honesty of the bonded person:

> Upon appointment of an individual to any office . . . provided the applicant be found a person of moral worth, the Society are willing to incur the risk of becoming his bondsmen: the individual contributing to the funds of the Society a small percentage proportionate to the amount proposed to be named in the surety bond. *This percentage, however, is not calculated upon the degree of honesty he may be supposed to possess: if his reputation for strict integrity and morality present any blemish, he is rejected* altogether. Independently of the personal character of the individual, the Society is also guided by the nature of the engagement, and the description of employment or business in which the bond of suretyship is required—the character of the referred and their connection with the party—the check under which the person will be placed for whom the security is sought, and the evidence the Society may obtain, that his conduct under these frequent and periodical checks will be observed by a wise and vigilant superior, and not abandoned to the common influence by which he may be surrounded.
>
> (Charles Saunderson, cited in Morgan 1927:167)

Honesty of the employee and opportunities for dishonesty were apparently considered during the application phase, but this information was not used to determine premiums. Though it is unclear whether this later statement represents a deviation from DeMorgan's initial position, it is quite clear that the earliest bonding companies had a different view of the matter than did later bonding companies. And while it is unclear whether the Guarantee Society ever based *individual* premiums on expected losses, it is clear that the overall premium level was based on an estimate of the expected losses of the whole group.

Later companies were unwilling to concede even this much. By the 1900s, differences in opportunities for dishonesty were reflected in the rates, but the bonding companies retained the emphasis on outright rejection of anyone whose reputation was not completely above reproach, and developed a rhetoric about not expecting any losses.

Although in many cases surety and fidelity writers simply assert that no losses are expected, in other cases this assertion is linked to arguments about the policyholder's control over losses, the consequences of assuming that there will be losses, or the functions of suretyship. Often the controllable nature of surety losses is contrasted with the accidental and inevitable nature of losses in other lines of insurance:

> The Surety should theoretically suffer no losses since the risk is within the control of the Principal, whereas the Insurer expects losses, due to the fortuitous events over which it has no control, in accord with a table of averages or experience.
>
> (Cross 1963:17)

Sometimes this comparison of bonding with insurance leads authors to conclude that if they anticipate losses they will somehow convey this expectation to their policyholders, who will then behave less responsibly. For this reason, perhaps, bonding company literature stresses that the principal continues to have the primary obligation to pay for a loss.

In other cases, authors suggest that the increase in losses would be due to changes in the behavior of the bonding companies. For example, Spalding (1967:10) asks:

> If he [the surety writer] did assume the "certainty of loss" principle as applying to contract bonds, would his investigation of the contractor,

his operation and finances, really be as thorough as if he operated on the conventional principle which pre-supposes no loss at all?

A more convoluted argument suggests that surety bonds are a mechanism to eliminate weaker and less responsible businesses. If underwriters became more lax because they expected losses and were charging premiums high enough to cover them, then the weak companies would continue to flourish to the detriment of everyone:

> Accordingly, it could reasonably be anticipated that the bonding of contractors at slightly higher rates because of certain weaknesses which would prevent their bondability at "regular" rates, would bring about far more losses than would otherwise be the case, and the aggregate size of these losses in dollars would probably increase geometrically rather than arithmetically from the number of contractors who caused them.
>
> (Spalding 1967:11)

The most extreme form of this argument suggests that insurance is a mechanism to distribute losses over a large group, while suretyship is not:

> Suretyship does not contemplate bonding of all members of a class, so as to distribute equally among all of them the derelictions of a few. On the contrary it is founded on the opposite principle, namely that suretyship shall be given only for those selected applicants who are responsible and who are expected to fulfill their engagements, keep their promises, and perform their contracts. These are the selected members of a class; not all its members as in the case of insurance.
>
> (Towner, cited in Spalding 1967:16)

If surety rates were set assuming that losses would occur and bonds were granted more freely, then suretyship

> would cease to be a guarantee of the contractor's financial responsibility and would break down under the weight of losses that would ensue. Responsible contractors finding themselves no better able to obtain a bond than the most irresponsible dummy who paid the same premium rate, would cease to bid or apply for bonds in their own names. All proposals for contract work and all applications for contract bonds, would be made by irresponsible persons who, on a purely insurance basis, would procure suretyship by the payment of a premium.
>
> (Towner, cited by Spalding 1967:16–17)

Note that in painting his gloomy picture of the effects of treating suretyship as insurance and calculating premiums on the assumption that some losses will occur, Towner also assumes that the rates for good and bad contractors will be identical, though it is far from obvious that this is a necessary result of counting on losses. Whatever the exact mechanism, surety writers make it clear that if they set rates as if losses were anticipated, losses will in fact occur. Towner's description of the effects of information asymmetry bears a striking resemblance to Akerlof's (1970) analysis of the same problem in used car markets.

A further justification for surety bonders' refusal to admit that they anticipated losses and to peg rates to them is that losses are supposed to be paid primarily out of the assets of the bonded person. Backman's (1948:63) view on this is typical:

> One of the fundamental distinctions between insurance and suretyship is that by insurance the insured is indemnified against loss with the premium fund used to pay the losses. Under a contract of suretyship, on the other hand, the person indemnified against loss is a third party known as the obligee, while the resources from which losses are to be paid are the assets of the principal, the collateral he has deposited, or the indemnity he has furnished, and only when these are inadequate to meet the claim promptly, the resources of the surety.

Authors continually stress that the assets of the principal are the more important of the two loss-paying funds and also that the surety's funds will be drawn on only after the principal's resources are exhausted.[4]

But Backman, at least, admits that losses will occur from time to time even when sound underwriting has eliminated those least likely to meet their obligations. According to Backman (1948:34–35) losses usually are due to conditions that the principal cannot control (such as fluctuations in economic conditions), and the principal retains a responsibility to meet such losses:

> If a loss does occur and the principal cannot meet it, then the surety makes good. But in effect the surety company often is merely telescoping time. It pays today, with full right to recover from the prin-

4. See especially Towner (1924), who continually refers to the resources of the principal as "the largest and most important fund" for the payment of losses, and Crist (1950, especially pp. 175–79).

cipal tomorrow. In the vast majority of cases, the principal meets his obligation or makes good the financial obligation he incurs so the surety company pays no losses.

Still, if policyholders really do repay losses when they occur, then the bonding companies are only providing a service, not insurance, and should charge to cover the service, not the loss.

We have seen then that the belief that bonding rates should not reflect losses because none are to be expected seems to have been due in some cases to a belief that if the underwriters selected policyholders properly there would be very few losses and these few would be fully repaid. In other cases, the writers believed that assuming that losses would occur would *cause* them to occur. The increase in losses would result either from increased irresponsibility among policyholders, who would know they were buying insurance rather than a service, or from decreased selectivity by underwriters. If bonding underwriters were less selective, then the insurance equivalent of natural selection would cease to operate, and weak companies would flourish along with the strong ones (there seems to be no possibility of elimination of weak companies through any other means); perhaps the good companies would cease to operate because of the demoralizing effect of subsidizing their less competent competitors.

There are several problems with this theory that surety rates should not be pegged to anticipated losses. First, losses do occur. Second, at least up until the late 1940s, salvage accounted for only about a third of all losses (Backman 1948:72–75), and losses are in fact often paid from the surety company's funds before drawing on the resources of the principal, since salvage is often not collected until years after the loss occurs (see Backman 1948:66–67, for statistics on this).

As a result of this confusion about the appropriate relation between surety rates and losses, ratemakers developed a rather complex ideology about the differences between insurance and bonding and argued that surety rates should be made on a "scientific" rather than a "statistical" basis (Towner 1924; Crist 1950:187). Though based on extremely naive notions of both science and statistics, the idea seems to have been that surety bonders, for the various reasons outlined above (and because of the inadequacies of past experience as a guide to the future in bonding; see Heimer 1981:390–92) could not use the rating formulas employed in other lines of insurance.

Despite their belief that surety and fidelity rates should not be set in the conventional manner, surety and fidelity ratemakers still had to face many of the problems faced by ratemakers in other lines. At the very least they had to figure out how to come up with good estimates of future losses and how to calculate the proportion that could be expected to be recovered from the assets of the principal. And they also had to decide whether the decisions to expect losses and to expect not to recoup them completely from salvage would somehow, magically or mechanically, cause the losses to grow. Finally, fidelity and surety ratemakers had to decide what to do if surety and fidelity losses did grow. In the short run surety bonders responded to this dilemma by refusing to rely on their statistics and by stressing "judgment" instead. Towner (cited in Backman 1948:332) summarized his view of the matter in this way: "I have over 18 years experience in the surety business to guide me not only in using figures but in disregarding them."

The surety companies did eventually start to take losses into consideration in calculating their rates, though this change has never been reflected in their discussions of their procedures. Largely because of state rating laws and pressure from state insurance departments, surety bonders were forced to substitute statistical methods for judgment.[5] But because the stubborn insistence that surety bonding is not insurance has only grudgingly given way to the use of an insurance methodology, surety bonders never really faced their dilemma head on. This means that they never arrived at a clear formulation of their anxiety that risks that are under the control of the principal might actually grow in response to risk-management techniques that either admit that losses might occur or that not all principals will repay sureties for them. It also means that as they adopted techniques that implicitly concede that losses are expected, they did not collect evidence necessary to assess the effects of such changes in technique.[6]

5. For accounts of the role of the Towner Rating Bureau and investigations of this bureau by the New York Insurance Department, see *Insurance Advocate* (1944, 1945), State of New York Department of Insurance (1914, 1945a, 1945b), and *Weekly Underwriter* (1934).

6. For other discussions of how bonds are rated, see Brodsky (1934), Fosket (1955), Gaffney (1965), and Murray (1964).

Organizational Correlates
of Surety and Fidelity Losses

Throughout this book I have argued that it should not be possible to calculate very exactly what losses will be when the events leading to loss are controlled (or partially controlled) by people whose motivation to prevent losses will decrease when the insurer agrees to bear the cost of losses. According to this argument, it should be impossible to set rates in fidelity and surety bonding, since the main causes of loss are dishonesty and failure to abide by contracts. My conclusion in this case coincides with the argument of insurers, discussed in the previous section, that it is unwise to *expect* losses in fidelity and surety bonding since this will *cause* losses to occur more frequently.

In fact, though, modern fidelity and surety bonding companies do anticipate losses and do charge premiums that are more than just service charges. In this section I will explain how this is possible. My basic argument will be that rating of bonds is possible largely because bonding companies have come to recognize that the magnitude of losses varies both with organizational susceptibility to loss and with individuals' tendencies toward dishonest and unreliable behavior, and that even if it is impossible to base rates on variations in tendencies toward dishonesty it is entirely possible to use variations in organizational control structures as a basis for ratemaking. This means that it will be easier to set rates in those types of bonds that most resemble true insurance.

Fidelity bonds are in general more insurance-like than are surety bonds. In order to understand why this is so, one must know something about the distinctions between these two major groups of bonds.

One of the main ways different kinds of insurance are distinguished from each other is by the *causes* of the losses (perils) for which compensation is given. While in other lines of insurance physical phenomena are the main causes of loss, in corporate surety bonding human actions are the most important causes. That is, surety bonds compensate people for losses due to the unreliability of other people.

Bonding companies therefore divide bonds into two main groups, according to the sort of reliability with which they are concerned. As pointed out above, fidelity bonds provide compensation for the dishonest acts of the bonded persons, while surety bonds compensate for failures to perform promised acts. Another distinction between surety and fidelity bonds has to do with whether the obligations of the bonded person are implied (honesty) or expressed (especially in a written contract). This distinction applies primarily to public official bonds, which often cover "faithful performance" as well as honesty but which are still classified as fidelity bonds.

Further distinctions have little to do with differences in the causes of loss. Instead, bonds are subdivided into categories that offer more or less homogeneous coverages to similar sorts of organizations to cover specified relations with particular individuals, groups of individuals, or organizations. What is involved in honesty or faithful performance varies with the nature of the obligations, and this varies a good deal from one line of business to another. For example, there are important variations in the scope of the bonded person's obligations to carry out a performance or to deal honestly and the ways in which these are spelled out. In some cases, for example, public officials are responsible for the honesty of their subordinates in the public administration. This responsibility for subordinates is usually not part of the requirement that a bank worker deal honestly. And the performance guaranteed in a contract bond is quite different than that guaranteed in a license bond since the obligations in the first case are spelled out in an individual contract, whereas in the latter case they are dictated by law, established in a professional code of ethics, and/or institutionalized through standard operating procedures and customs of a particular trade.

These categories of bonds are important because bonds that fall into the same category are rated the same way. The 1979 edition of the Surety Association of America's rate manual (Surety Association of America n.d., j) groups bonds into nine categories (with color-coded pages): fidelity bonds (mostly for mercantile establishments), financial institution bonds, forgery bonds, judicial bonds, contract bonds, miscellaneous bonds, license and permit bonds, federal bonds, and (state and local) public official bonds.[7] Within each of these categories there are often two or three forms of the bond (for example, fidelity bonds can be blanket, position, or individual bonds, and pub-

---

7. See the appendix for brief descriptions of each of these bonds and for a table outlining how each is rated.

lic official bonds can cover either honesty alone or honesty and faithful performance), optional packages that include special coverages, and variations in rates according to traits of the insured parties or characteristics of the agreement between them. However, one does not find the same kinds of variations in each of the nine categories.

Among these nine categories of bonds, fidelity, financial institution, and contract bonds are the most important. Besides the evidence on the proportion of premiums derived from these lines (contract bonds alone provide a third of all the premium income in bonding), this fact is evident from the systematization of the rating schemes for these bonds. The following discussion is therefore based mainly on a contrast between rating in fidelity and financial institution bonds (both sub-types of fidelity bonds), on the one hand, and contract bonds (a sub-type of surety bonds), on the other.

Fidelity bonds cover mainly the dishonest or fraudulent actions of employees in many different kinds of businesses. Financial institution bonds are fairly similar to fidelity bonds except that they cover the losses of banks, savings and loan associations, stock and commodity brokers, and other similar organizations (Schmidt 1931). But since the objects used in everyday business in financial institutions are objects that most people find useful and that can be stolen relatively easily, the likelihood of loss is higher in financial institutions than in other organizations. People are more likely to steal money than baked goods or dentists' tools.

A contract bond is an agreement that if the contractor fails to carry out the activities specified in the contract, the surety will either pay the compensation or attempt to carry out the activities (or find someone else to carry them out) in the contractor's place (Surety Association of America n.d., a, b). This bond guarantees that owners will get what they have paid for; it is a performance bond as opposed to an honesty bond.

Given that people usually have more control over their honesty than over their ability to meet contractual obligations, particularly when these depend on the performances of subcontractors, it is somewhat surprising that the problems of calculating rates are more easily overcome in fidelity bonding than in surety bonding.[8] The reason for

8. Because public official and public employee bonds can be bought as simple honesty bonds or as honesty and performance bonds, it is possible to compare the losses due to each type of peril. The ratio of the honesty bond premium to the faithful

this has mainly to do with *whose* honesty is usually covered in a bond and what the relation is between this person and the policyholder. In most fidelity bonding, the bond covers the behavior of a subunit—an employee of a firm—rather than of the unit itself, and the policyholder who purchases the bond is not the entity that controls the loss.[9] In surety bonding, in contrast, the bond covers the behavior of the entity as a whole (this is usually an organization, though many small contractors involve primarily a single individual) and is purchased by that same entity. That is, fidelity bonds are usually bought by employers to cover their employees, while most surety bonds are bought by organizations to cover their own performance.[10]

Just as was the case in marine insurance, then, it is easier to calculate a rate and safer to sell insurance when the policyholder does not directly control the loss-causing events. When there is considerable distance between the policyholder and the individual covered by a bond (e.g., when a large organization carries the bond and the person covered is a low-ranking employee), the potential thief will not be much inclined to steal just because the employer can recoup the losses from the insurance company. Very likely potential thieves will be unaware that their thefts would be covered by a bond.

---

performance (which includes honesty) bond premium is 1:1.25 (1:1.33 for public utility employees). This means that although faithful performance is harder to come by than honesty (the premium is a quarter to a third extra), important prerequisites of faithful performance are honesty and good intentions. But we should also remember that the definition of honesty in public official bonds is one of the most encompassing—honesty includes responsibility for the honesty of one's subordinates.

Still, these ratios are suggestive. They suggest that bonding companies believe that faithful performance of one's duties is largely under one's control and that failure to meet one's obligations is not really an accident. This helps explain why bonding companies have been reluctant to assume that any losses need occur and have been stubborn in their insistence that they should not rate as if losses were inevitable.

9. This arrangement is a fairly recent innovation. Individual employees once arranged for their own bonds and paid the premiums themselves.

10. A further distinction has to do with *who is the beneficiary* of the bond. In most cases, the beneficiary of a fidelity bond is the policyholder, while the beneficiary of a surety bond is the actor for whom the policyholder is carrying out some set of performances. It is because surety bonds are three-party contracts (the surety company agrees to compensate the beneficiary for the policyholder's defaults) that insurers often do not classify these bonds as insurance. Since fidelity bonds are now often two-party contracts (i.e., the policyholder is the beneficiary), insurers concede that fidelity bonds are more like insurance. From our perspective, though, the insurers' emphasis is misplaced, and the most important question is not whether the beneficiary and the policyholder are the same actor, but whether the policyholder is the actor who controls the loss-causing events, since this is where the problem of decreased incentive to prevent losses really matters.

Although the distance between the policyholder and the person controlling the loss makes the risk less reactive than might otherwise be the case, this does not solve a second problem. A second obstacle in setting rates for bonds is the inadequacy of theories about what causes loss.[11] As the history of fire insurance redlining shows, insurers have not done too well when they have tried to predict which categories of policyholders are moral hazards (see Heimer 1982).

In fidelity bonding this particular problem was circumvented when insurers began to rate the settings in which potential thieves were embedded rather than rating the people themselves. One of the first innovations of this sort was the substitution of position bonds for individual bonds. Position bonds, of which there are many varieties, cover whatever individuals occupy the specified positions in an organization. Rates for position bonds are based only on the characteristics of the position, while premiums (and even the decision to give or withhold the bond) for individual bonds can be based on the characteristics of the individuals as well as of the positions they occupy.

Position bonds were first developed for bonds covering the officers of fraternal orders (Joyce 1945:1A, 15A). Since new officers were elected every year, new bonds and new investigations were required even though the risks being covered had changed only trivially. At the time of this innovation, insurers and employers believed that the chief advantage of the position bond was that it obviated the need to file a new bond every time an employee quit and was replaced. With high turnover, position bonds substantially reduced paperwork.

Perhaps more important, though, this shift paved the way for rating based on organizational control mechanisms rather than on individual honesty. Because the loss record and the inspection pertained to the position rather than to individual incumbents of that position, insurers' attention shifted from variations between individuals to variations between positions.

When insurers began to look for situational traits that might account for variations in fidelity losses, they apparently found two important ones, since these two factors are used in rating a wide variety of bonds. The first could be regarded as a standardized measure of the number of potential thieves.

11. See Klimon (1979) for an attempt to define dishonesty.

If there are many employees, then the pool of potential thieves is larger, and one should expect the odds of a loss to go up. Since employees with certain kinds of jobs have more opportunities to steal than those in other kinds of jobs, we might expect that the odds of loss would vary with whether employees in general handled money, had access to valuable inventories, worked unsupervised, and so on. Because of these variations, bonding companies count only certain kinds of employees when relating the premium rate to the number of employees. These are called ratable employees, and the method for calculating the number of ratable employees varies from one type of bond to another (Surety Association of America n.d., j; Heimer 1981:348–83, 427–35).

For example, when insurers are counting the number of ratable employees to be covered by a fidelity bond, insurers group them as class 1 and class 2 employees. But it is no simple matter to count up the number of class 1 employees. The number of class 1 employees is the sum of all class A employees, which includes those with substantial opportunity to steal, plus 5 percent of the first hundred of the rest of the employees, plus 1 percent of the remaining employees. Class 2 employees are not counted for most kinds of business. This group seems to include employees who do not have formal control over very much money or inventory but who are relatively unsupervised—janitors, drivers, and so on. In effect, this way of counting employees says that insurers believe some employees have about twenty times as much (or a hundred times as much) opportunity to steal as others. People with little opportunity for theft are then counted as 1/20 (or 1/100) of a person each.

The second measure of the likelihood of loss has to do with the directness of the supervision of the employees. In general, as I argued in the chapter on marine insurance, the odds of loss will go up when supervision is more indirect. This problem is partly taken care of in the classification of employees as ratable or not, but a further cause of difficulties in supervision is having employees located in several different branches. A special charge for having more than a single office is intended to reflect the extra losses that will occur because of the indirect supervision of branch offices.

Although insurers write of the shift from individual to position bonds as if this were a simple matter of convenience, early essays on the benefits of corporate surety bonding stressed the importance of checking to see whether potential employees were indeed honest people. This suggests either that the change to position bonds involved a major philosophical reorientation, combined with a substantial reworking of rating and underwriting methods, or else that bonding companies had long ago given up most checking of the credentials of individual employees, and were simply bringing rhetoric and details of coverage into line with rating and underwriting practice. Early writings also stressed the prophylactic effect of employees knowing that their records were being checked. In other varieties of surety bonds, the bonds still tend to cover specified individuals, and presumably bonding companies still make checks on these individuals.[12]

But this new emphasis on situational correlates of fidelity losses does not mean that insurers ignore the problem of rating honesty or good intentions themselves. In practice, though, when insurers are setting rates for businesses rather than individuals and are selling position bonds rather than individual ones, they must rate not the morality of any individual but instead the morality of the *average* employee in that industry, taking into account all those factors (such as moral climate, temptations, and so on) that might influence such things and that might vary between businesses. This, in effect, is aggregate-level experience rating. Insurers do not have a theory about why there are fewer fidelity losses in churches than in liquor stores; they just know that they have gotten fewer claims from churches.

Many of these residual causes of variations in loss are captured in the rate adjustment for the kind of business being bonded. For forgery bonds, the distinction is a simple one between private bonds and business bonds. In a business setting, one is more likely to be taking checks from strangers than in a private setting. In mercantile establishment and financial institution bonds, the rate modification adjusts the rate to take into account such diverse factors as the kind of people who work in that sort of business (church as opposed to bank), the typical supervisory structure (dental office compared to bakery), the sort of inventory on hand to be stolen (dry cleaners compared with a jewelry store), and so on.

In the case of contract bonds, the variation has to do with the difficulty of the work. Rates are higher for heavy contract work (such as

12. See Risler (1963) on further changes in bonds.

constructing buildings) than for light contracting work (such as furnishing buildings). Presumably, these variations have more to do with the difficulty of meeting contract deadlines than with honesty. Heavy contract work may be more uncertain because of dependence on weather, on price of raw materials, on work of subcontractors, and so forth. But, in addition, this difference in rates may be partly due to differences in contractors' organizational structures, in the kinds of people who work in heavy contracting, and so on.

When insurers use these sorts of gross rate modifications, this means that they have no theory about the cause of loss, but instead have had to build the rate out of aggregate loss experiences. This sort of aggregate-level experience rating makes for a somewhat rigid system. Since the bonding companies cannot predict what traits of companies will be associated with losses, they cannot adjust the rate of a costume jewelry store that has nothing anyone wants to steal to be more like the rate of the dry cleaning shop; they cannot adjust the rate of a bakery with a supervisory structure more like that of a dental office to be in line with the rate of the dental office; and they cannot adjust the rate of a labor union with a bunch of staff members who are all saints to be more like that of a church and alter the rate of a labor union with staff members who are thugs to be closer to the rate of an adult bookstore.

Again, this problem is similar to Akerlof's (1970) market for "lemons" in the sense that the "blue book" price is the only estimate available. One difference, though, is that while former owners of used cars know whether they have a "peach" or a "lemon," we would not necessarily expect a similar level of awareness of the quality of their employees in the owners of jewelry stores. The latter do not have access to the "blue book" (only bonding companies would), and *Consumer Reports* does not publish a list of average fidelity losses comparable to their lists of repair experiences for automobiles for policyholders to use in judging their own establishments.

When we compare this set of factors with those used in other lines of insurance, we see that in fidelity and surety bonding the rate increases with increased likelihood of loss just as it does in other lines of insurance. And, just as in marine and fire insurance, the *variations in rates reflect not just variations in ability to minimize or withstand loss but also variations in the likelihood of an accident that will cause a loss.* That is, in marine insurance, rates are higher when ships are old and lack modern safety equipment and also when they will be sailing during winter months or in seas where storms are more likely. In fire insurance, rates are related both to combustibility and to the likelihood of sparks and ignition. In fidelity and surety bonding, the rates also respond both to the equivalent of combustibility or of seaworthiness of the vessel, on the one hand, and to the equivalent of sparks or storms, on the other. It is not organizational design or indirect supervision or access to money that leads to a loss in fidelity or surety bonding. Instead, these factors make it easier or more difficult for a person to steal or to fail to live up to obligations. The efficient cause of the loss is always an individual act. Rates cannot be directly related to the likelihood of such individual acts because of a lack of understanding of the motivation for such actions. But insurers have learned that the moral character of the average employee varies from one kind of enterprise to another, and they use this information to calculate about variations in the functional equivalent of sparks or storms.

Finally, employers are expected to make some checks on potential employees, and bonds are likely to be contingent on making such checks; compensation for a loss is usually also contingent on the employer not having failed to report previous incidents involving that employee. This means that the insurer requires the policyholder to make reasonable efforts to control the source of the risk, in this case the person or position bonded. These requirements are rather like the rules in marine insurance that the ship be seaworthy (in this case, it is the position that must be kept "seaworthy") and that the policyholder exercise due diligence, or the rules in fire insurance that safety devices must be inspected periodically.

Thus far, I have argued that the rating of bonds is possible because of three innovations. First, when bonds are bought by the beneficiary rather than the principal, they are more "insurance-like" in the sense that the person holding the bond does not directly control the loss. With this arrangement, fidelity bonding is in principle no different than marine insurance coverage of barratry. (Note, though, that insurers worry that an owner's interest in controlling the actions of a captain might decrease if barratry were covered by insurance.) More important, we have moved quite a distance on the continuum from perfect control by the policyholder to no control by the policyholder. As I argued earlier, the more losses are out of control of the policyholder, the more possible insurance is.

A second innovation was the change from bonding of individuals to the bonding of positions. This was important because it shifted attention from the characteristics of individuals to the characteristics of organizations and the positions in them. While bonding companies may have been uncomfortable trying to predict whether *individuals*, even those with unblemished records, would continue to behave honestly, they were less reluctant to say which characteristics of positions and organizations made fidelity losses more or less likely. Inadequate supervision or access to valuable products, bonders believed, made fidelity losses more likely.

But bonders still had to face the fact that the moral character of employees played a big role. They have, in effect, concluded that the moral character of the average employee varies from one kind of enterprise to another, and they have used experience-based data to modify rates accordingly.

When it is not possible to do one of the things outlined above, bonding companies are forced to treat premiums as service fees. But just as banks base interest payments on the size of a loan, so bonding companies base their premiums on some measure of the largest possible loss. This is done in other lines of insurance, where the face value of a policy depends on the value at stake and the premium depends (among other things) on the face value.

The bond penalty or contract price is a measure of the amount at stake, and this is the equivalent of the face value of the insurance policy in fire or marine insurance. This value serves two functions— it places a limit on the amount that can be recovered, but it also should serve as an estimate of how much is at stake. In fidelity and surety bonding (except for contract bonding where the bond penalty is usually set equal to the value of the contract), there is often no independent measure of how much really is at stake, so pegging the premium to the penalty is a bit awkward. As has been shown over and over again in other lines of insurance, how much is lost in any given accident depends heavily on the original value at stake. All other things being equal, a bill for fire damage to a $100,000 home is likely to be higher than one for damage to a $50,000 home. Similarly, it is easier to steal $10,000 worth of jewelry from a jewelry store that sells gold and diamond rings than from one that sells costume jewelry. But it is harder to know exactly what the relation is between the value of a business and the likely size of fidelity losses. That is, it is not all that obvious how large a bond the owner of the business should carry. Only in financial institution bonds (where the minimum bond varies with the size of the organization measured by assets, number of employees, and so on) and contract bonds does there seem to be any agreement about how bond size should be related to other measures of exposure. What is clear is that small losses are considerably more likely than large losses, so in general the premium rate drops with increases in the size of the bond penalty. No matter how much is at stake, small losses are more likely than large ones.

In an effort to provide an appropriate measure of exposure (or the amount at stake), the Surety Association made a study of losses of $10,000 or more actually sustained by policyholders over a period of ten years. This information was used to construct an "exposure index," relating current assets and gross sales to minimum coverage appropriate for the enterprise in question. An insured who had bought a bond of the size specified by the formula would have been fully protected in 95 percent of the losses covered by the study.[13] But while insurers may recommend that their policyholders carry adequate bonds, premiums are still not pegged to carrying a bond penalty of the appropriate size. That is, there are no provisions for coinsurance in fidelity and surety lines as there are in marine and fire insurance.

Finally, the premium is adjusted to the amount of time the bond is in force, just as the borrower pays more interest if he or she keeps the debt for a longer time. More thefts occur in longer periods of time; it is harder to meet all of a series of contract obligations spread over a long period of time than to meet a smaller number of deadlines in a shorter period. Even if the premium is mainly a service charge, we would expect premiums to vary with the time span covered by the bond.

Underwriting: Matching Policyholders with Rates

The fact that insurers have learned how to set surety and fidelity rates does not mean that further calculations about the honesty of individuals are unnecessary. The underwriter, the person respon-

---

13. This study is discussed in Surety Association of America (n.d., e), Beardsley (1965:826), and Porter (1966:25). The general issue of how large a bond is required is discussed in Conner (1951) and *National Underwriter* (1961).

sible for accepting or declining applicants for coverage, still has to decide which organizations and individuals should receive bonds, determine which rates apply to them, and engineer the contracts to keep losses low. In this section, I will discuss how it is possible to select policyholders, given that no one knows how to sort the honest from the dishonest, and how underwriters provide incentives for honesty.

One reads over and over again that "if the surety has any doubt about the integrity of an applicant, it will not bond him under any condition" (Surety Association of America n.d., g:2). The problem, of course, is how to determine which applicants are honest and capable. In making a decision about whether to accept or reject an applicant, an underwriter assesses the information given in the application and does some additional investigating, checking references, seeing whether the surety company's files contain prejudicial information about the applicant, and so on.

In fidelity bonding, both the traits of individual employees and the characteristics of the position are covered in the application forms and investigations. In going through the standard questions one by one and explaining the purpose of each, Crist stresses that underwriters

> do not presume to judge the priceless integrity of a human being, but they do attempt to determine whether they shall insure the continuity of that integrity in the face of whatever temptations.
>
> The art of fidelity-bond underwriting does not contemplate an exact analysis of the component parts of the moral fiber of the individual applicant. That would be impossible. All the underwriters do, all they can hope to do, is to realize that some human beings (which ones they do not know) are weaker than others; that some yield more readily to temptation than others. The underwriting problem resolves itself into *weighing the factors which might make for the pressure of temptation, and appraising the hazards which might yield an opportunity wrongfully to convert an employer's funds—and to get away with it.*
>
> (1950:214; emphasis added)

Crist consistently emphasizes questions that provide evidence about discrepancies between people's needs and their income (such as the number of dependents, the income from the job, and other sources of income) or that tell something about special temptations on the job that are not matched with special checks (such as responsibility for writing large checks with no requirement that checks be co-signed).

Also important are questions about the assets of the bonded person and of other family members, since these are important sources of salvage either through legal action or because a relative wishes to "clear the family name." Questions about past business endeavors and failures are useful because many people apparently attempt to justify or cover up past indiscretions and end up providing enough information to get caught at it.

Not all of the questions and investigation procedures are very useful, according to Crist (1950:254–58). He devotes a couple of pages to bemoaning the fact that "there is no safety engineering of human honesty, as there is of boilers or elevators" and speculating, in a manner reminiscent of Goffman's (1969) distinction between communicating and giving off information, about which biographical characteristics might be used to predict honesty. Noting that letters of recommendation are uniformly uninformative, Crist searches for clues whose connection to honesty is sufficiently subtle that it will not occur to the applicant to manufacture appropriate evidence.[14]

But while these writers admit that they cannot really tell which people will remain honest and that there are few good indicators of integrity, they continue to argue that, in addition to investigating situational factors, the underwriter should attempt to determine which applicants are most likely to remain honest. Presumably that elusive goal of no losses would be attainable if only the underwriter could figure out which people would continue to resist temptations.

Actually, the problem is even more complex, since fidelity underwriters usually have to be concerned about the integrity of two people; losses can be caused either by dishonest employees or employers, or by a combination of the two. The underwriter thus investigates the employer's application (as well as the employee's), partly in an attempt to uncover dishonest employers who may get employees

---

14. Economists also have been concerned with this issue. The general problem is to find actions outside a market (e.g., an insurance or a labor market) that will yield information uncorrupted by market incentives. This pre-existing information can then be used in the market by actors who would otherwise have to base their decisions on inadequate and biased information since more reliable information will only be revealed later (e.g., after an insurance contract is signed or over the course of an employment relation). Education is sometimes discussed as a signal of a worker's "type" (that is, as an indicator of whether the worker is reliable and disciplined; Spence 1973 and Weiss 1982). As Spence (1973) points out, though, when individuals are aware that they are providing this information, their choices (e.g., about how much education they want) may well be affected.

bonded as a source of easy cash, as well as to discover unwise management practices that may increase the opportunities for employee dishonesty.

The situation is a bit different in contract bonds and in other performance bonds. In these cases, the underwriters are supposed to investigate the "three Cs": character, capacity, and capability. The descriptions of what one does to check character are especially abbreviated in accounts of contract bond underwriting, perhaps because in these cases, unlike in other sorts of fidelity and surety bonds, there is a very close tie between the interests of the bonded person and the interests of the enterprise.

In contract bonding, much more emphasis is placed on the ability of the contractor to carry out the contract. Much attention is given to the adequacy of the bid, which must be "in line" with the other bids (Burgoon 1965:836). The amount of dependence on subcontractors and the quality of such subcontractors are also considered. In addition, the bonding company is likely to examine up-to-date financial information indicating the ability of the contractors to finance the projects in question, to pay labor and materials bills whether they have been paid themselves, and to cushion losses due to unexpected cost increases or other mishaps. The debt-paying record of the contractor is also investigated. And the surety company will be interested in the contractor's responsibility for other work on hand, experience in similar undertakings, and ownership of appropriate equipment. Finally, the contract documents are a very important source of information, since they specify the responsibilities of the contractor, the payment schedules, and so on.

Presumably, the reason for this heavy emphasis on ability rather than on character is that contractors often have considerably more invested in their businesses than most employees have in their jobs. It is easier to get another job (even with a bad record) than to set up a whole new construction business. This means that one can more justifiably assume the good intentions of the contractor (at least as far as getting the work done more or less as agreed in the contract) than one can assume the good intentions of others covered by bonds. Fiduciaries such as executors of wills, for example, do not usually have sunk costs in their roles, nor do they so directly benefit by living up to their obligations.

Because fiduciaries, public officials, and others sometimes covered by performance bonds rather than honesty bonds benefit less directly from their performances (that is, income and other rewards are not so closely tied to performances, at least in the short run), underwriting their bonds is in some ways more similar to underwriting honesty bonds (mercantile fidelity and financial institution bonds) than to underwriting contract bonds. Specifically, more attention is paid to information about character and especially to information about the adequacy of the principal's income, the principal's financial needs, opportunities for theft inherent in the position, and checks against exploiting such opportunities.

Though investigation of the applicant is still an important part of the decision to give a bond, there is some evidence that its importance has declined, particularly in fidelity, financial institution, and public official bonds. Much of this change, in fact, occurred long ago with the advent of blanket and position bonds.[15]

During the time when the uses of fidelity bonds were considerably more limited and, in particular, when only individual or schedule bonds (covering several listed individuals) were used,

> every slightest suggestion of underwriting peril was run down and cleared up if possible; and when a man was finally accepted, at the end perhaps of weeks of research, his fidelity bond was instantaneously honored by St. Peter as a pass to Paradise.
>
> (Lunt, in Law 1924: 13)

When blanket bonds began to be used, practices changed dramatically. The blanket bond (covering all of the officers and employees) "eliminates at one stroke the old individual investigations . . . eliminates them by making them impossible" (Lunt, in Law 1924: 13). The surety is usually not even given the names of the bonded people, much less fidelity applications from them. These blanket bonds were first used in banks, but the position bond, "a form of bond equally fatal to the old underwriting system" (Lunt, in Law 1924: 14), was adopted in other fields. Since no specific individuals are named, there is no possibility of investigation.[16]

15. See Law (1924) for a series of letters about the shocking laxity of investigation procedures.
16. One could argue that surety companies have continued to make investigations. But since they are insuring *positions* rather than individuals, they investigate to see that whoever occupies that position is adequately supervised, required to follow appropriate procedures, and so on. Investigation of individuals who fill the positions is then left to the employer's personnel department.

The primary purpose of the investigation is, of course, to determine whether the applicant should be bonded. But even in the harsh light of a surety underwriter's inspection, the world is not neatly divided into black and white; instead there are many ambiguous cases in which an underwriter believes it is probably safe to bond the applicant though he or she is nervous about doing so. According to all the advertising, the underwriter would refuse the bond in these cases. The reason that underwriters do not refuse all ambiguous cases is not, as some authors would have us believe, that they are doing a sloppy job or that they have somehow failed to realize that their job is to exclude all those bad risks. Instead it is that underwriters have considerable flexibility and can vary the conditions of the bond to suit the situation. It is true that the underwriter has relatively little control over the rate, but varying the conditions of the bond in effect varies the service given for the fixed rate (which is really the same thing as varying the rate).

One important question asked in an investigation concerns the assets of the person seeking a bond, and also the assets of his or her relatives. Underwriters are interested in a principal's assets because they can be used to pay the obligee directly or to repay the surety company. One way both to reduce the likelihood of loss and to increase the likelihood of repayment is to freeze the principal's assets. A very common way to do this is to require the principal to deposit collateral. The rate manual specifies how much the premium rate should be reduced when collateral is given and what sort of collateral is acceptable. Usually the premium is reduced by 50 percent when collateral is given (though the rules about minimum bonds remain the same), and usually only cash and government bonds are acceptable as collateral, though according to Crist (1950:203) underwriters can choose to accept other assets. The rate manual is completely silent on the question of *when* the underwriter should require collateral, though. Obviously, one is more likely to require collateral when one is unsure that a bond should be given; so requiring collateral is a way for the underwriter to give a bond in an ambiguous case without substantially increasing the odds of having to pay a loss. Collateral is often *required* for court bonds (Backman 1948:178). The reasons for this are discussed further in the section on loss prevention.

When a policyholder has a bad record, especially when the policyholder has experienced a series of small losses, the underwriter can require what is known as an "underwriting deductible." This deductible can be applied to the entire coverage or to specific classes of employees or even to subgroups within a class. Credit is given for the deductible, so the policyholder pays a lower rate. But the main point is that the surety company is able to avoid small recurrent losses and to encourage loss prevention by forcing the policyholder at least to share the losses. Underwriting deductibles are not available in all lines; the underwriter has this flexibility only in fidelity (including financial institution) and forgery bonding. (This is discussed mainly in Travelers Insurance Company 1956:9 and in Beardsley 1965: 824-25.)

A corresponding option is available in public official and contract bonds, where the likelihood of loss depends substantially on others not covered by the bond (lower-level employees in one case, subcontractors in the other). The underwriter can insist that these principals require bonds of those on whom they depend. If a contractor has required that subcontractors have surety bonds naming the contractor as the obligee, then the subcontractors' defaults will be less likely to result in the contractor defaulting as well. And if the contractor is still forced to default, there will be some funds to help cover the loss. Similarly, public officials are often legally liable for losses due to the acts of lower-level employees. It has become common to bond public employees who are subordinate to liable higher officials in order to protect the higher-level officials (and, of course, to protect their sureties). When such lower-level bonding is not common, an underwriter can make it a condition of bonding the applicant, particularly if the contract is poorly designed or if the subcontractor has a bad reputation, in the one case, or if the obligations of the public official are diffuse or ill-defined or if his or her underlings control large sums of money, in the other. Though such lower-level bonding is common in these two areas, there is in principle no reason why the underwriter cannot use this loss-prevention technique in other areas as well.

Underwriters can in effect charge bad risks a higher rate by forcing them to carry especially large bonds. How well this strategy works depends on how much the insurer can control the bond penalty carried by the policyholder, and what the relation is between bond penalty and premium rates, as I will explain below.

In contract bonds the premium is based either on the bond penalty or on the contract price, whichever is larger. In other cases, for example in public official and fiduciary bonds, there are legal requirements about bond penalty size. And, of course, there is little question about the size of a bail bond, since this is fixed by a judge. In fidelity bonding, though, there is no obvious way to determine how large a bond needs to be, and it is clear that policyholders do not know how much insurance they need and often purchase too little. In the Surety Association study only 15 percent of the losses of $125,000 or less were fully covered (Beardsley 1965:826).

Such underinsurance hurts both the policyholder, who suffers the loss, and the bonding company, which cannot sell big bonds. As in other lines of insurance, small losses are more likely than large losses. That is, if a house is worth $40,000, losses of $5,000 in fire damage are considerably more likely than $35,000 losses. Knowing this, the owner of a $40,000 house might buy only $5,000 worth of insurance. The problem with this is that the odds of a $5,000 loss are the same (unless the owner intervenes) whether the owner purchases a small or a large amount of insurance. Insurance rates have traditionally been set assuming that people will insure the full value (or almost—at least 80 percent) of their property or else that they will receive only partial payment for losses.[17] Under this rating system, it is unfair for an owner of a $40,000 home insured for $5,000 (who has therefore paid a relatively small premium) to recover as much for a $5,000 fire as a similar homeowner who has insured the entire value of the house.

The point is that *if* losses have the same relation to exposure in bonding as in fire insurance (that is, if loss size is only weakly related to exposure and if small losses occur more frequently than large losses, so that *most* losses on a $50,000 bond will be under $10,000, just as they would on a $10,000 bond), then policyholders buying small bonds would be receiving a subsidy from those buying larger ones if rates do not vary by size of the bond penalty. Though none of the literature discusses this question explicitly, the combination of the structure of the rates (which decrease with the size of the bond penalty, indicating that small losses are more frequent) and the elements of the Surety Association exposure index (which indicate

17. The relevant rule in fire insurance is called the 80 percent coinsurance rule and is discussed in the section on face values in chapter 3.

that the size of losses is weakly related to the size of the enterprise) suggests that losses are related to exposure in the same way in bonding as in fire insurance. But the experience rating formulas provide for larger percentage reductions to policyholders carrying larger bonds, indicating that the current rates are somewhat inequitable, involving some subsidy of small bonds by large bonds.

What all this means is that if underwriters have doubts about applicants, they may want to require them to carry larger bonds. There is more "underwriting fat" on the large bonds than on small ones, so if one compares losses to premiums, one might well find that the loss ratio is smaller and therefore that the rate being charged per dollar of loss is considerably higher. In this way, then, an underwriter can charge a higher premium to a bad risk. (The danger, of course, is making oneself vulnerable to a large loss rather than a small one.)

The last important option available to the underwriter is experience rating. Experience rating is a refinement of a rate to reflect the actual loss experience of an insured. Through experience rating one in effect rewards good risks for keeping losses down and penalizes bad risks for allowing losses to occur. Actually in many lines of bonding the rating plans are "all credit plans"; so policyholders are rewarded with larger or smaller decreases in premiums, and no one is punished with higher rates (or actually, everyone is penalized by having to pay too much at the start; see State of New York Department of Insurance [1945a:73] for a comment on this practice). Credits vary between 0 and 50 percent and are given for loss ratios below 40 percent. Credits also vary with the size of the bond penalty (or premium).

The second reason that experience rating is so significant is that the adjustments offered are substantial—up to 50 percent of the premium (with a rule requiring a $25 minimum premium). Adjustments for experience rating are not nearly so substantial in other lines of insurance. What this suggests is that a substantial portion of the variation in likelihood of loss is not captured by the rates. That is, the measures of opportunity for dishonest behavior, average honesty of employees, and so on, are inadequate predictors of actual behavior and are worse, predictors of losses than are those used in other fields. Presumably another reason for this emphasis on experience rating is that where losses are somewhat under the control of the policyholder, one wants to provide significant incentives for loss prevention. Even if losses could be predicted, one still might choose to emphasize experience rating. Any other system would entail the danger of encouraging laxity, and the predictions might end up being grossly wrong after all.

Who benefits from the cut in premiums from experience rating, and therefore who gets an incentive for loss prevention, is different for different kinds of bonds. In the case of financial institution or mercantile establishment bonds, for example, a dishonest employee is "experience rated" either by being fired or by not being hired to begin with. However, the bank or mercantile establishment that employed (or refused to employ) this person (the principal) receives the monetary incentive to screen potential employees and to control their behavior. That is, since the premium on a fidelity bond is usually not paid by the principal but instead by the obligee, the incentive offered is not an incentive for the principal to behave properly but for the obligee to *control* the principal. This is less true in surety bonds, since in most cases the principal—the person licensed or the contractor—actually pays for the bond. Experience rating therefore tends to provide an incentive for *self*-control in surety bonds and for indirect control by someone else in fidelity bonds.

To summarize, then, we have found that underwriting is indeed crucial in surety and fidelity bonding, just as the early writers claimed. But we have argued that it is important for different reasons. Underwriting is important not because the underwriter can eliminate all the bad risks and therefore make it feasible for the ratemakers to base their rates on an assumption of no losses; instead it is critical because the underwriter adapts the rates and coverages to adjust for the fact that "all men are not equal, even at conception" (Crist 1950:244) and to encourage them to behave honestly and live up to their obligations despite that.

Loss Prevention: Compensating for Information Asymmetries

Surety loss prevention differs from that in other lines of insurance both in the *degree* and the *purpose* of the insurer's intervention. Bonding companies intervene more frequently and more directly than other insurers do, and their purpose is often as much to collect information about whether the coverage should be continued as to deter loss.

In this section we will see that when information asymmetries are especially severe, and when losses are almost entirely controllable, insurers move several steps away from pure market solutions. In some cases they overcome information asymmetries by requiring policyholders to share information with them or with specified third parties. In especially troublesome cases they require that some of the policyholders' activities be carried out with supervision from the insurer. If we were to abstract from insurers' behavior, we would say that markets only work when risks are fixed, that supplementary information must be supplied through contractual agreements where information asymmetries are moderate, and that temporary penetration of the policyholder organization is necessary when information asymmetries are severe and where losses are almost completely under the control of the policyholder.

Because fidelity and surety loss prevention depends primarily on getting people to behave properly, rather than on installing equipment and then leaving it to function with only occasional inspections and maintenance, the motivation of those who might cause losses is crucial. Bonding companies stress their right to try to collect from whoever is responsible for the loss, and they admit that this emphasis on salvage is intended to warn the bonded contractor, employees, or public officials that they really do intend to come after them.[18] "They [the employees] also are aware that if they default they must answer to the impersonal surety company for their defalcations, and this understanding has frequently deterred a bonded employee from taking his first misstep" (Surety Association of America n.d., k:23). Note that the collection of salvage differs from loss-sharing arrangements (such as deductibles) in other lines of insurance in two respects. First, the bonding company tries to make a person responsible for the loss repay the *entire* loss, not just a portion of it.[19]

18. Whatever the bonding company recovers from a thief or defaulting contractor is called salvage.

19. Insofar as there is justification in bonding companies' traditionally stubborn insistence that they are not selling insurance, but a service instead, it is that they expect to pursue defaulting contractors and dishonest employees and to recover their losses. Ideally, then, the bonding company is only "loaning" the obligee funds until it recovers the losses from the guilty bonded person or organization. But this is an excessively optimistic view of the chances of recovering the entire loss.

According to Backman (1948) salvage is substantial; it averaged around a third of all losses for the period up to 1946. This means that there is a substantial probability that a bonding company will recover from a bonded principal and that the odds of a bonding company "punishing" a wrongdoer are substantially greater than the odds of

Perhaps more importantly, though, the loss is to be borne by whoever caused the loss, whether this is the policyholder or someone
else. With this latter policy the surety company extends itself into the
policyholder's organization, attempting, for example, to influence
employees directly rather than rely on the employer to provide appropriate incentives. Fire and marine insurers do not intervene so directly, offering rewards to policyholders' employees neither for preventing fires nor for averting marine disasters.

One of the main loss-prevention methods employed by bonding
companies is the threat or promise of investigation and record keeping. When a person or company applies for a bond, a thorough investigation (the bonding companies' terminology) is conducted. Often
such an investigation involves checking not just employment history
but also personal habits, since these provide motivations for dishonesty and theft.

These sorts of investigations are made in other lines of insurance
as well (mainly for commercial customers), but there are several differences. First, since surety and fidelity losses are more subject to
control than are losses in other lines of insurance, any questionable
fact in someone's record is reason enough to refuse a bond. Therefore, the investigation of the potential insured carries considerably
more weight in surety and fidelity lines than in others. A second difference, which reinforces the first, is that the bond can be nullified by
an employer's failure to report new evidence about the moral character of a bonded employee. If an employee is caught filching even trivial amounts and this is not reported to the bonding company, then
subsequent losses in which this employee is implicated will not be
covered.

What this really means is that to the extent that surety and fidelity

---

the courts doing so. Of course, this is partly because many of the losses covered by
bonds are not "crimes." Even though a principal has some control, and is in some
senses responsible for a loss, he or she may not have been able to avert it. This is often
the case, for example, in contract bonding during periods of widespread economic
difficulty and also for public officials whose subordinates are either dishonest or in-
competent. In such cases, having to pay back the bonding company's "loan" is certainly a burden, but it may be one that the individual or company would have assumed
voluntarily. It is unclear whether the threat of the bonding company only reinforces the
sense of moral obligation of those who would be inclined to make good the losses, or
whether bonding companies actually pursue those less willing to repay and "teach
them a lesson."

losses, especially, are due to traits of the bonded person, information about these traits must be given a lot of weight. But human character is not permanently fixed, so bonding companies must keep updating their information. An efficient way to do this is to motivate an employer (the policyholder and beneficiary) to provide any information indicating that the risk is *worse* than had been assumed. The provision that the employer must notify the bonding company of minor thefts has much the same function as warranties do in marine insurance. Dangerous conditions are specified, and recovery for losses depends on the policyholder following the insurer's instructions.

Bonding companies' stress on the importance of following sound business practices is rather like marine insurers' emphasis on seaworthiness. Both are flexible standards that change as standard practices evolve. And in both cases there are inspections by outsiders to see that the policyholders' affairs are in order. But in surety bonding this intervention takes place more frequently than the annual classification society inspection in marine insurance, and it often involves deeper penetration of the policyholder's organization. Exactly how this intervention is arranged varies from one line of bonding to another and also depends on the extent of the insurer's reservations about the policyholder.

In Williamson's (1975) terms, surety and fidelity bonding companies are a step closer to an organizational solution than are marine or fire insurers. Though bonding companies will be more able to predict the performance of their policyholders, they (and especially their policyholders) will start to incur the *costs* of organizational solutions.

In fiduciary bonds, the bonding company sometimes supervises the activities of the principal, or arranges for a bank to perform this same function by acting as a co-fiduciary. Under "joint control," a written agreement is made between the fiduciary, the bonding company, and banks, safe deposit companies, and so on, that assets are subject only to *joint* action by the surety company and the fiduciary. This means that withdrawal slips have to be signed by an agent of the surety company as well as by the fiduciary, that access to the safe deposit box is only permitted in the presence of both parties, and so forth. Surety company literature stresses that the need for joint control is based primarily on the complexity of the duties rather than on bad intentions:

The real function of joint control is to guard against improper acts arising from inexperience, ignorance of the law, careless handling, premature distribution (of assets), or laxity.

(Surety Association of America n.d., c:4)

Bonding companies also stress the symbiotic relation between lawyers and themselves, noting that since so many of the losses they pay are due to ignorance of the law, their clients must be encouraged (or forced) to seek good legal advice (Surety Association of America n.d., c:6).

Given this insistence on good legal advice, it is unclear why joint control would still be necessary to make certain that the fiduciaries are not ignorant of the legal requirements of their jobs.[20] The answer, of course, is that joint control has other functions that are at least as important. In another pamphlet, the Surety Association (n.d., g:2) asserts that "joint control enables surety companies to execute many fiduciary bonds which they might otherwise be forced to decline for reasons of sound underwriting judgment." Still, the exercise of joint control is not seen as a reflection upon the honesty of the fiduciary, since the bond would be refused if there were any doubt about the applicant's integrity. The point is rather that "many fiduciaries of high character but without financial strength thus may procure substantial surety bonds which, without the exercise of joint control, would be unavailable to them" (Surety Association of America n.d., g:8). What this suggests is that bonding companies are most motivated to prevent losses by close supervision when there is least opportunity for them to recover their losses.

Joint control is the most extreme example of this interventionist strategy. Milder forms include "periodic review" and "close supervision," which are discussed less fully in the pamphlets. According to one account, most fiduciary losses arise from embezzlements that occur over a period of years (Surety Association of America n.d., c:5). An examination of the periodic accounts required by the state is intended both to deter theft and to nip it in the bud when it does occur.

That such methods of control are actually effective is suggested by

20. They investigate the attorneys as well (Surety Association of America n.d., c:17).

the facts that bonding rates are lower when a bank is a co-fiduciary (the discount is 33⅓ percent; Surety Association of America n.d., j:CF-30) and that there is no charge for the extra services provided in joint control. The latter suggests that the decrease in losses at least makes up for the cost of the extra service.

Though these requirements seem to be somewhat less formal (than, for example, in court bonds), surety bonding companies also encourage equivalent loss-prevention techniques in businesses. To avert fidelity losses, they stress that a business should be audited regularly by an outsider and should have a good system of internal control.[21] There is some attempt to screen out clearly dishonest types (through personnel selection and training programs), but mainly these systems attempt to limit severely the opportunities for dishonesty (through an organization plan that establishes lines of control and that separates accounting from operating functions, and through division of duties, so that no single person is responsible for a transaction from start to finish) and to provide evidence that can be reviewed periodically to determine whether people are behaving themselves (through charts of accounts and records designed to show whether control procedures have been followed). Such a system of internal control is in many ways similar to the practice of joint control, except that the controller in this case is also the policyholder.

Presumably there are similar requirements for contract bonds, though since the period of time over which a bond runs is shorter, there may be less need for this sort of supervision. In large contracts, surety companies try to help the contractor avoid default. They provide funds themselves; arrange loans with banks (guaranteed by the surety companies); provide engineering, accounting, special consulting, and other technical services; and in some cases take over the management of the contractor's organization (see, for example, the cases discussed in Surety Association of America [n.d., b] and advocated by Fredericks [1965]). In the worst cases, the surety companies must either pay the owner the bond penalty or find new contractors to do the job. Perhaps one reason that there is less emphasis on supervision in contract bonding is that it is less clear that a surety company's supervision really would assist in ensuring *performance*. Though su-

21. Surety Association of America (n.d., k:3–4) discusses the components of an internal control system, and *National Underwriter* (1963) advocates using accountants on fidelity claims.

pervision may truly reduce opportunities for dishonesty, the supervision of an expert by someone relatively ignorant of the task is less likely to enhance performance.

When it is not possible to intervene to prevent or curtail losses, bonding companies often require collateral. The deposit of collateral is almost always an option available to the principal as a way of reducing the premium. But collateral is quite often *required* in types of bonds (e.g., immigrant or judicial proceeding bonds) where supervision is impossible or in cases in which the bonding company is reluctant to give a bond.

Thus far, I have been discussing how bonding companies collect information about the intentions and behavior of policyholders and their agents and how they provide incentives for trustworthiness. But there are still cases in which bonding companies are unwilling to grant bonds at all. These are cases in which the bonding company either has *no* information or else negative information. In such cases, though bonding companies typically refuse to give bonds, they have recently agreed to allow other organizations to act as co-sureties during a probationary period. After this period, the bonding company will consider the new evidence about the policyholder and perhaps provide a bond. In this way the reliability of corporate suretyship is combined with the flexibility of personal suretyship.

Corporate suretyship was not developed until around the middle of the nineteenth century, even though personal sureties had provided a wide variety of guarantees since antiquity (Mason 1924; Morgan 1927; Insurance Institute of London n.d.; Powell 1944; Lunt 1940; McMahon 1941; Mobley 1961; Russell 1951; Surety Association of America 1946; Weichelt 1934; Zimmerman 1963). It is unclear why corporate suretyship developed at this time. From the obligee's point of view, the guarantee of the corporate surety is probably better than that of the personal surety. The corporate surety will be more likely to be able to meet the obligations of the defaulting principal, as insurance writers are quick to point out (see Nichols 1939:7–9; Conlon 1938:397; Lesy 1973:2/1; and Mobley 1961:127 for examples of problems with personal sureties who were unable to meet their obligations).[22] The corporate surety is also better equipped than the per-

22. Ability to compensate an obligee is not enough in itself. Mobley (1961:131) mentions that people frequently complain that surety companies engage in litigation to

sonal surety to carry out loss-prevention activities. Corporate sureties are more likely than personal sureties to investigate the records of principals; to help administer a failing business; or to teach the policyholder how to keep records, set up systems of internal control, select employees, and so on. Insofar as nonperformance is due to incompetence or ignorance, the corporate surety is more likely than the individual one to correct the situation. And insofar as losses due to dishonesty are really due to poor control systems within an organization, the corporate surety is more likely than the personal surety to be able to help prevent losses.

Judicial and legislative actions may have encouraged the development of corporate bonding. Realizing that suretyship is a heavy honor, the courts have tended to treat personal sureties as "favorites of the court," making the personal surety's guarantee even less reliable (Brodsky 1940:141; Arnold 1926:171–89). Some authors have also argued that when legislatures have tried to make personal suretyship "safer" (for example by requiring personal sureties to keep the courts informed about the disposition of their wealth, by putting liens on their property so that funds would be available in the case of a loss, or by requiring more than one personal surety [Nichols 1939: 11–17; Millikan 1940:5 and 10–11]), they made an already onerous obligation even more burdensome, therefore making corporate suretyship more attractive by comparison. The substitution of corporate bonds for personal ones may also have been encouraged by legislation either permitting government organizations to accept corporate bonds in lieu of personal ones or requiring corporate bonds (Mobley 1961:127–28). Judges also have a good deal of leeway in deciding whether to accept personal or corporate bonds; so changing judicial views on personal suretyship may also have had some effect.

But not all advantages are on the side of the corporate surety. Personal suretyship is a much more egalitarian institution than corporate suretyship. Since personal suretyship depends primarily on friendship and family ties, and since almost everyone has some friends and some family, this sort of guarantee is available to most. Family and friendship ties are more evenly distributed over the population than are the good credit ratings and reserves of assets on which corporate sureties base their decisions to grant or to refuse bonds.

---

delay payment. If this is true, then the fact that the surety company is financially sound may make little difference to the obligee.

What this suggests is that the corporate surety is more concerned about ability to meet a loss than with honesty and the likelihood of carrying out a contract, while personal sureties rely on their ability to influence the principals to meet their obligations. Because a personal surety usually cannot *afford* to compensate the obligee, he or she must somehow influence the principal to avoid causing a loss. While a corporate surety may be able to offer advice and give business assistance, personal sureties should be at least as adept as corporate sureties at motivating the policyholder to deal honestly or to try to do the work.

One of the most important advantages of personal suretyship is that it facilitates building a good reputation. A good reputation need not be based on public knowledge or on records that have been kept by credit bureaus or other business organizations, but instead can be based on the knowledge that friends or relatives have. This means that a person with a blemished record might not be permanently marked, since individuals might be more willing to guarantee the performance of a repentant thief than a corporation would be. (Presumably, this is partly because the individuals would be more likely than corporations to be affected by the repentant thief's bad reputation. For example, a relative might have to support the reformed thief if employment were unavailable.) Also, personal suretyship might mean that people who are "outsiders" would have less trouble breaking into the system. Race, ethnicity, and sex have been grounds for refusing corporate bonds.[23] This means that blacks, for example, have had difficulty getting licenses to operate businesses, that they have been unable to get the performance bonds necessary to win large contracts, and so on.

In order to deal with these sorts of problems, some organizations (mostly governmental bodies) have devised programs that combine personal suretyship with corporate suretyship or that provide two layers of corporate suretyship. One program for ex-convicts provided that the insurance company (Aetna) would compensate employers only after the funds of the group bonding program were exhausted (*The National Underwriter* 1967:1, 4). The program was operated by an ex-convict group that was intended to function much like Alcoholics Anonymous in providing mutual support.

23. Fire insurance was often refused to applicants who were the wrong race or ethnicity or who were located in predominantly minority neighborhoods (Heimer 1982).

A second program, also for ex-convicts, combined the resources of the Department of Health, Education, and Welfare with those of Aetna (*The National Underwriter* 1967:4). H.E.W. sponsored the program and paid the premiums for the participants, and it was sufficiently successful that it became a national service, funded under Title III of the Comprehensive Employment and Training Act (*The National Underwriter* 1979:58). Though the bonds were originally provided only for ex-convicts, later they began to be provided for others who could not get bonds because they lacked credit references.

A third program provided surety bonds for small contractors (*The National Underwriter* 1973:3, 13). Over a third of the participants in the program were minority contractors. Under this program, called the Surety Bond Guarantee (S.B.G.) program, the participating surety company paid only 10 percent of any loss. The rest was paid by the Small Business Administration. Local organizations, such as the Metropolitan Contractors Association in Detroit, worked with the contractors to teach them record-keeping techniques and to help out in other problem areas. The main idea was to "help the small contractor establish a track record," according to an executive in one of the participating surety companies (*The National Underwriter* 1973:13).

What these programs really do is provide a link between the personal suretyship arrangement and a corporate suretyship arrangement. As long as the principal (either an ex-convict, a person without credit references, or a small contractor) has no record or a bad record, the intermediary takes the responsibility. In some cases this means that the intermediary bears most of the financial losses, but in all cases it means that the intermediary is responsible for selecting the principals and for doing all of the loss-prevention work. During this introduction or probation period, the corporate surety has little responsibility. Its primary responsibility, really, is to agree to take seriously the evidence produced during this period so that the principal can develop a reputation.

It is in this area of trust-building or reputation-building that personal sureties have traditionally been superior to corporate ones, but it is not quite fair to say that corporate sureties have made no attempt to cope with this problem. More precisely, bonding companies will refuse bonds to less "desirable" applicants when they can pick and choose among them. But when the choice is between bonding a particular applicant or no one (as is the case in many kinds of court bonds), they have developed considerable flexibility. By requiring joint control or collateral, for example, a bonding company can reduce expected losses while bonding less "desirable" applicants. Joint control and collateral are common in court bonds, but they are still not in other kinds of bonds in which it is not economically necessary to figure out how to bond people about whom the guarantor has little information. Government organizations have stepped in to fill the void by acting as intermediate guarantors. But there is no particular reason that bonding companies could not have developed probationary bonding programs on their own.

Corporate sureties are more reliable (because more financially sound) than personal sureties, and corporate sureties are more likely to be able to reduce losses by guiding their policyholders through the intricacies of the legal system, by helping them set up systems of internal control, or by hiring consultants to help them with difficult technical problems. However, personal sureties are equally likely to be able to motivate principals to deal honestly or to perform as well as possible, and in addition they have traditionally excelled in helping "outsiders" to build or reestablish reputations. This suggests that corporate sureties have made little progress with the core problems of figuring out who will steal or default and of motivating people to behave more reliably.

The economics literature on information asymmetries has little to say about the problem of reformed criminals. Economists have usually been concerned with the problem of getting information about goods whose quality is fixed—once a "lemon," always a "lemon"— and knowing what price one should be willing to pay for the goods. The information problem is even more complex when "lemons" can become "peaches" (perhaps water turning into wine would be a more appropriate metaphor). In such a case, information asymmetries could only be overcome in a close and long-term relation between the two parties. At the very least a contractual relation will be required, since changes in insurance prices must be *contingent on* changes in policyholder behavior.

Conclusion

Many of the problems of reactivity that insurers face in fire and marine insurance are also problems in fidelity and surety bonding, and many of the techniques used in fire and marine insurance to control reactivity are also used in bonding. Besides confirming some of what we learned in our investigation of fire and marine insurance and showing how the strategies for managing reactive risks are modified by the routine requirements of bonding, an examination of fidelity and surety bonding is important for two further reasons. First, because bonding developed in a context in which it was insisted that it is impossible to provide true insurance coverage of losses that people can control, the literature on bonding contains explicit discussions of the problem of calculating rates given the reactivity of risks. This tends to confirm the argument that calculation is a central difficulty.

Second, because the insurer is often trying to influence a policyholder to avoid losses, rather than trying to influence the policyholder to influence *someone else* to avoid losses, the analogy between insurance management of reactive risks and the management of such risks in everyday life is stronger. Reactive risk plays two different roles in fidelity and surety bonds. First, the *perils* covered by these forms of insurance—theft and nonperformance—are under human control. But at the same time, moral and morale *hazards* increase the likelihood of loss from the covered perils. Once the employers have bought fidelity bonds, they may no longer keep close watch over subordinates, or they may become more lax in the screening of new employees. Or a contractor who has purchased a surety bond may worry a bit less about completing the contract when times are hard. But since the losses themselves are due to human behavior, sometimes with only a single step between the insurer and the person controlling the loss-causing action, moral and morale hazards have a bigger effect on the likelihood of loss in bonding than in other lines of insurance. The problem of the insurer in bonding is essentially the same as the problem of the *policyholder* in other lines of insurance. The bonding company has almost the same relation to fidelity or surety losses as the uninsured shipowner has to pilferage or barratry.

Bonding companies once argued that their rates should be only service charges since no losses are expected. This was, in part at least, an argument that it is in principle impossible to calculate expected losses when those losses are under the control of policyholders and their agents and when incentives for loss prevention decrease with insurance coverage.

But surety and fidelity bonders have learned to circumvent this difficulty. They have learned which organizational characteristics on the average are correlated with losses. They have learned to intervene (or to have others intervene) to restructure and supervise so that theft and nonperformance are less likely. They have learned to collect information about individual policyholders and their agents and to adjust their rates and contracts as this new information becomes available. And they have recognized that the problems of reactivity are less likely to be serious when the distance between the policyholder and the person controlling the loss increases and when volitional control over losses decreases. All of these innovations serve to make calculation about reactive risk possible, ultimately making insurance markets possible.

6

A Theory
of
Reactive Risk

When social scientists write about decision making under risk, they argue that the actors who are facing the risks first have to collect information about the likelihoods of various outcomes and then, in essence, have to place their bets appropriately. Translating these conclusions into insurance terminology, one would say that insurers, facing the unpredictable loss experiences of their clients, must underwrite and rate carefully. That is, they must collect information about potential policyholders so that they can make some sensible estimates of the probabilities of loss, and then they must charge rates that are set according to estimates of the (aggregate-level) probabilities of loss.

While this advice would work reasonably well if insurers faced only fixed risks, in actuality insurance companies would never remain solvent if this were all they did. Reactive risks must be dealt with through other methods.

In our examination of fire insurance, marine insurance, and fidelity and surety bonding, we have seen that insurers do in fact use supplementary strategies to cope with reactive risks. In particular, they employ four distinct sorts of strategies, all of which serve to ensure that the likelihood of loss does not increase once the insurance agreement is signed. In addition to collecting information on the odds of loss and setting prices appropriately (underwriting and rating), insurers first try to judge the extent to which policyholders really can control losses. In some cases, a risk that appears to be reactive because it is under human control turns out to be fixed because the *policyholder* has only very indirect or imperfect control over the loss-causing events. In these cases (which occur most frequently in large organizations), an ordinary insurance solution based entirely on rating and underwriting is possible. A second strategy involves the creation of a community of fate between policyholders and insurers. By forcing the policyholder to share losses and by making the rate contingent on participating in loss-prevention programs, for example, the insurer offers an incentive to keep losses down. Third, insurers try to reduce losses by giving control over crucial loss-prevention activities to third parties who will not benefit from failing to carry them out. Finally, insurers and policyholders must renegotiate frequently in order to make sure that the policyholders' incentive structures are adequately represented in the insurance contract. This fourth strategy for managing reactive risks is primarily important in preventing insurance fraud.

In this concluding chapter, I will first discuss insurers' attempts to manage reactive risk through rating and underwriting. Then I will discuss the supplementary strategies for managing reactive risk, drawing examples from fire and marine insurance and fidelity and surety bonding. Finally, in an afterword I will show how these strategies are used both by individuals who are trying to manage the risks of sexual relationships and by those who are responsible for designing legal systems.

We should note here that almost all of these strategies to control reactive risk take the form of institutional policies and standard provisions in contracts. In older books about underwriting one finds accounts of cables to policyholders canceling coverage when the value of property takes a sudden dip. But modern insurance companies build these strategies into fairly rigid routines, and the quaint eighteenth-century language in the provisions to combat moral hazard in marine insurance contracts merely indicates a long institutional history. "Strategies" here then does not mean the quick calculation and rapid response of a battlefield officer fighting moral hazard; instead it means providing a supply of standard operating procedures from far behind the lines.

Estimating the Odds
and Placing the Bets:
Rating and Underwriting

A rating scheme is essentially a pricing system.[1] In setting rates, insurers try to determine which policyholder traits are associated with high losses and which with low losses. The premium rates for particular policyholders will then be determined by the combination of characteristics they possess. Because frame buildings burn more frequently than brick buildings, the owners of frame buildings usually will be charged a higher rate than the owners of brick buildings. Because fresh fruit is more perishable than canned fruit, the owner of a cargo of fresh fruit will have to pay a higher price for cargo insurance than will the owner of a cargo of canned fruit. Because thefts from banks are more common and larger than thefts from dry cleaning outfits, the owner of a bank has to pay more for fidelity bonding than does the owner of a dry cleaning store.

The underwriter's job is to apply this pricing system to individual policyholders. In order to do this, the underwriter must collect the information necessary to assign the policyholder to a rating category. In addition, though, the underwriter must determine whether the policyholder is a better-than-average, average, or worse-than-average member of that category. If the owner of a frame building were an especially fastidious housekeeper, the underwriter might expect the fire losses to be lower than the average for frame buildings. If the owner of the cargo of fresh fruit had a reputation for packaging the cargo sloppily, the marine insurer might expect higher than normal losses. If the dry cleaner specialized in cleaning furs and did not

1. We will be abstracting from the forces of supply and demand and of state regulation that tend to force rates to correspond to the actual risk of loss. But we should note that insurance sales departments create a constant pressure on rates and on underwriting decisions. Salespeople have a short-run interest in getting a fixed risk classified into a lower category in order to give a competitive price. But they have a similar incentive to ignore problems of moral hazard, to collect their commissions on policies sold to shady characters, and to sell these policies at the same rates and with the same underwriting decisions as apply to upright citizens. Only in the long run, as poorly classified risks and moral hazards force their rates above competitors' rates, do salespeople have an interest in correct rating and underwriting. We ignore this problem of morale hazard within the insurance industry itself in the following discussion of rating and underwriting.

screen personnel carefully, then the underwriter might anticipate that fidelity losses might be higher than was usual for dry cleaning establishments.

Insurers have traditionally argued that reactive risks (such as moral and morale hazard) should be the concern of the underwriters and not of the ratemakers. Insurance rates are built primarily around fixed risks, and insurers believe that behavioral factors only determine whether policyholders are good or bad bets compared with others in their particular rating categories.

There are two problems with this view that behavioral factors should be dealt with only by underwriters. First, it assumes that moral and morale hazard enter the loss-causing chain of events only as hazards. In fact, as I pointed out in chapter 2, behavioral factors function both as *hazards* (factors that increase the likelihood of loss) and as *perils* (events that directly cause loss). For example, while the carelessness of a worker who handles gasoline may be a hazard that increases the likelihood of loss due to fire (the peril), barratry and pilferage may be direct causes of loss in marine insurance, and theft is a direct cause of loss in fidelity bonding. This means that reactivity must be, and is, taken into account in ratemaking as well as underwriting. In some cases (e.g., in fidelity and surety bonding), reactive risks are explicitly included in the rating scheme; in other cases (e.g., in marine insurance), rates are adjusted when perils involving controllable human actions are added to the list of perils covered by the policy; in still other cases, reactive risks are only implicitly taken into account through their connection with other factors that are explicitly included in the rating scheme.

The second problem with the argument that underwriters, rather than ratemakers, should deal with reactive risk is that underwriters are not very good at detecting moral hazard. That is, underwriters are not very good at determining which policyholders are likely to be careless, which ones are likely to steal from the insurance company, which ones are likely to be bad at their business and to end up insolvent, and so on.

Thus, the traditional position is wrong on two counts. First, reactive risks have to be included in the rates since behavioral factors function as perils as well as hazards; second, the problem cannot be handed over to underwriters because they cannot solve it either. The problems of underwriters and ratemakers are related. Insurers' theories about behavioral risk are inadequate. If one does not know very well how to predict who will either intentionally or inadvertently cause losses, then one can neither set rates to take account of variations in the likelihood of loss due to human action nor identify individual policyholders possessing traits associated with higher losses due to behavioral factors. The same sort of theory about human behavior would be required for underwriting and for ratemaking, and insurers simply do not have an adequate theory.

Because insurers have only rudimentary theories about how policyholder traits are associated with reactive risk, they have not been very successful at sorting policyholders into groups according to expected losses due to behavioral factors, and they cannot charge rates commensurate with expected losses. Therefore, it is not possible to collect information about likely outcomes and then to act accordingly, as social scientists would normally argue they should do.

Those who take insurance markets for granted would expect that insurers' activities would be restricted to rating and (limited) underwriting. But it is in principle impossible to manage reactive risks in this way. Since loss experiences ultimately depend on the reactions of actors who are (by definition) capable of adjusting their behavior to take account of insurers' risk-management strategies, it is not possible to calculate as if the possibilities of loss were fixed. In managing reactive risks, then, the problem is much more to *fix* the probabilities of loss. In the rest of this conclusion I will discuss methods for stabilizing the probabilities of loss. Without such institutions insurance markets could not exist.

Distance and Reactivity

At several points I have argued that the most important difference between reactive and fixed risk is that reactive risk responds to attempts to manage it while fixed risk does not. From the perspective of the risk manager or insurer, the crucial point is that attempts to reduce losses are often ineffective if one is dealing with reactive risk. If the reactivity itself can be reduced, then insurers can manage reactive risks in much the same way that they manage fixed ones. If they can isolate those situations in which risks under human control should not be reactive, then such risks can be managed as social scientists have argued they could be, by collecting information about the likelihood of losses, choosing the best bets, and setting prices appropriately.

In adjusting their strategies to the actions and reactions of others, purposive actors, including insurers and policyholders, only calculate about the behavior of those who are relatively close to them. They do not formulate strategies that take account of the behavior of actors with whom they are only indirectly linked, even though they are fully aware that they are affected by the behavior of these actors. Part of the reason that actors tend not to take into account those who are several steps removed is that they lack information about them. It is rather difficult to formulate a plan that includes others' reactions if one has no inkling about their goals, resources, or plans. Similarly, it is rather difficult to try to influence someone about whom one has no information. In addition, though, one can assume that an actor who is several steps away will be unlikely to adjust his or her strategy to take account of one's own behavior. This means that reactivity (which is really a continuous variable rather than a dichotomous one) decreases with distance, and a reactive risk that is several steps removed and over which one has no control or only very indirect control is essentially a fixed risk. The likelihood of loss neither increases nor decreases as a result of one's calculations; therefore, reactive risk at a distance can safely be treated as nonreactive.

In large organizations with several levels of hierarchy, those actors who control the loss-causing events are often sufficiently far removed from both the insurer and the beneficiary of the insurance policy that they will not be affected by the insurance agreement. Presumably this is why insurers agree to cover barratry and pilferage in marine insurance and why fire insurers will compensate for fire damage even when it is due to the carelessness of an employee in a factory.

Presumably this is also the logic behind the change in the insurance arrangements in fidelity bonding over the last few decades. Part of the reason that bonding companies feel comfortable pegging rates to expected losses (and are willing to concede that they do expect losses) is that the policyholder is now often the beneficiary rather than the principal (who could cause the loss); several extra links often lie between the policyholder and the person who actually causes the loss. The policyholder may be a large company, for example a bank, and the person who causes the loss may be a low-level employee, for example a teller, not personally known to the employee who arranged the insurance and therefore not likely to be cognizant of the arrangements. Therefore, the person who might cause the loss is unlikely to be able to calculate around the risk-management plans of an insurer or policyholder because he or she is not close enough to these actors to be aware of the details of the arrangements they have made. This means that it will be difficult for policyholders, or their agents, or insurers, to do anything to influence those who might cause the loss, and it may help explain why bonding companies have so cheerfully accepted these new forms of bonds despite their initial dissatisfaction with the fact that they can no longer investigate the individuals covered by them.

Risk-management plans for large organizations may therefore need to include strategies to manage reactive risks, strategies to manage intermediate ones, and strategies to manage risks that are sufficiently distant that they will not react to the risk-management program but instead will remain fixed. While low-level employees may not calculate around the insurer's or management's attempts to control them and will not benefit from the company having insurance, higher-level employees may be lulled by their knowledge about the insurance arrangements. High-level executives may believe that their bosses will not be hurt by an embezzlement, and they also may believe that a company that is covered with a generous bond will be less likely to prosecute. At the very highest level, a policyholder who is an individual owner of a company may be able to reap a handsome profit by stealing from the company and claiming a fidelity loss at the same time.

These observations about the relation between distance and reactivity do not point the way to a novel strategy for keeping losses low. Instead they suggest that the dangers of the odds of loss increasing when a policyholder has insurance coverage are considerably smaller when the policyholder does not directly control the loss-causing events. This in turn suggests that it may be safe to give insurance coverage and to use conventional insurance methods (those used to cover fixed risks) when the distance between the policyholder (and/ or the person who arranges the insurance agreement) and the actors controlling loss-causing events is large. The larger the distance, the less likely it is that the odds of loss will rise once an insurance agreement is signed. The same logic applies to situations where volitional control is decreased for other reasons, for example in cases involving negligence or inattention, as I argued in chapter 4. Distance may change over time, of course, with organizational changes in control procedures, technological changes in communication systems, and so forth. In such cases, the question of insurability must be reevaluated.

Creating a Community of Fate

Loss prevention is partly a matter of motivating policyholders to continue to act like uninsured owners, but it is also partly a matter of convincing them to act like *well-informed* ones. The insurer wants the policyholder to be careful but also to adopt innovations that will reduce the likelihood of loss. Since the insurers are often willing to provide the information about what needs to be done to keep losses low, they see loss prevention as a matter of incentive and of morale hazard. In studying loss prevention, then, we must ask how an insurer can motivate a policyholder to make efforts on the insurer's behalf, to act so as to reduce losses that ultimately will be borne by the insurer.

The main solution to this problem has been to make the policyholders' outcomes *contingent* on their continuing to act like prudent uninsured owners. How this is done varies from one line of insurance to another. In some cases the standard that the prudent uninsured owner is supposed to meet is well specified, in other cases not. In some cases the contigency is a contingent punishment (not letting the policyholder recover for the loss), while in other cases it is a contingent reward (giving policyholders discounts on their premiums if they have good loss records or adopt specific loss-prevention methods). Almost always such contingent rewards and punishments are coupled with deductibles. While contingent rewards and punishments can be used when the insurer knows what the policyholder should do to decrease losses, deductibles can be used when such information is lacking and the idea is just to motivate carefulness. How exactly one structures contingencies and deductibles depends on what is known about causes of loss, how frequently losses occur, and on the cost of loss prevention compared with the premium volume. When losses are relatively rare, rewards and punishments must be made contingent on loss-prevention activity; when losses are more frequent insurers can make them contingent on outcomes as well as on activity. In either case the insurer is attempting to fix the probability of loss at the pre-contractual level by forcing policyholders to engage in activities that would usually not directly benefit them once the insurance contract has been signed.

Loss-prevention efforts are perhaps most developed in marine insurance, where recovery for a loss is contingent on meeting a long series of requirements. Policyholders must have met the requirements of the classification society; vessels must have been seaworthy; vessels must have followed specified routes; policyholders and their agents must have "sued and labored" to try to reduce the losses to the insurer. Only when all of these conditions have been met—that is, only when the policyholder has acted as the insurer would have acted if given the chance—can the policyholder recover for the loss. In some cases it is clear what the standard is (for example, when routes are clearly specified), but in others the standard is not fixed but instead fluctuates with the season, with weather conditions, with the type of trade in which the vessel is engaged, and with current practices of those engaged in that trade. This, then, is a rather demanding standard—in effect it holds the policyholder responsible for keeping abreast of new techniques, paying attention to current conditions, and acting appropriately. Otherwise the insurer need not repay losses.

But marine policyholders are not just punished for their lapses. Because marine losses occur quite frequently, it is possible to use a second sort of contingency to motivate loss prevention and to stabilize the probability of loss. In marine insurance rates vary with the loss experience of the policyholder. In addition to the incentive introduced by contingent recovery, policyholders will also be motivated by the contingent reward or punishment provided by the decrease or increase in premiums when their losses drop or rise. This means that marine policyholders are rewarded not only for engaging in specific activities; they also are rewarded (or punished) for outcomes.

In fire insurance losses occur considerably less frequently, so it does not work to reward policyholders for good loss records. Rather than offering such contingent rewards, insurers offer rewards (lower premiums) for the adoption of loss-prevention devices or methods that are known, in the aggregate, to decrease fire losses. Premiums then depend not on having good loss experiences but instead on installing sprinklers and smoke alarms, having one's own water pumps, and so on. Because continual vigilance is needed, loss-prevention programs usually include inspections and maintenance schedules.

One of the main difficulties with contingency as a way of stabilizing the probability of loss is that it cannot be used in all situations. Because the cost of loss-prevention equipment is relatively high compared with the premiums paid by private citizens, it is not feasible for the insurance company to offer to reduce fire insurance premiums to compensate for the expenses of loss prevention. In addition, in order to verify that loss-prevention equipment has in fact been installed and is in working order, the insurers need to make inspections (as they do for commercial customers). But the relatively small premiums from personal lines customers are not sufficient to cover this expense. Unless loss-prevention equipment becomes cheaper and insurers find an inexpensive way to verify that such equipment has been installed, fire insurers will not be able to offer incentives for private individuals to cut fire losses. The only kinds of loss-prevention efforts that are recognized for individual policyholders are their choices to buy homes built of fire-resistant materials and their decisions to locate in areas in which fire losses are low. But such decisions are made before fire insurance is purchased, and rewarding these decisions does little to solve the problems associated with the reactivity of risk.

This analysis is a bit misleading, though, because it understates the amount of loss-prevention effort in fire insurance. Much of the fire-prevention effort is collective. Building codes and zoning laws serve many of the functions that classification society rules serve in marine insurance. The difference is that in marine insurance the policyholder has some control over compliance with such rules and therefore has to be motivated to meet the standards, while in fire insurance the policyholder usually has little control in these matters. Builders, electricians, and city councils have the control, so there is little point in making recovery for fire losses contingent on meeting these regulations. This will be discussed further in the section on collective loss prevention.

In fidelity and surety bonding, loss-prevention efforts are motivated in three different ways. First, insurers make recovery for losses contingent on policyholder behavior by prohibiting recovery when policyholders have failed to follow the rules about informing the bonding company when trivial losses occur, or when policyholders have not informed the bonding company about the backgrounds of key employees, or perhaps when policyholders have failed to notify the bonding company of turnovers in personnel or of changes in the responsibilities associated with important positions.

In addition, rates for many kinds of bonds are contingent on loss experience. For example, if a bank experiences few losses, its rate in subsequent years will be lower.

A third method, used in both bonding and in marine insurance, is to refuse to grant an insurance policy unless certain conditions are met. In fidelity and surety bonding, insurers might require policy-holders to undergo audits periodically, for example. But bonding companies carry these requirements a step further than they are carried in other lines of insurance: in some cases a bond will not be given unless the bonding company is given permission to intervene directly in the affairs of the policyholder. In essence what the bond-ing company does is to try to make its control over loss-causing events more direct. In some cases this means that bonding com-panies will intervene to manage failing businesses; in other cases it means that fiduciaries will get bonds only if they agree to joint con-trol by the bonding company. In this way the policyholder is pre-vented from making mistakes out of ignorance of proper procedures or of the law, but also the insurance company has an opportunity to check very frequently on the honesty and performance of the policy-holder. Insurance coverage in these cases is contingent on agreeing to let the insurance company assist in the management of the operation.

While in other lines of insurance, recovery is often contingent on the policyholder behaving like a prudent uninsured owner and in this way taking the interests of the insurer into account, such an arrange-ment does not always make sense in fidelity and surety bonding. What is covered in the insurance contract in these lines is often not the policyholder's interest but instead the interest of a third party. This means that the incentives for proper behavior may be reduced. In essence, policyholders do not have to imagine themselves in the situation of being without insurance, but instead have to imagine themselves in the shoes of an uninsured third party. For the policy-holder losses are thus two steps, rather than just one step, removed. It is perhaps for this reason that insurers sometimes insist on direct intervention. By making insurance coverage contingent on the right to intervene, the bonding company stabilizes expected losses at the pre-contractual level by decreasing both the likelihood of loss and the magnitude of losses should they occur.

In the first part of this section I argued that insurers try to fix the probabilities of loss by encouraging specific loss-preventing activities. They do this by making recovery for losses contingent on having met certain requirements, by offering discounts that are pegged to loss-prevention efforts, or by making premium rates contingent on loss experiences. But it is not always possible to make policyholder outcomes contingent on loss-prevention efforts in this way. In lines of insurance in which losses are infrequent, insurers cannot motivate policyholders with the threat (or promise) of higher (or lower) premiums. It is also not practical to peg premiums to loss experience when premiums are relatively small, because this arrangement requires a substantial amount of bookkeeping, and it is not cost effective to offer policyholders discounts for investing in loss prevention. And insurers cannot require policyholders to meet specified standards if the premium will not cover the cost of inspections or if they are not paid for in some other way. Finally, it is not always practical to threaten punishments when the policyholder can easily purchase insurance elsewhere if the insurer threatens to raise premiums too much.

In these cases, if insurers want to alter policyholder incentives so that policyholders will try to keep losses low, they must use another method. One common method is the deductible clause, which forces the policyholder to share all losses. If policyholders must bear some portion of each loss, then presumably they will be more inclined to behave like prudent uninsured owners, since in effect they are uninsured for part of the loss. An important advantage of this arrangement is that it can be used with both large and small policyholders, regardless of the size of the premium. Furthermore, if the insurer has evidence indicating that the policyholder is especially loss prone, the size of the deductible can be increased to increase the incentive for carefulness. And since the policyholder's loss is tied very directly to the insurer's loss, the policyholder cannot help but be aware of the insurer's interest. Deductibles are used in fire insurance, in marine insurance (in some cases arranged as "franchises"), and in some kinds of fidelity and surety bonds.

In summary, insurers seem to have concluded that the best way to get people to try to reduce or prevent losses is to structure their incentives so that they, as well as their insurers, benefit from the loss-prevention efforts or suffer from their negligence. Insurers hope that they can give the policyholders some reason to keep losses low even though the policyholders no longer pay for the losses. The insurers are trying to keep the probabilities of loss fixed at the pre-insurance level. Though this system of incentives is far from perfect—not everyone who is negligent gets punished, and not everyone who is careful ends up with a good loss record—this should not matter since these incentives are only intended as supplements to an already unbalanced system. Fire insurers assume that their policyholders will already be motivated to maintain their homes and businesses because fire damage leads to costs, such as inconvenience or loss of business reputation, which are not compensated by insurance money. Similarly, marine insurers assume that the possibility of losing one's customers motivates shipowners to be careful with their vessels even though the main costs of an accident can be recovered from the insurer. And contractors covered by surety bonds will still be careful not to default because this will ruin their reputations. So the problem faced by insurers does not have so much to do with big losses. Instead these incentives (deductibles and contingent rewards for loss prevention) are intended to control the problem of insurers being "nickel-and-dimed to death" with small claims. Notice that since losses that lead to these small claims often do not substantially affect the functioning of the policyholder, concern about loss of reputation or of customers does not provide much incentive to avoid them. The methods discussed in this last section therefore are intended mainly to stabilize the likelihood of small claims.

Third-Party Control and Collective Loss Prevention

Not all loss-prevention efforts can be carried out most effectively at the individual level or by the policyholder. It is sometimes cheaper to collectivize loss-prevention efforts, and it is often easier to make sure that the loss-prevention activities are actually carried out if someone other than the policyholder controls them. Likewise, loss-prevention activities are more easily adapted to changing conditions if they are collectively organized. Third-party control can solve many incentive problems, and collective loss-prevention often involves economies of scale.

Collective loss-prevention efforts include a wide variety of phenomena, for example, the development of municipal organizations such as fire departments or national ones like the Coast Guard, but also the centralization of key functions, such as standard setting, inspection, or safety research. In fire insurance, centralized waterworks, municipal fire departments, and building codes and zoning laws are some of the most important methods of collective loss prevention. Other sorts of collective fire prevention, such as research and certification of the safety of products, are less closely connected with fire insurance. In marine insurance, international salvage laws and classification societies (which set standards, carry out inspections, and do research on safety) are the main forms of collective loss prevention. Collective loss-prevention efforts are less developed in fidelity and surety bonding, though the standardization of financial procedures, the passage of laws about financial requirements for fiduciaries, and the existence of organizations that do credit checks and keep records are steps in the direction of collective loss prevention.

One of the chief advantages of collectivized standard setting is that it takes the policing problem out of the hands of the insurer. When marine insurers require their policyholders to be classed with particular classification societies, they have little further responsibility for the nature of the standards that the policyholders must meet in order to be certified or for determining whether policyholder losses are due to failures to keep things in order. Similarly, when fire insurers have supported moves to develop building codes and zoning laws, they were working toward a situation in which individual policyholders would not have to be motivated to meet standards themselves and would not have to encourage building contractors to do so. Once these various regulations become law, the fire insurers do not have to negotiate with individual policyholders about which requirements they have to meet in order to get coverage and which ones they can be excused from meeting for the time being.

Since the standards are not controlled (directly) by insurers, the minimum standards can be changed without lengthy negotiations between the policyholder and the insurer. If one has an arrangement in which insurance coverage is contingent on meeting the standards of another organization—either a governmental body or a classification society—then one can require that policyholders meet these standards without writing into the insurance contract exactly what the standards will be (Heimer 1980). When these outside organizations adjust their standards because of technical innovation or because new information about loss prevention has become available, policy-holders are automatically required to adopt this new standard. Be-cause policyholders have already invested considerable time and money in arranging insurance contracts, they will have a strong in-terest in complying with the new regulations so that the contract will continue to be valid.

Though both insurers and policyholders will be able to pressure the standard-setting organization to set regulations that they believe are appropriate, there are still advantages to having the issue decided outside the insurer/policyholder relation. In addition to providing flexibility and eliminating some of the policing problems, this ar-rangement means that insurers can assume that policyholders will be uniform in certain important respects. If they can assume that every-one will meet some set of minimum standards, then fire and marine contracts can be designed and rates set in terms of these standards, and this provides an important saving for insurers. Uniform con-tracts are considerably cheaper to arrange than individualized ones, and they make calculation about expected losses much easier.

In fidelity and surety bonding, the relevant standards are in gen-eral not set by standard-setting organizations, or even by govern-ments, but instead are based on "good business practice." The stan-dardization of accounting procedures and the quasi-legal status accorded such rules because of their role in taxation both serve to put a floor under bonding companies. Bonding companies can then insist that their policyholders adopt good business practices or comply with IRS regulations in these areas. In addition, codes of ethics adopted in particular professions and standard practices used in other lines of business make it easier for the insurer to know what to expect, and they make it possible to argue that the policyholder is not behaving properly. Finally, surety companies have lobbied for laws requiring checks on the financial standing of fiduciaries and laws encouraging joint control. If state laws encourage joint control, for example, it is considerably easier for the insurer to insist on this arrangement.[2]

Though such arrangements do not really exist in fidelity and surety bonding, in both fire and marine insurance there are collective

2. Though most arrangements giving control to third parties are collectively orga-nized, this is not always true. For example, in fidelity and surety bonding, co-fiduci-aries and joint control make loss prevention the responsibility of someone other than the policyholder, but these are arranged for individual cases rather than collectively provided.

provisions to cut losses while they are occurring. Fire insurers supported the development of municipal fire departments partly because such departments were cheaper and more effective than individual fire-fighting efforts, but also because the insurers did not have to worry about motivating city firemen to do their job. In one case (described in Factory Mutuals 1935:149), the factory's volunteer firemen abandoned their work in order to go save their families and homes when the fire spread beyond the factory. In that instance, the factory was entirely destroyed.

Since it is not really possible to have the equivalent of the fire department to save vessels in distress—though the Coast Guard does have a similar function—marine insurers have encouraged the court system to reward heavily those who will save vessels in distress. The awards given by the admiralty courts, or arranged by arbitration, are intended to encourage the development of commercial rescue services and also to encourage those who happen to be in the vicinity to turn aside from their voyages in order to assist vessels in difficulty. Though the assistance itself is not collectively organized, it is collectively rewarded. This collective reward is arranged through the legal system so that no one can choose to abstain from participation in what all agree is ultimately to the collective benefit.

Though individual policyholders may benefit from a failure to carry out loss-prevention activities—it is costly to install and maintain the equipment and to develop appropriate organizational routines—collective loss-prevention organizations do not have the same sort of incentive to fail to do these things. The fire department does not usually increase its profits by doing a shoddy job of putting out fires, while a factory may benefit by concentrating on production rather than on fire drills. By relocating loss-prevention efforts in organizations that do not benefit from neglecting them, insurers increase the likelihood that loss-prevention activities will get carried out even though policyholders themselves would neglect loss-prevention. This system helps stabilize the probabilities of loss.

Insurance Fraud
and Outdated Bargains

Insurance fraud apparently costs billions of dollars; estimates of the cost of insurance fraud vary between $1.5 billion (Insurance Crime Prevention Institute n.d.) and $3.5 billion (Van Slambrouck 1978:B8). The most common sort of insurance fraud is claims fraud, which seems to be concentrated in fire and auto insurance. Marine insurers are sufficiently alarmed about the levels of fraud in their area that a United Nations committee (FERIT) has been formed to investigate the problem.[3]

Fraudulent claims are clearly a case in which the insurer has failed to fix the probability of loss at its pre-insurance level. In this section, I will try to explain how such a failure is possible given all of the strategies that insurers have already employed to fix the likelihood of loss. Since fidelity and surety bonding are so much concerned with the problem of dishonesty, policyholder fraud is not really distinguished from other causes of loss in those lines. For this reason, fraud in fidelity and surety bonding will not be discussed in this section.

While insurers tend to categorize insurance fraud by the line in which it occurs (e.g., auto or personal injury or fire), it may be more profitable to group instances of insurance fraud by the *motivation* of the insureds. Insurance crime is then divisible into two main categories: (1) *premeditated insurance crime*, in which the insurance is procured (or sold) with the intention of defrauding the insurance company (or policyholder); and (2) *opportunistic insurance crime*, in which the insurance is procured for legitimate purposes but in which the policyholder later decides to defraud the insurance company.

The latter situation is especially interesting because it falls into neither of the categories that insurers usually discuss. As discussed in more detail in chapter 2, a *hazard*, in insurance terminology, is something that increases the likelihood of a loss. Insurers further distinguish between physical hazards and moral ones. The category of *physical hazards* is a catch-all that includes everything from a badly wired house to living in a hurricane zone. *Moral hazards* are conditions that are not precisely physical hazards but that nevertheless increase the odds of loss. Insurers sometimes attribute moral hazard to bad character. Insurers also discuss *morale hazard*, which is a decline in vigilance (loss-prevention activity) once one has insurance. For example, in auto insurance, worn brakeshoes or a slippery road

---

3. Barnard (1978), *Journal of Commerce* (1977), Lovell (1980), and Unsworth (1980a, 1980b) discuss the increases in marine losses and speculate about possible causes.

are physical hazards, inebriation or a history of alcoholism and lack of respect for traffic rules are moral hazards, and the discontinuing of a long-established habit of locking the car door after buying theft insurance is due to morale hazard.

When human behavior increases or decreases the risk, insurers customarily explain this as due to moral hazard or morale hazard. Note, however, that as insurers use it, moral hazard is a condition that exists at the time the insurance contract is made (and so could theoretically be estimated and underwritten), while morale hazard is a response to the purchase of an insurance policy. Note also that while moral hazard *may* explain a premeditated insurance crime, it cannot explain an opportunistic one. And, as I will argue below, the change that does explain the second category (opportunistic insurance crime) does not correspond to morale hazard. What changes is the *objective situation* of the policyholder, not his or her vigilance.

Since in this case of insurance crime, the increase in the likelihood of loss is due to behavioral rather than physical causes, we have to look for behavioral explanations. Since the usual explanations in the insurance literature (moral and morale hazard) cannot account for policyholders changing their minds and deciding to defraud the insurance company, the problem is to figure out what would make someone who had taken out an insurance policy for legitimate reasons decide later to defraud the insurance company. The argument below will be that such decisions are responses to outdated bargains and are examples of a process that occurs quite commonly in everyday life.

Insurers stress that insurance is *not* wagering. One of the main concerns of insurers has been to make sure that policyholders cannot gain more than they have lost. This idea is embodied in the legal doctrine of indemnity (discussed in chapter 2), which has led to many court decisions about the inappropriateness of recovering from more than one insurance company, of recovering more than actually lost, and so on. But while insurers have done pretty well in figuring out how to keep people from recovering more than the loss was worth at the time the insurance was taken out, they have done less well in figuring out what to do about unexpected changes in the value of the object insured. The classic arson case is one in which a business is failing because of a widespread change in the market or because of the cancelation of a large order. Suddenly, the buildings and merchandise are worth considerably less than their insured value. Given the option of exchanging them fraudulently for their previously higher policy value, it is often economically sound to take the cash and try some new business.

Such discrepancies between current market value and insured value can arise in many ways. Sometimes the discrepancy arises because previously profitable contracts are no longer profitable or have fallen through. For example, a toy manufacturer in the Philadelphia area had two terrible fires. The first, a $3.5 million blaze, destroyed all the toys he had contracted to a retail chain that was about to collapse. The second fire, a small $2.5 million job, occurred just after the toymaker learned that a sale to a leading discount-store chain was about to fall through (McKinley 1979:170). Other possible reasons for arson might include a need for cash, a need to relocate a business, or a need to terminate a lease. In each of these cases, the use value of the current business is suddenly lower than its insured value, so the executive may prefer the cash.

But not all factors leading to this discrepancy between market and insured value are idiosyncratic. A fairly high proportion of these cases of opportunistic insurance fraud seems to be due to system-wide problems (see chapter 3, pp. 76–88, and chapter 4, pp. 127–47). For example, the rate of arson goes up when there is a recession.[4] Insurers frequently discuss the sharp increase in arson and other types of insurance fraud during the Great Depression (e.g., Bainbridge 1952). One Canadian insurer blamed the increase in auto losses on higher gasoline prices (*The Canadian Underwriter* 1979: 10). And when freight rates drop, ships are damaged more frequently (and so collect insurance money for loss of freight payments during the repair period).[5]

Probably the most severe problems occur when technological changes are added to general economic recession. In the late 1860s, the combination of a depression, technological changes in shipping,

4. According to the U.S. Department of Commerce (n.d.:5), the arson rate rose 70 percent per year in the late 1970s, rather than the 20–30 percent that would be expected on the basis of earlier experience. Stevenson (1977) argues that these increases in arson call for insurance reform.

5. Not surprisingly, fidelity and surety losses also rise when economic conditions become difficult. See Evert (1975), Bennem (1950), and *Rough Notes* (1950) on this subject.

and an archaic evaluation system provided powerful incentives to sink Norwegian ships. At that time the Norwegian standard-setting and evaluating organization, Det norske Veritas, did not set the insured value of a ship at its market value. Instead, the values were fixed by the ships' categories of seaworthiness, size, function, and so on. One result of this was that wooden sailing ships were insured at far above their market value; they were being classified along with metal steamships that were worth considerably more, and that were taking business away from sailing ships. One author cites a case in which a ship was evaluated at 150 percent of its market value, and comments that in such a case the loss of a ship could bring a handsome profit (Færden 1967:143–44).

When the change in the value of a business affects all of the businesses in a particular area, insurance companies can protect themselves by altering the face value of the policy in accordance with economic indicators of the current market for goods similar to those insured rather than pegging insurance rates and reimbursements just to the value of the insured object. If such a policy were instituted, when the shipping market is depressed, the value of ships (and perhaps freights) would be automatically deflated, while they would be automatically inflated in a booming market. Note that this solves two problems encountered by insurers: (1) the problem of incentives to cause losses, and (2) the problem of people not keeping their insurance up to the right value.[6]

Something similar to this was done in Norwegian fire insurance. Because property values were changing rapidly, the insurance company altered its regulations about the evaluation of insured buildings. The new regulations required that insured property be inspected and evaluated at least once in every twenty years. More importantly, though, insured buildings could be inspected and reevaluated considerably more frequently, and the insurance company retained the right to choose the reevaluation date so that policyholders could not have their property evaluated at a time when prices were especially high (Færden 1967). Such regulations discourage arson for profit.

What we have learned so far, then, is that because the insurance

6. Of course one could allow policyholders the option of providing evidence that the deflated rate was inappropriate since their particular businesses were booming despite the general depression.

mechanism is poorly designed, it sometimes turns pure risks into speculative ones. People would not burn down their businesses or electrocute race horses that were no longer winning if they could not collect insurance money (Insurance Crime Prevention Institute 1979: 1). But what this says is that this class of insurance crime is not really primarily a problem of moral or morale hazard. The insurance was bought in good faith, but the situation changed since then without the bargain being renegotiated. The general lesson to be drawn from this is that bargains need to be renegotiated in the light of changing circumstances. If we can trust people to behave appropriately, not to burn down their businesses, for example, it is often because it is in their own interest to preserve their property. When this is no longer the case, we must reexamine the bargain. The decision about whether to renegotiate then depends on the magnitude of the imbalance, on whether the imbalance is permanent or temporary, on whether this imbalance is embedded in a long-term or short-term relation, and on whether there are other interdependencies. Besides these situational analyses, we may also make an estimate of the moral makeup of the person or firm.

To be a little more explicit about why the bargain becomes problematic, let me note that there are two values involved in the bargain. One is the market value of whatever is at stake and the other is the bargain value. At the time when the bargain is struck, the two are equal, and often the bargain makes provisions about changes in the market value. So, for example, insurance agreements often incorporate depreciation. But sometimes such accounting estimates of changes in market value are really inadequate (for example, when there is a rapid technological change, a general depression, and so on).

In insurance, the relevant changes in value occur when the market value drops below the bargain value. The odds of someone violating the agreement (i.e., committing an insurance crime) then rise. For example, arsons occur when businesses are not worth their insured value. Similarly, insurers cancel insurance if a business does not raise its insurance when the value goes up.

Note that this analysis applies only to one kind of insurance crime, that is, opportunistic insurance crime. It does not apply to all those cases of premeditated insurance crime in which the person buys (or sells) insurance with the express intention of defrauding the insurance company (or the policyholder) later.

Calculation and Control
in Imperfect Markets

In the cases we have been considering in this book, threats of market failure are due to excessive control by one of the parties. In the insurance case, the *cost* of providing insurance depends on the behavior of the policyholder, but it is hard to make the *price* reflect that dependence since the behavior of the policyholder cannot be observed by the insurer and often changes as a result of coverage. The policyholder has some control over losses, and because the likelihood of losses changes as a result of coverage, the insurer has difficulty estimating them and setting an appropriate price for coverage. But insurance markets continue to exist, and we must therefore ask what makes it possible for insurers to sell policies *despite* the fact that policyholders control losses and have different interests than insurers.

What I have argued is that there are abundant possibilities, but that they all have in common a single condition. While the primary condition for a simple market is that the likelihood of an outcome not change as a result of decision making (that is, that the cost of providing some commodity not depend on the behavior of the purchaser), the primary condition for an effective if imperfect market is that *control not interfere with calculation*. Otherwise actors will be unable to make choices in the usual way. (This does not mean they will not make any choices, but only that the logic of such solutions will be different than in cases where market failure has been averted. In particular, they may choose so as to minimize transaction costs or to maximize the number of goods they can look over rather than try to choose an optimal product or service.)

I have tried to show that this condition can be secured primarily by arranging for some overlap between the interests of the person who must make the calculation (the person who sets the price in insurance) and the person who controls the outcome (the policyholder who can avoid or cause losses). When authors like Williamson address this question, they tell us (correctly) that the fusion of the two parties in an organization or hierarchy will solve the problem. It is also true that intermediate solutions such as contracts (as documented by Stinchcombe 1983) will also work. But what such authors have failed to note is that *any arrangement that gives control to*

*someone whose interests are in line with those of the party who must
make the calculation* (and who does not control the outcome) will
avert market failure. A particularly important case here is the third-
party loss preventer (fire department, marine classification society,
or auditor), an organization or role designed to have relatively unmixed motives. I have tried to show the variety of institutions that
will serve this purpose, how exactly they function, and some of the
conditions under which one arrangement will be more appropriate
than another.

A secondary aim of this book has been to bring insurance institutions to the attention of social scientists. Insurance and insurance-
like institutions abound in modern societies. Many of the relations of
interest to economists and organizational sociologists are mediated
by insurers. For example, in many products liability cases the ultimate defendant is an insurance company, not the manufacturer; insurance availability and conditions imposed by insurers have an important impact on the design of new high-risk projects such as oil
exploration, construction, and production projects in the North Sea;
and the urban housing problem and bank mortgage redlining are
often blamed on practices of those selling homeowners' insurance. If
we can illuminate the workings of insurance organizations themselves, we will be better equipped to understand their influence on
our society.

Though there are many benefits to insurance and insurance-like
institutions, those responsible for designing them must become more
sensitive to their effects on incentives. A recent news story illustrates
the problem (Sinclair 1984). California farmers received subsidies
(through a federal payment-in-kind program) to take farm land out of
production to avoid grain and cotton surpluses. But the land that they
agreed to idle could not have been planted anyway because it was
flooded, so the effect of the subsidy on production (though not on
farmers' income) must have been trivial. Furthermore, the farmers
collected government flood insurance on the same idled land. (One
wonders whether recent increases in productivity per acre might not
be accounted for in the same way: the government pays farmers to
idle land; they idle the least productive land; productivity per acre
shoots up.) Flood water has traditionally been shifted to more arid
areas or stored for future irrigation. But because farmers are eligible
for financial disaster aid to pump out the water, they did little to avert

the flooding and are now planning to drain the flooded land (with possible unfortunate environmental impacts such as the transfer of predatory white bass to waters containing other species). Finally, the Small Business Administration agreed to guarantee loans to California farm businesses that can show that they lost business when farmers participating in land-idling schemes did not buy seed, pesticide, machinery, and so on, insuring them against the risks of governmental policies affecting their customers.

Such outcomes would not have occurred in the absence of farm subsidies, disaster aid, or guaranteed loans, all insurance-like risk-management strategies, and would be difficult to predict. If we can understand the effects on human and organizational incentives of having some outcomes guaranteed, then we will be better equipped to decide when we want insurance-like institutions and how we want to design them.

Afterword:
Noninsurance Settings

I argued earlier that the main value of this book would lie in its articulation of universal strategies for the management of reactive risk. Thus far I have outlined what strategies exist in insurance and have tried to suggest the conditions under which insurers have found it strategic to employ one method rather than another. Now I would like to make the case for the generality of my argument by showing how these strategies appear in two other areas, the management of contraceptive risks and negotiations about virginity by couples, and the design of a legal system to deal with tort liability, especially for defective products.

This book has been about strategies for managing reactive risk, but it has also been about how such strategies are institutionalized in insurance. Because risk-management strategies are thoroughly institutionalized in insurance, we have not been able to examine risk management and institutionalization separately. But the two are separate phenomena, and the pressures that produce institutions are not the same as those that lead actors to adopt one risk-management strategy rather than another. The same risk-management strategy can be more or less institutionalized (building codes are more so than good business practices) or institutionalized in different ways (classification societies serve roughly the same function for marine insurance that building codes serve for fire insurance). My concern has not been with the question of when a strategy will be institutionalized or when the institution will take one particular form rather than another, but instead has been focused on questions such as what strategies can be used to stabilize reactive risk and to make calculation possible, and when one type of strategy will work better than another.

Given my assertion that institutionalization and choice of strategy are really two different variables, I am also arguing that we would expect to find the same types of risk-management strategies used in settings with little institutionalization as in settings with well-developed institutions. Where there are conflicts of interest between interdependent actors, those actors will need to figure out how to make their interests more congruent so plans can be made and outcomes reliably predicted.

The examples of sexual negotiations and betrayals and products liability law were chosen to illustrate how my analysis can be extended to settings with varying degrees of institutional development. Though sexuality itself is governed by well-defined norms, in our society decisions about whether to begin a sexual relationship and how to avoid pregnancy occur in an institutional vacuum. (In other societies the virginity of a young woman is often the responsibility of her kin group, whose status is adversely affected by her indiscretions; sexual initiation and contraception are then embedded in an institutional structure [Paige and Paige 1981].) This is a setting in which institutions are either vestigial or, in some cases, decaying. In contrast, products liability is a setting in which institutions are of intermediate importance—they exist but are changing. Though products liability has long been a legal issue, the law in this area has been undergoing a transformation in recent decades.

Despite these variations in institutional development, the same types of strategies are used to manage reactive risks in negotiations about virginity and contraception, in products liability law, and in insurance. The question of why strategies are institutionalized in some settings but not in others is important and complex, but is not one that can be addressed responsibly by the research here.

To demonstrate the utility of my scheme in each of these areas I will do two things. First I will try to show how some risk faced by those in each area is a *reactive* risk, and how people face decisions about strategy when others have some control over outcomes. Next I will try to demonstrate that some of the strategies that are or might be used to overcome these difficulties are analogous to those discussed earlier in the sense that they have the effect of fixing risk so that calculation is possible.

Controlling Reactive Risk
in Sexual Relations

A central dilemma in courtship is when to engage in sexual activity for the first time. The traditional view has been that males will be willing, even eager, to have intercourse whenever they can persuade the woman to permit it, but that women will try to postpone intercourse until the man is committed to the relationship. Traditional morality supports the eagerness of the male and the reluctance of the female by blaming women for yielding but not blaming men for urging (exceptions include incest, statutory rape, and taking indecent liberties with children). When couples negotiate about their sexual activity, and when individuals think about contraception in the context of particular relationships, they necessarily must calculate about the probable reactions of their partners and others concerned. Though no contracts are made and though individuals often make their decisions without consulting their partners, this is still a case of reactive risk because of the dependence of each one's outcomes on the decisions of the other and because the decisions of each change with the other's behavior.

For a woman the stakes are high: possible pregnancy, loss of reputation with a corresponding decrease in marriage possibilities and a change in how she can expect to be treated in marriage, and at the same time a possibility of keeping a man attached and so increasing his commitment by providing sexual services, and finally, her own sexual satisfaction. For a man the stakes are less high but not trivial: the possibility of pregnancy and community pressure to marry, enhancement of reputation as a man able to seduce a woman, increased commitment of the woman to him since her reputation will be adversely affected if she is known to have had sexual relations with more than a single partner, and, of course, sexual satisfaction. The conventional wisdom is that "a man's gain is a young woman's loss" (Horowitz 1983:117). Obviously this formulation is too simplistic since there are possible gains and losses for both partners. But what the conventional statement does emphasize is that there is a distinct possibility that the woman will lose a great deal and the man will not; the risks are not distributed equally.

What must happen, then, is that the man must persuade the woman that she *will not* lose so much, and she must find some way to make him keep his part of the bargain. She must, for example, figure out some way to persuade him to keep the secret that she is sleeping with him despite the fact that he (superficially) gains more by talking. He in turn must persuade her, for example, that there is some point in remaining faithful to him despite the fact that she has already ruined her reputation by yielding.

When deciding which people to have relationships with, men and women presumably try to estimate the odds that they will get what they want out of the relationship (Heimer and Stinchcombe 1980).[1] But this calculation about the odds of one's partner protecting one's reputation as a virgin or as a man able to control his woman will not be enough. Once the relationship has started, the odds will change. Though a man may be able to persuade a woman that he loves her and respects her, she may nevertheless discover a few days after yielding to her suitor that he has told all of his friends about his conquest. In such a situation, he should not be surprised if she does not remain faithful to him, and he gets a reputation as a cuckold. Knowing about these possible outcomes, young people do considerably more than collect information about prospective partners before they make their decisions about how to act. (This would be the equivalent of setting rates in insurance.) They also engage in substantial loss-preventing activity to fix the reactive risks so that reliable estimates of losses and gains can be made. In the rest of this section I will give examples of how couples (and their families) use the same types of techniques as are used by insurers.

Third-party control of sexuality is the ideal of parents who wish their daughters to remain chaste until marriage. But this third-party control is hard to achieve when chaperones are no longer fashionable. When adolescents can skip school and spend an afternoon in some friend's or relative's deserted apartment, and when there is no consensus about how closely young people should be supervised, parental control of children's sexuality becomes precarious. But the role of chaperone, where it exists, is clearly designed to put control

1. Becker (1964) argues that we should look at situational pressures for consistency (rather than personality variables). He argues that the side-bets people make (for example in the friends and relatives of a spouse) produce commitment to behavioral consistency (for example in continuing a relation with a spouse). This suggests that people should assess the extent to which another person's side-bets are in line or in conflict with an action when estimating its likelihood.

in the hands of one who has unmixed motives, removing it from the groping fingers of those who are both less experienced and more ambivalent.

Another sort of third-party control involves a division of labor between the lover and the contraceptor. Contraceptives like the pill and the IUD, and to some degree the sponge and diaphragm, allow separation of the contraceptive act from the sexual act. Contraception can be removed from the control of the impassioned lover to the control of the cool, collected person who wishes to avoid pregnancy. Perhaps some of the failures of condoms, diaphragms, spermicides, and especially rhythm and withdrawal are due to the fact that these methods of birth control require attention to loss-prevention routines at a time when other goals are more pressing. The choice between abstaining from or delaying intercourse and making love "unprotected" is rather like the choice faced by a factory with back orders and defective fire-protection equipment or an ill-trained fire brigade. Given that the odds of an accident are low in both cases, we should expect that loss-prevention activities will be neglected in favor of other activities *unless* loss prevention is made the responsibility of someone who is not forced to choose between seeking sure gains and avoiding unlikely losses.

But while one could argue that the fire insurer rather than the factory is the loser in one case, one cannot really argue that someone other than the young couple bears the main costs in the other. It is true that humiliated parents usually get considerably less of the pleasure that led to a daughter's pregnancy, but it is not true that she gets less of the pain. What may be true, though, is that her lover gets less pain than she does. This suggests that if one wants reliable protection of virginity or prevention of pregnancy, one should usually put control in the hands of parents, daughters, and suitors, in that order.

If parents are no longer very effective as third-party loss preventers, daughters may also be ineffective for different reasons. Both Luker (1975), discussing why women who "knew better" failed to use contraceptives and wound up having abortions, and Horowitz (1983), discussing why young Chicanas so often end up premaritally pregnant despite knowledge of birth control and strong community pressure to remain virgin, argue that when women are calculating the chances of pregnancy and deciding whether to use contraceptives, and what kind to use, factors other than contraceptive effectiveness enter into their thinking. There are sometimes good reasons *not* to use contraception despite the increased risk of pregnancy. A woman may be trying to achieve several goals besides the avoidance of pregnancy. As Luker points out, pregnancy has an important role in modern courtship; it provides an opportunity for decision making about marriage. Horowitz also reports that couples often married just before the birth of a child and that, although fathers no longer chase down daughters' seducers with shotguns, there was considerable community pressure for marriage.

But even if a woman is not able to secure this desirable outcome, in many communities and in the context of many relationships, there are fates worse than unwed motherhood or an unwanted pregnancy and an abortion. Young women from Catholic backgrounds may worry about compounding the sin of illicit intercourse with premeditation of the sin (as evidenced in the securing of contraceptives) and the sin of contraception itself (Luker 1975:45). Or a young woman may not want to seem like someone who is too experienced, since this decreases her chances of marriage. Though forty years and a sexual revolution separate the work of Whyte (1943) on an Italian slum and Horowitz (1983) on the Chicano community, both authors describe how the marriageability of a woman varies with her reputation as a virgin, a woman who has been intimate with only a single man, a woman who has had several partners but has been faithful to each in turn, and a woman who is available to anyone. One way to maintain a reputation as a woman whose sexuality is "bounded" (in Horowitz's terminology) is to show that one has not planned to engage in sexual activity. Further, in the community that Horowitz (1983) studied, a woman's sexual activity could be justified as submission to a man she loved since submission of women to men was also valued in this community. But one does not *plan* to submit to a lover; so if one is going to justify sexual activity on grounds of submission to a man one loves, one cannot use contraceptives. Finally, in the Chicano community, a woman who has lost her virginity and has not managed to negotiate a marriage can still save her reputation by becoming a mother (Horowitz 1983). Since motherhood is highly valued, a woman can redeem herself by devoting herself to her child. But such a strategy of minimizing the maximum loss precludes the use of contraception, and devotion to the child does not completely solve the problem of finding a husband.

The classical solution to these problems of sexual and contraceptive risk is the formation of a community of fate, either through marriage or through some less formal commitment. But there are other communities of fate involved here as well. Parents and siblings share a girl's shame if she becomes pregnant or acquires a reputation as a sexually active woman. In the Chicano community, tension about virginity reaches a high point when the family must decide whether or not to have a cotillion to celebrate the girl's fifteenth birthday. The cotillion is regarded as a public affirmation of the daughter's virginity; so the daughter and parents will be embarrassed not to have a cotillion, but the parents will also be embarrassed if they stage the celebration only to discover a few months later that their daughter is pregnant. As Horowitz (1983:53) points out, "rumors often claim that a young woman holding a cotillion is trying to prove that she is still a virgin when she no longer is. On the other hand, failing to have a cotillion is frequently considered a good indicator that a young woman is no longer a virgin and may even be pregnant." Because parents also lose when daughters are unchaste, they can be counted on to try to control their daughters' sexuality.

This same sort of solution is used by formerly married people trying to avoid contracting herpes. According to Benjamin (1983), formerly married people collect information about the social settings in which they encounter potential sexual partners and about the behavior of these people in order to assess the likelihood that a person has a sexually transmitted disease. In order to increase the chance of being informed of a potential partner's sexually transmitted disease, Benjamin's informants usually limited themselves to sexual contacts with people they had gotten to know and had developed emotional attachments to. That is, they tried to control the risk by first developing a community of fate in which the partner would also be harmed by damaging someone he or she loved.

Renegotiation of outdated bargains also occurs when couples are trying to avoid pregnancy or decide whether to make love. Only a demographer, talking about an abstraction of a marriage or a cohort of women, can think that the likelihood of pregnancy is a fixed probability, given some particular method of contraception. The rest of us know all too well that the probability of pregnancy depends on whether a couple can find an effective method of contraception that fits into their sexual routines and whether their bargains about these things are kept current. In many couples' negotiations about contraception there is an explicit agreement very early in the sexual relationship that pregnancy is to be avoided. But an unwanted pregnancy is more disastrous at some times (and for one member of the couple) than at others. A man or woman who has decided to marry someone who eventually wants to have children may begin to be less careful about contraception, even though this change in behavior may be in violation of the agreement and opposed by the other person. What has happened is that the current value of an unwanted pregnancy is different than the bargain value. Of course this can work the other way too—when a previously stable marriage becomes unstable, the value of an unwanted pregnancy may change in either direction. One may want to have a child to try to keep the spouse, or one may be worried about having a child and then splitting up. These are not matters of *false* promises, but only of outdated ones.

Finally, people do take distance into account both negatively and positively. Realizing that casual acquaintances are *socially* distant even though they have had sexual relations, people compensate by taking extra precautions about contraception and venereal disease when sleeping with relative strangers. Prostitutes never rely on their customers to use contraceptives or to be disease-free. But people who are socially distant also do not enforce the norms of one's home community and cannot as easily ruin one's reputation. When a community tries too hard to protect young women's virginity, they may go elsewhere for their premarital sexual relationships (Horowitz 1983).

Schelling (1978:35–36) discusses the extent to which marriage is a market relation, at least in the U.S. Since "marriage is a voluntary contractual relation between people who are free to shop around," courting couples have to be able to calculate about the likelihood of getting what they want out of marriage. They have to decide about appropriate prices to pay for the benefits they expect to receive from each other.

I have tried to illustrate how people might use the strategies outlined in this book in decision making about sexual relationships. We find, for example, that families use chaperones as third-party loss-preventers and that young women may use a psychological split between their roles as contraceptors and lovers in the same way. We find reactive risk controlled by communities of fate between young women and their lovers (e.g., in marriage or "steady" relationships).

And "accidents" tend to occur when couples do not renegotiate their bargains about contraception when the value of a new baby changes— for example, when a couple decides to marry or to divorce. Finally, we find people taking distance into account in their calculations about contraceptive and disease-preventing strategies. We should expect to find the same kinds of processes in other areas of marital relations as well.

Managing Reactive Risk in Products Liability

When we buy goods we usually assume that there is some correspondence between the advertised and the actual qualities of products. At the very least, we hope that we will not give birth to deformed babies from taking prescribed drugs, be maimed by the tools we use, get cancer from the additives in our food, or be seriously burned from wearing flammable clothing. Similarly, when we go to doctors, we assume that they will not leave surgical sponges in us. We also assume that when other people choose what kinds of cars to purchase and how to drive them, they will take into consideration the costs of possible injuries and property damage to others as well as to themselves. Finally, we hope that industries will take into account not only the costs and benefits to themselves, their employees, and their customers, but also the costs of pollution and noise to others who cannot avoid being affected. But if it happens that we are injured by the actions of producers and sellers of goods, by other drivers, or by our own doctors, we at least want them to help cover the costs of our misfortunes. We may even hope that having to bear the cost of accidents will "teach them a lesson" so that they will be more careful next time.

These are problems of reactive risk, and when as a society we try to decide how to allocate the costs of accidents we are concerned partly with motivating loss prevention. We believe that if Proctor and Gamble has to bear some of the costs of illness and death from toxic shock syndrome due to the use of Rely tampons, they will be more careful about marketing dangerous products. And by assigning Ford some of the costs of accidental deaths due to the location of the gas tanks in the Pintos, we hope to convince Ford Motor Company that our chances of being burned to death should be evaluated at more than $200,000 per life lost (Strobel 1980) so that it would be worth their while to construct the cars more safely.

In the case of products liability, the general question is how to arrange the law so that companies will have an incentive to be truthful and to exercise care when the usual situation is that they sell their products and then have nothing further to do with their customers. We want to design the situation so that they will have an incentive to take into account the interests of their customers as users, not just purchasers, of the goods in question. If in the insurance case we want policyholders to continue to act like prudent uninsured owners, in the products liability case we want manufacturers and sellers to act as if they themselves were prudent purchasers and users of the goods they manufacture and sell. And we want manufacturers to behave as if all those affected were potential customers who have to be pleased not only with the product but with the total effect of the industry on their lives. In the malpractice case, we want the practitioners to act as if they would suffer the costs of not exercising appropriate care—in this case we want them to behave as if they were treating their own family members. In the auto liability case, we want people to drive as if they bore the full costs of injuries and damage to others. The problem of reactive risk in these areas is, in short, to provide incentives for people to follow the Golden Rule.

This suggests that tort law, sales law, and contract law should be concerned not just with providing fair compensation to the victims of mishaps or punishing wrongdoers, but should also try to allocate the costs of accidents to provide incentives for loss prevention, remedial action, and insurance by those who can provide it most cheaply.[2] Quite often the losses do not naturally fall on the manufacturers and sellers, careless drivers, or medical practitioners who might be able to reduce losses. We thus face the familiar problem of the separation of incentive and control that we encountered in insurance, and we are asking, once again, how to adjust the incentive system so that incentive and control are fused. When we try to decide who should

2. Good introductions to these issues can be found in Rabin (1976), McKean (1970; the Fall 1970 issue of the *University of Chicago Law Review* is devoted to products liability), Posner (1977), and the Spring 1980 issue of the *Hofstra Law Review* (vol. 8, no. 3). Much of the debate here centers on whether legal decisions are made on an economic basis (e.g., whether judges really assign the costs of accidents to those able to reduce the costs most efficiently), and whether that is desirable.

pay the costs of accidents, we want the burden of loss reduction to be assigned to whoever can take care of the problem most cheaply and effectively. This is analogous to the question of whether loss prevention in fire or marine insurance should be turned over to some third party or whether insurers should try to motivate policyholders themselves to reduce losses individually. We do not much care whether manufacturers, insurers, regulatory agencies, or sellers pass on the costs of loss prevention, as long as they reduce losses when the general welfare is increased by doing so.[3]

In the rest of this section we will be examining some alternative ways of dividing responsibility for preventing losses, pointing out some of the conditions that make one system more effective than another. I will also show how these alternatives are related to the types of techniques for managing reactive risk that are used in insurance.

The old warning that the buyer should beware is essentially a statement about how to divide the costs of accidents. The manufacturer and seller have no further responsibilities once the product passes into the hands of the purchaser. From the point of view of the purchaser, this amounts to a strict market system—the purchaser estimates the odds that the goods are worth the money and will do what is wanted, and then decides whether or not to buy. If it looks like a good bet, the purchaser buys the goods and bears the consequences if this turns out not to be true. Such an allocation of responsibility fits neatly into a rational decision-making framework—the buyer collects information and decides what to do, with the assumption that the incentives of the manufacturers and sellers are relatively fixed and transparent. (This is equivalent to rating and underwriting in insurance.)

But when buyers cannot easily determine whether products will satisfactorily meet their needs or when they cannot pressure manufacturers and sellers by threatening to take their custom elsewhere, the incentives of manufacturers and sellers will not be fixed and neutral, and consumers will often be defrauded when manufacturers provide goods that are not what they appear to be. Posner (1973:8–9) summarizes the characteristics of products, sellers, and buyers that

---

3. Calabresi and Bobbitt (1978) ask when we will decide that it is worthwhile to bear the "tragic costs" of accidents in order to increase the general welfare and how such costs can be allocated fairly.

make consumer fraud most likely. He argues that fraud is likely when the performance of the product or service in question is highly uncertain, when the seller can go out of business relatively easily, when the seller or manufacturer has no competitors to offer better goods and services or to point out the defects of the available products, and when it is impossible for the buyers of goods and services to collect sufficient information to make sensible decisions. Stone (1975:88–92) gives a more disturbing list of situations in which market pressures will not serve to keep corporations in line. He points out that we often have no idea that we are being injured and so cannot adjust our patronage accordingly. We often have no inkling of where to apply pressure since we do not know who really makes the products we use. Because we have not kept up with the ownership patterns and products lists, we will often continue to purchase products from the offending company. Even when we know which organization to pressure we may not be able to because we do not use its products or because we have no choice but to use them. And finally, organizations may not react to pressure by changing their behavior in the ways we want (for example, they may decide on advertising campaigns to convince us that kids can be taught to open the dangerous metal lids of canned puddings rather than deciding to replace the metal lids with snap-off or screw-off tops).

How do we make producers and sellers of goods and services take into account the interests of their customers and other affected people in situations like those described above? Our earlier analysis provides some guidance. First, the principle that reactivity decreases with distance applies in reverse here. Here we are trying to make organizations and people take into account the interests of others, rather than trying to *prevent* them from responding to the fact that their losses are covered by insurance.

What this says is that when there is great distance between those who are affected by something and those who can influence the outcome, it will be relatively difficult to make those with power take into account the interests of those affected. Distance can come about in a number of ways. Organizations commonly increase the distance between themselves and outsiders by trying to seal off their core processes from disruptive influences (Thompson 1967). If it requires more adjustment to change the way that puddings are packaged than to try to teach kids to open them without cutting themselves, then we can expect that the organization will be unwilling to hear the message that consumers are trying to transmit about their preferences. Because the problems may be in a component of a product rather than in the product itself, consumers may find that they have to pressure the manufacturer of the end-product to pressure the manufacturer of the component. Both information and incentive may decay when they have to pass through intermediaries, but the signals may also be unclear in the first place. The manufacturer may be uncertain about whether consumers are patronizing another company because they like the alternative product better, are attracted by flashy packaging, were tempted away by a discount, or disapprove of the manufacturer's employment practices. Finally, it is difficult to influence other actors when you do not control anything of interest to them (Coleman 1973). Industrial polluters pay little attention to the interests of those who are not their customers but who nevertheless hear the noise, breathe the polluted air, or cannot catch any edible fish. Similarly, patients cannot get hospitals to modify offensive or dangerous routines unless they go through their physicians. When there is great distance between those with control and those affected, we cannot rely on market pressures to cause responsible behavior.

Distance is sometimes subject to legal manipulation. Part of the reason that manufacturers and sellers have been unresponsive is that they have not been legally required to respond to consumers who did not *themselves* purchase the goods in question or who had bought them from an *intermediary*. Until early in the twentieth century, manufacturers and sellers were not held liable for defective products unless there was a direct contractual relationship between the injured person and the manufacturer or seller.[4] Over the years this rule has been relaxed in several ways. First, manufacturers began to be held liable for defects in foods, "inherently or imminently dangerous," and "ultradangerous" products (McKean 1970:8). In these cases courts held that no contractual relationship was required. Alternatively, if there was evidence of negligence, a manufacturer could be held liable even though there was no contractual relation. Usually these cases were ones involving serious physical injuries. But gradually negligence began to be taken for granted when products were

4. See McKean (1970:6–13) for a discussion of these developments in products liability.

defective; so injured parties were required to prove neither the existence of a contractual relation nor the negligence of the manufacturer or seller. Distance can be reduced in other ways as well—courts have held that a manufacturer may be liable even though the spouse or guest of the person purchasing the product was the injured party and that advertising directly to consumers can create warranties to them (McKean 1970: 10–11, 13).

We might expect that the question of how controllable losses are would enter into legal decisions about distance, just as it entered into insurers' decisions about when to grant insurance coverage. In the law these issues would be raised in the context of rulings about strict liability (the manufacturer is held liable whether or not it could have prevented the problem), negligence (the manufacturer is held liable only when its carelessness led to the problem), and recklessness (the manufacturer was fully aware of the potential problem and chose not to adjust for it).[5]

Those who can most easily protect themselves from consumer fraud are those who are involved in a community of fate with the producers or sellers of the goods they use. The most common form that such a community of fate takes is a contract. If two parties negotiate the terms of the contract, each can see that its interests are represented; because contracts are legally enforceable, the bargain can be made to stick (there is also a third-party loss preventer—the court system). When people or organizations have long-term, continuous interactions they will be more able to work out appropriate protections for both parties. Each will be interested in the other's welfare since the two are interdependent. In short, the farther we move along the continuum from simple markets to contracts to organizations, the easier it is to protect one's interests (Stinchcombe 1983). This means that large purchasers of complex goods will be more able to protect themselves than will small single-time purchasers of inexpensive goods. The problems of small numbers bargaining start to enter in, though, and this may limit the extent to which a contractual community of fate is a solution *unless* the two parties really are *equally* dependent on each other.

In the case of malpractice, these principles suggest that fee-for-

---

5. This was one of the issues in the Indiana case in which Ford was charged with reckless manslaughter (Strobel 1980). Ford was acquitted.

service systems without insurance should make physicians behave more responsibly, just as the conventional wisdom suggests. Here two principles apply. There is little distance between physician and patient—the connection between physician outcome and patient outcome is not mediated by an insurance company or health maintenance organization (HMO). The direct tie should make the physician more sensitive to patient preferences and outcomes. Further, when an insurer pays for medical care, the patient and the provider are not really in a community of fate. The physician's outcome depends not on whether he or she has satisfied the patient but on whether he or she has done something that fits into a category specified by the insurer. Physicians negotiate with insurers, not with patients, about how much they will be paid and for what.[6] This suggests an important motive for deductibles in medical insurance. The usual argument is that when patients have to share the cost, they are less likely to go to the doctor for frivolous reasons. An alternative possibility is that deductibles make physicians more sensitive to the fact that their patients are the ultimate consumers of health care (and they give patients a legitimate way to express preferences about treatment).[7]

In auto liability, equivalent methods would include deductibles in insurance contracts to make people pay part of the costs of accidents, the arrangement that rates increase when a person has too many accidents (experience rating), and fault arrangements that would make people pay a higher proportion of the costs of an accident when they were in some way negligent.

Collective or third-party loss prevention also makes sense some of the time for products liability and corporate responsibility problems. The usual objection to such solutions is that they are more costly than either market or contractual solutions. Such objections seem less important, though, when we realize that usually we are not choosing between a free market and regulation but instead between two differ-

---

6. If this sounds too crass, see Hadley, Holahan, and Scanlon (1979) for evidence that physicians provided more of the more expensive services when their incomes were threatened by freezes on the prices that could be charged.

7. In fact I do not believe that they function this way. In order for deductibles to work like this, billing systems would probably have to be rearranged so that patients did not see themselves as merely loaning an uncertain quantity of money to the insurance company when they paid their medical bills, and physicians would have to be made aware that patients might not come back to pay their 5 percent to physicians they did not like.

ent methods of public control—a common-law system of privately enforced rights and an administrative system with direct public control (Posner 1977:271). Direct public regulation seems to be the only solution when there is great distance between the responsible parties and those who bear the costs, and this is especially true when the costs are dispersed over a large group.

Collective loss prevention typically occurs through governmental bodies like the Federal Trade Commission, the Federal Aviation Administration, the Food and Drug Administration, and the Transportation Department's Bureau of Motor Carrier Safety. The latter has been cut back in recent years, and though accidents have not yet risen, this seems to be only because states have taken over some of the inspections. In those states in which inspections have been stepped up, trucking accidents have dropped 30 percent (Feaver 1983). It is hard to imagine how private citizens could make trucking companies take into account their worries about accidents.

In insurance we saw that third-party loss prevention was needed when the motives of policyholders were too mixed, so that they would neglect loss prevention (even if on the average this did not make sense) when business was booming. Regulatory agencies presumably supply these same sorts of unmixed motives in situations in which companies may skimp on safety even to their own long-run disadvantage. When consumers cannot choose to reduce accidents, but can only choose to purchase cheaper goods without knowing whether the low price comes from cost-cutting measures or from accident reductions, or, more important, when the full costs of accidents are not borne by the company (but are externalized) and so not passed on to consumers who might then apply pressure by buying cheaper goods, regulatory agencies will be important.

Collective loss prevention will be important, then, in those cases in which there is no community of fate because customers are not the only ones damaged or because customers cannot (for the reasons outlined in Posner 1973 and Stone 1975) punish bad manufacturers or sellers. The Food and Drug Administration provides a good illustration of collective loss prevention in a situation in which the characteristics of products are not known for some time and in which it is difficult for consumers to collect information about products. When special expertise is required to discriminate between good and bad products, collective loss prevention by regulatory agencies will be important. Consumer magazines, certification organizations like Underwriters' Laboratories, laws requiring the disclosure of product information, the Uniform Commercial Code, and class-action suits are all forms of collective loss prevention.

Federal standards are supposed to serve a collective loss-prevention function in auto liability, as are departments of motor vehicles in testing and certifying driving ability, insurance companies in refusing insurance coverage to unsafe drivers, police departments and courts in apprehending and punishing unsafe drivers, and state legislatures in enacting driving rules.

In theory, professional organizations like the American Medical Association and the American Bar Association are supposed to act as collective loss-prevention organizations by policing their members and certifying their competence. But such societies are less divorced from the individual members they are supposed to be policing than are, for example, the certification societies in shipping. Because of the close relationship between the regulatory body and the professional (or organization in the case of governmental regulatory agencies) whose behavior is to be controlled, reactive risk becomes important again. A regulatory agency may be able to decrease the distance between the vulnerable consumer and the producer or seller of the product or service, but the regulatory agency may not have the hoped-for neutral incentives if there is not sufficient distance between it and the profession or industry it is supposed to regulate. We have to worry about changes in the incentives of regulatory bodies as well.

Renegotiation of outdated bargains is only possible in those cases in which there is some relation between the party that might inflict losses and the one that must bear them. Traditionally this has meant that only when there were contracts or implied contracts was it possible to have renegotiation. But third-party loss prevention often makes renegotiation possible. The relatively new phenomena of product recalls and corrective advertising about the true dangers of a product or the true virtues of some drug (the advertisements that admit Listerine will not prevent colds since it is only antibacterial, not antiviral) are essentially renegotiations of outdated bargains.

When we ask how reactive risk has been controlled in the area of products liability, we find that distance is a crucial variable. Because the distance between manufacturer and consumer is often very great, consumers find it hard to apply pressure to manufacturers. Third-party loss preventers, such as regulatory agencies and professional associations, sometimes fill the gap here. In other cases, when the distance between producer and consumer is not so great, communities of fate are formed, often through contracts. Renegotiation of outdated bargains also occurs either in communities of fate or when regulatory agencies or other third-party loss preventers require powerful producers to "renegotiate" their bargains with weaker consumers.

Perverse Uses of Strategies

Young women worrying that their lovers will kiss and tell and consumers worrying that manufacturers are misrepresenting their products must figure out some way to make the other party take their interests into account. In arguing that risk-management strategies help fix the behavior of lovers and manufacturers and make it possible for young women and consumers to calculate the odds of loss or gain, we want to be careful not to sound like functionalist Pollyannas. Risk-management strategies can be abused as well as used. Just as Goffman's spies (1967) chose to fake those signs that are regarded as most reliable because they are hard to fake, so we can expect that some actors will use the principles outlined above to encourage people to believe that they can calculate and make decisions when they really cannot.

Such a perverse use of these strategies can be found in used-car markets (Browne 1973). First, salesmen try to prevent buyers from collecting further information. By offering an especially low price on a car ("low ball") or by offering a high price for a trade-in ("high ball") they try to make sure a customer will come back. In order to make sure a customer goes directly home a salesperson might give the customer a carton of ice cream that needs to go into a refrigerator. Owners of dealerships protect themselves by increasing the distance between the "house" and the customer. The salesperson is kept ignorant of the price for which a car has been bought and the amount for which it should be sold. Such an arrangement means that there are at least two steps between the buyer and seller (buyer/salesman/ "house" or dealer), and *both* of them are across organizational boundaries. In this way the house protects itself from customer pressure. Similarly, the house can claim ignorance of such practices as appearance reconditioning and rolling back of mileage (the illegality of this act may lull customers into believing the odometer) because it can claim that it cannot influence the actions of previous owners, especially if the used car was bought at an auction. Finally, dealerships often appear to create a community of fate by giving a warranty, but these warranties are usually not worth the paper they are written on.

Used cars are exactly the sorts of products that make third-party loss prevention necessary. Because it is not possible to judge the quality of the car until considerably later, the buyer cannot choose sensibly. Blue books and consumer magazines provide some help, but they give information about a *class* of cars rather than about an *individual* car. State laws about "knocking the clock" (turning back the odometer) are attempts at collective loss-prevention that have failed because registration papers can be laundered in states that have not passed such legislation.

Despite the information asymmetries, used-car markets continue to exist. This is true for three reasons. First, many people cannot afford new cars, so they have to buy used cars. Dealers have a wider selection and will take one's old car as a trade-in. This helps explain why individuals buy used cars and buy them from dealers. Second, the problem of uncertainty about the quality of the used car is less important to the dealer than to the customer. The dealer can adjust the prices on both new and used cars to compensate for uncertainty about the quality of used cars (either being traded in or being sold). Standardization in new cars makes it possible to have a real market for them, and the market for used cars can then be hinged to this. Third, many of the tactics employed by used-car dealers and sellers seem to be designed to con the other party. These tactics make people *believe* that they can calculate but in fact make them calculate *incorrectly*. In this case, then, the theory would predict that people would make inappropriate calculations that would nevertheless lead them to *act*, rather than predicting that such calculations would lead people to act *rationally*.

Such problems are considerably less serious when customers can form long-term relations with dealerships and salespeople. In such cases a community of fate develops, and we would again predict a sensible outcome.

We have found that the strategies insurers use to control reactive risks are also used by individuals in negotiations about virginity and contraception and by individuals and organizations trying to control the producers and sellers of goods and services. In discussing the control of reactive risk in sexual relationships and in the relations between manufacturers and consumers I have tried to give some sense of the range of empirical settings in which these issues might fruitfully be studied and of the different guises in which the risk-management strategies might appear. At the same time I used the example of used-car markets to suggest that happy outcomes are by no means inevitable since risk-management strategies can be used to exploit as easily as to improve the general welfare.

Appendix:
Major Categories of
Fidelity and Surety Bonds

In this appendix I will discuss briefly the six categories of bonds *not* covered in the main body of the book. (See chapter 5, pp. 162–72, for the general discussion of the rating of fidelity and surety bonds and for specific comments on contract, fidelity, and financial institution bonds.) The accompanying chart summarizes information from the rate manual on important subtypes of bonds, what the bonds cover, what the rates are based on, and so forth.

Forgery bonds offer a rather different coverage than that provided by fidelity and financial institution bonds because the dishonesty covered is usually the dishonest act of some unknown person (Roberts 1965). The relation covered is often a relation between strangers rather than between employer and employee.

Court bonds are a different matter yet (Surety Association of America n.d., 1). Court bonds are bonds required by law, and they cover two very different kinds of risks. Fiduciary bonds cover the faithful performance of administrators, executors, guardians, and others appointed by the courts to carry out specified activities to benefit other people on whose behalf they act. The terms of the bonds are fixed by statute and cover not only honesty but also competent performance. Judicial proceeding bonds protect the rights of other litigants or interested parties and include appeal, attachment, replevin, costs, injunction, and bail bonds. A judicial proceeding bond is in essence a guarantee that the dispute will not end up being simply an academic matter because one side or the other has used up whatever is in dispute, for example by selling a house and spending the proceeds when the ownership of the house is in dispute. It therefore covers not just honesty and faithful performance, but financial responsibility as well.

License and permit bonds are bonds required by public bodies (Surety Association of America n.d., h). In general, a business enterprise is required by the relevant government body (federal, state, county, or municipal) to get a license to carry out its business, and it is also required to get a surety bond to back up this license. The license is an agreement to comply with the laws and to perform the business in the accustomed manner without violating the rights or interests of other parties. The purpose of the bond, then, is threefold: (1) the bond indemnifies the public body against direct damages and guarantees that taxes will be paid (so it makes government revenues more stable); (2) because the bonding company assumes these obligations, the government is spared the trouble of investigating the qualifications (financial, moral, and educational) of the licensees; and (3) the bond allows resources to be used more efficiently since the licensee does not have to make a cash deposit to guarantee compliance with the law. In some cases, the bond also has a fourth function: to guarantee the payment of losses to third parties resulting from the licensee's failure to meet obligations.

U.S. Government bonds (also called federal bonds) are also bonds that are required either by law or at the discretion of a government official. Coverage also is specified by the government. There are four main kinds of federal bonds: (1) official bonds, which can be either name or position bonds, and which guarantee the faithful performance of government employees, especially high officials; (2) immigration bonds, which can be either individual or blanket bonds, and which are sometimes required of immigrants to assure that they will not become public charges, will pay their fines and debts, will maintain the status that was the basis for the visa, will depart on schedule, and so on; (3) excise bonds (also called internal revenue bonds), which guarantee that the bonded persons (or organizations) will pay all taxes and fines (in some cases the *entire* bond is forfeited for failure to pay taxes promptly); and (4) customs bonds, which guarantee the redelivery of illegally imported goods, the payment of fines and duties, and compliance with the laws and regulations of the customs bureau.

Public official bonds are required by law for the officers, agents, and employees of states and political subdivisions (Surety Association of America n.d., e, i). Such bonds come in two forms, one that guarantees only the honesty of the public official, and one that guarantees both honesty and faithful performance. Bonds for high officials almost always are faithful performance bonds, though there are some variations in how closely this is specified. Sometimes the meaning of faithful performance is given in the law and sometimes it has a common-law meaning. Very often the public official is personally liable for the actions of lower-level employees, for burglaries, for investments that are not in accordance with the law, and so on. In this sense public official bonds are somewhat similar to fiduciary bonds in that in both cases the person bonded is held responsible for a complete knowledge of and compliance with the relevant laws. For this reason, bonds are often required (by higher officials) of lower-level employees as a way to protect the higher official from the consequences of other people's mistakes.

Finally, miscellaneous bonds are those bonds that do not fit into any of the previous eight categories. Some of these are bonds required by law, in which case the conditions are often, though not always, specified by law. Others are purely voluntary bonds with the specifications designed by the principal and obligee. Among the sorts of bonds included in this category are lost instrument bonds (which cover the problems a company faces in issuing a duplicate of a stock certificate, insurance policy, or whatever), income tax bonds for individuals, sales promotion bonds (covering guarantees for used cars, for example), and patent infringement bonds.

Summary of Information from the 1979 Rate Manual of the Surety Association of America

Type of bond	Coverage	Main variants	Rating considerations
Fidelity bonds *Eligibility*: any employer (except those covered by other kinds of bonds listed below). (ME-6 to ME-11)[a]	Mainly dishonesty; also disappearance and destruction of property; also extortion, on-premises, and in-transit losses. (ME-1 to ME-5[a])	(1) Variations in units covered: individual bonds, name schedule bonds, blanket fidelity bonds, commercial blanket bonds, and blanket position bonds. (2) Package deals for different kinds of businesses.	(1) Amount of bond penalty. (2) Classification of insured (gives class rate modification). (3) Number of employees (calculated by including all employees of a certain class and a proportion of other employees). (4) Charges for extra locations or branches. (5) Extra coverage or exclusions. (6) Experience modifications. (ME-15ff.)
Financial institution bonds *Eligibility*: banks, credit unions, insurance companies, personal finance companies, stockbrokers, etc., but eligibility varies by bond and is rigidly limited. (FI-5 to FI-11)	Losses due to dishonesty of employees; extortion; on-premises and in-transit coverage (larceny, robbery, destruction); forgery; redemption of U.S. Savings Bonds; court costs and attorneys' fees. (FI-2 to FI-3)	(1) Variation in units covered: individual, schedule, or blanket bonds. (2) Special purpose "standard forms" and "insuring agreements." (FI-5 to FI-8)	(1) Coverage charge for amount of bond. (2) Employee charge (in some cases all employees counted; in others only "ratable employees"). (3) Charge for branch offices, facilities, mobile branch units, etc. (4) Deductibles: underwriting and self-insurance. (5) Form-of-coverage modification for type of business.

Type	Coverage	Subtypes	Rating
Forgery bonds *Eligibility*: any person, firm, or corporation except banks (and bank-like organizations). (FOR-3)	Losses due to forgery, counterfeit currency, extensions of credit, etc.	Depositors, credit card, securities, postal employees, family, merchants check cashing, comprehensive, or combination forms.	(1) Amount of the bond. (2) Form of bond. (3) Deductibles. (4) Business or private coverage. (5) Adjustment for type of business. (6) Extra coverage. (7) Experience rating. (FI-22 to FI-30)
Court bonds *Eligibility*: required by law. (CF-1, CF-20)	Prescribed by law: fiduciary bonds cover loss due to failure faithfully to perform duty; judicial proceeding bonds protect rights of other litigants or interested parties. (CF-1, CF-21)	(1) Fiduciary: long-term and short-term. (2) Judicial proceedings: civil proceedings; admiralty proceedings; release-of-defendant bonds.	(1) General rate is based on amount of bond (declines with increase in bond) and is given for civil and admiralty proceedings, bail, and fiduciary bonds. (CF-12[a], CF-17, CF-18) (2) Collateral: fixed or open penalty; relation between bond and assets; co-fiduciary; discount for particular types of bonds; no extra charge for joint control. (3) Specific rates for bonds rated separately. (4) No experience rating.

Summary of Information from the 1979 Rate Manual of the Surety Association of America (continued)

Type of bond	Coverage	Main variants	Rating considerations
Contract bonds *Eligibility:* any person entering into written contract.	Specified by obligee or by statute, not by principal or surety. (C-1) Corresponding to four main variants: (1) Bidder will enter into contract and supply required bonds. (2) Principal will carry out duties of written contract (often includes payment and maintenance). (3) Contractor will pay for labor and materials. (4) Guarantee against defective workmanship and materials (may include efficient or successful operation). (C-2)	(1) Bid or proposal. (2) Performance. (3) Payment of labor or materials. (4) Maintenance. (For various sorts of contracts listed above: class A-1, A, B construction contracts; supply contracts; miscellaneous contracts.)	(1) General rate: (a) contract price or bond price, whichever is higher; (b) supplement for periods over 24 months; (c) difficulty of contract (B, A, A-1) or other variation in work (rate is higher on maintenance if successful operation is guaranteed). (2) Specific rates, especially for miscellaneous contracts. (3) No experience rating. (4) Where rate fits two categories, the higher is used. (C-10, C-12, C-14, C-15, C-18 to C-21)
Miscellaneous bonds *Eligibility:* no specified requirements.	In accordance with statute where bond is legally required; otherwise not standardized. (M-1)	(1) Bonds required by federal government. (2) Bonds required by other political subunits. (3) Bonds required by persons, firms, corporations, associations, or other legal entities. (M-1)	(1) Tied to bond penalty (per annum or per term legally required). (2) Where not tied to penalty (e.g., open-penalty bonds), tied to some other unit, such as shipments. (M-7) (3) Variations with locale or lo-

	Coverage	Beneficiaries / Subclasses	Rating factors
(continued from previous row)			cal law (e.g., with workers' compensation self-insurer's guarantee). (M-23) (4) Reduction with collateral. (M-2a) (5) No experience rating.
License and permit bonds *Eligibility:* those needing permits or licenses to engage in particular activities.	(1) Indemnification to government body for loss or damage resulting from failure to comply with law or regulation (including tax payment). (2) Losses or damages to third parties resulting from failure to meet obligations. (3) Coverage is specified by law. (LP-1)	(1) Only state or other government gets benefit. (2) Third-party beneficiaries as well.	(1) Tied to penalty (and sometimes decreased with increase in penalty); no general rates. (2) State variations override general rates. (LP-1) (3) Collateral reduces bond. (4) Amount of time.
U.S. Government bonds *Eligibility:* required by law (though immigration bonds seem to be at the discretion of officials).	Coverage specified by government. Corresponding to four main variants: (1) Guarantees faithful performance. (2) Guarantees not becoming a public charge, payment of fines, maintenance of status, departure, etc. (3) Guarantees payment of all taxes, fines, etc.; in some cases bond is forfeited if there is failure to comply with law.	(1) Official bonds (individual or position bonds). (US-1) (2) Immigrant bonds (individual or blanket). (US-19) (3) Excise bonds. (US-27) (4) Custom bonds. (US-43)	(1) Amount of coverage (in some cases decreases with increase in bond penalty); period of coverage (per annum or term); other measures of size (e.g., number of trucks in some custom bonds). (2) Collateral (for immigrant bonds, excise bonds, and custom bonds). (3) Variation with subject of bond. (4) Maximum bonds on excise.

Summary of Information from the 1979 Rate Manual of the Surety Association of America (continued)

Type of bond	Coverage	Main variants	Rating considerations
	(4) Guarantees redelivery of illegally imported goods; payment of fines, duties, charges, etc.; compliance with all laws and regulations of Bureau of Customs.		
Public official bonds *Eligibility:* officers, agents, employees of state or political subdivisions, required by law or voluntary. (See fidelity bonds for bonds covering officers and employees of libraries, hospitals, and charitable and religious institutions, unless owned by a state or political subdivision.) (All States 122, All States 122a)	Guarantees honesty or faithful performance of duties. Coverage not standardized: may be specified in law or may be "common law."	Public official bonds, public employee blanket bonds.	Public official bonds: (1) computed on bond penalty unless another method is prescribed; (2) per annum or per term; (3) variations with position. Public employee blanket bonds: (1) class or number of employees; (2) class rate modification; (3) additional indemnity charge; (4) experience rating; (5) honesty or faithful performance; (6) number of days in force; (7) underwriting deductibles. (All States 122d, All States 122q)

ᵃAll page numbers (e.g., ME-6) refer to the Rate Manual of the Surety Association of America. Pages in the rate manual are numbered sequentially within each section.

Selected Bibliography

ADAM, JOHN, JR.
  1965 "Underwriting in Fire Insurance." In *Property and Liability Insurance Handbook*, edited by John D. Long and Davis W. Gregg, 190–205. Homewood, Ill.: Richard D. Irwin.
AETNA INSURANCE CO.
  1819 *Aetna Guide to Fire Insurance for the Representatives of the Aetna Insurance Company*. Hartford: Aetna.
  1979 "Summary: Report on Property Insurance Availability." Aetna Insurance Company, Hartford. Photocopy.
AKERLOF, GEORGE A.
  1970 "The Market for Lemons: Qualitative Uncertainty and the Market Mechanism." *Quarterly Journal of Economics* 84:485–500.
AMERICAN IRON AND STEEL INSTITUTE
  1971 *Fire Protection Through Modern Building Codes*. 4th ed. New York: American Iron and Steel Institute.
ARNOLD, EARL C.
  1926 "The Compensated Surety." *Columbia Law Review* 26 (February):171–89.
ARROW, KENNETH
  1963 "Uncertainty and the Welfare Economics of Medical Care." *American Economic Review* 53:941–69. Reprinted in Arrow (1971).
  1971 *Essays in the Theory of Risk Bearing*. Chicago: Markham.
BACKMAN, JULES
  1948 *Surety Rate-Making: A Study of the Economics of Suretyship*. New York: The Surety Association of America.
BAINBRIDGE, J.
  1952 *Biography of an Idea: The Story of Mutual Fire and Casualty Insurance*. New York: Doubleday.
BARLAUP, ASBJØRN, ED.
  1976 *Det norske Veritas, 1864–1964*. Oslo: Det norske Veritas.
BARNARD, BRUCE
  1978 "A Wave of Fraudulent Claims Hits Marine Insurance Industry." *Journal of Commerce* (September 14):1, 2.

BARZEL, YORAM
1983   "The Residual Claim as the Entrepreneur's Reward for Self-Policing." University of Washington, Seattle. Photocopy.
BAZAIRE, HOWARD A.
1979   "An Approach to the Market Value Homeowners' Concept by One Michigan Insurer." In *25th Annual Workshop*, 193–96. Boston: National Association of Independent Insurers.
BEARDSLEY, JOHN F.
1965   "Fidelity Bonds and Underwriting." In *Property and Liability Insurance Handbook*, edited by John D. Long and Davis W. Gregg, 816–28. Homewood, Ill.: Richard D. Irwin.
BECKER, HOWARD S.
1964   "Personal Changes in Adult Life." *Sociometry* 27 (March): 40–53.
BENDOR, JONATHAN
1985   *Parallel Systems: Redundancy in Government*. Berkeley and Los Angeles: University of California Press.
BENJAMIN, ESTHER
1983   "Herpes and the Formerly Married Adult: Risk Taking in Everyday Life." Paper presented at the Annual Meetings of the Society for the Study of Social Problems, Detroit.
BENNEM, W. H.
1950   "Fidelity Bonds in a War Economy." *The Casualty and Surety Journal* (November): 22–25.
BICKELHAUPT, DAVID LYNN
1961   *Transition to Multiple-Line Insurance Companies*. Homewood, Ill.: Richard D. Irwin.
BRODSKY, JOHN C.
1934   "How Surety Bond Rates Are Made." *The Weekly Underwriter* (March 24): 602–5.
1940   "Fidelity and Surety Bonds: Course No. 4, Chapter 1." *The Weekly Underwriter* (July 20): 140–43.
BROWNE, JOY
1973   *The Used Car Game: A Sociology of the Bargain*. Lexington, Mass.: D. C. Heath.
BURGOON, NORMAN A., JR.
1965   "Surety Bonds and Underwriting." In *Property and Liability Insurance Handbook*, edited by John D. Long and Davis W. Gregg, 829–40. Homewood, Ill.: Richard D. Irwin.
BURKE, NORMAN D.
1933   *Retail Company Reports on Dwelling Risks*. Address before the Insurance Library Association, February 7. N.p.: no publisher listed.
BUTLER, BEN M.
1965   "Loss Adjustment in Fire Insurance." In *Property and Liability*

Insurance Handbook, edited by John D. Long and Davis W. Gregg, 218–32. Homewood, Ill.: Richard D. Irwin.

CALABRESI, GUIDO
1970   *The Costs of Accidents: A Legal and Economic Analysis*. New Haven: Yale University Press.

CALABRESI, GUIDO, AND PHILIP BOBBITT
1978   *Tragic Choices*. New York: W. W. Norton.

Canadian Underwriter, The
1979   "Prevalence of Arson Cause for Concern in Canada." *The Canadian Underwriter* 46 (August): 10–11, 73.

CARR, WILLIAM H. A.
1975   *From Three Cents a Week . . . . : The Story of the Prudential Insurance Company of America*. Englewood Cliffs, N.J.: Prentice-Hall.

CHEUNG, STEVEN N. S.
1983   "The Contractual Nature of the Firm." *Journal of Law and Economics* 26 (April): 1–21.

CIALDINI, ROBERT B.
1984   *Influence: How and Why People Agree to Things*. New York: William Morrow.

COLEMAN, JAMES S.
1973   *The Mathematics of Collective Action*. Chicago: Aldine.

COLLINS, JOSEPH F.
1955   "Rate Regulation in Fire and Casualty Insurance." In *New York State Insurance Department: Examination of Insurance Companies*. Vol. 5, xv–xviii. Albany: State of New York.

CONLON, C. C.
1938   "Corporate Bonding Principle Growing in Favor." *The Weekly Underwriter* (August 27): 396–98.

CONNER, GEORGE A.
1951   "How Much is Enough Dishonesty Protection." *The Weekly Underwriter* (June 23): 1577–79.

COOPER, HARRY P.
1938   *A Brief History of the Indiana Farmers Mutual Insurance Company*. Indianapolis: Sabins Press.

CRIST, G. W., JR.
1950   *Corporate Suretyship*. 2nd ed. New York: McGraw-Hill.

CROSS, J. HARRY
1963   "Suretyship is Not Insurance." *The Journal of Insurance Information* (September-October): 14–17.

DEAN, A. F.
1925   *The Philosophy of Fire Insurance*. Edited by W. R. Townley. Chicago: Edward B. Hatch.

DENENBERG, HERBERT S.
1965   "History, Nature, and Uses of Suretyship." In *Property and Lia-*

bility Insurance Handbook, edited by John D. Long and Davis W. Gregg, 803–15. Homewood, Ill.: Richard D. Irwin.

DENENBERG, HERBERT S., ROBERT D. EILERS, G. WRIGHT HOFFMAN, CHESTER A. KLINE, JOSEPH J. MELONE, AND WAYNE SNIDER
1964   *Risk and Insurance.* Englewood Cliffs, N.J.: Prentice-Hall.

DE ROOVER, FLORENCE EDLER
1945   "Early Examples of Marine Insurance." *Journal of Economic History* 5 (November): 172–200.

DOHERTY, NEIL
1976   *Insurance Pricing and Loss Prevention.* Lexington, Mass.: D. C. Heath.

DONAHUE, RICHARD
1979   "Evils of Redlining Trotted Out at Press Conference in Chicago." *The National Underwriter* (March 2): 28–29.

DWELLY, ROBERT R.
1965   "Concepts Associated with Marine Insurance." In *Property and Liability Insurance Handbook*, edited by John D. Long and Davis W. Gregg, 252–68. Homewood, Ill.: Richard D. Irwin.

Eastern Underwriter, The
1925   "How Moral Hazard Reports Are Secured." *The Eastern Underwriter* (November 6): 24.
1950   "Associated Factory Mutuals Report $3,700,000 Loss Prevention Expense." *The Eastern Underwriter* (April 25): 30.

EVERT, DAVID R.
1975   "When Economic Conditions Become Difficult Fidelity Losses Increase." *The Weekly Underwriter* (April 5): 18–19, 25.

FACTORY MUTUALS
1935   *The Factory Mutuals, 1835–1935.* Providence, R.I.: Manufacturers Mutual Fire Insurance Co.

FÆRDEN, KARL
1967   *Forsikringsvesenets historie i Norge, 1814–1914.* N.p.: no publisher listed.

FEAVER, DOUGLAS B.
1983   "Those Trucks May Be As Dangerous As You Fear." *Washington Post* (Weekly Edition) 1 (December 19): 33–34.

FOSKET, GEORGE F.
1955   "Fidelity and Surety Insurance Rates." In *New York State Insurance Department: Examination of Insurance Companies.* Vol. 5, 189–99. Albany: State of New York.

FREDERICKS, ALANSON R.
1965   "Defaults in Suretyship." In *Property and Liability Insurance Handbook*, edited by John D. Long and Davis W. Gregg, 859–74. Homewood, Ill.: Richard D. Irwin.

FRITZEL, CHARLES H.
1979 "Legislative Reaction to Homeowners Underwriting." In *25th Annual Workshop*, 181–85. Boston: National Association of Independent Insurers.

FROLICH, NORMAN, AND JOE A. OPPENHEIMER
1978 *Modern Political Economy*. Englewood Cliffs, N.J.: Prentice-Hall.

GAFFNEY, WARREN N.
1965 "Fidelity and Surety Ratemaking." In *Property and Liability Insurance Handbook*, edited by John D. Long and Davis W. Gregg, 841–58. Homewood, Ill.: Richard D. Irwin.

GILMORE, GRANT, AND CHARLES L. BLACK, JR.
1957 *The Law of Admiralty*. Brooklyn, N.Y.: The Foundation Press.

GOFFMAN, ERVING
1969 *Strategic Interaction*. Philadelphia: University of Pennsylvania Press.

GREENE, MARK R.
1973 *Risk and Insurance*. 3rd ed. Cincinnati: South-Western.
1974 "Attitudes Toward Risk and a Theory of Insurance Consumption." In *Insurance Insights*, edited by Mark R. Greene and Paul Swadener, 59–80. Cincinnati: South-Western.

HADLEY, J., J. HOLAHAN, AND W. SCANLON
1979 "Can Fee for Service Reimbursement Coexist with Demand Creation?" *Inquiry* (Chicago, Blue Cross) 16 (Fall):247–58.

HANSON, JON S.
1977 "An Overview: State Insurance Regulation." *Chartered Life Underwriters Journal* 31 (April):20–31.

HARDY, EDWARD R.
1926 *The Making of the Fire Insurance Rate*. New York: The Spectator Insurance Co.

HARRIS, MILTON, AND BENGT HOLMSTRÖM
1982 "A Theory of Wage Dynamics." *Review of Economic Studies* 49:315–33.

HART, OLIVER D.
1982 *Optimal Labour Contracts Under Asymmetric Information: An Introduction*. Theoretical Economics Discussion Paper Series, no. 82142. London: London School of Economics and Political Science.

HEIMER, CAROL A.
1980 *Substitutes for Experience-Based Information: The Case of Offshore Oil Insurance in the North Sea*. Discussion Paper no. 1/81. Bergen, Norway: Institute of Industrial Economics.
1981 "Reactive Risk and Rational Action: Managing Behavioral Risk in Insurance." Ph.D. diss., University of Chicago.

1982   "The Racial and Organizational Origins of Insurance Redlining."
        The Journal of Intergroup Relations 10 (Autumn): 42–60.
HEIMER, CAROL A., AND ARTHUR L. STINCHCOMBE
1980   "Love and Irrationality: It's Got To Be Rational to Love You Be-
        cause It Makes Me So Happy." *Social Science Information* 19
        (4/5): 697–754.
HOGARTH, ROBIN M.
1982   *Decision Making in Organizations* and *the Organization of Deci-
        sion Making*. Chicago: Center for Decision Research, Graduate
        School of Business, University of Chicago.
HOLMSTRÖM, BENGT
1979   "Moral Hazard and Observability." *Bell Journal of Economics* 10
        (Spring): 74–91.
1982a   "Managerial Incentive Problems: A Dynamic Perspective." In *Es-
        says in Economics and Management in Honour of Lars Wahlbeck*,
        210–29. Helsinki: Swedish School of Economics.
1982b   "Moral Hazard in Teams." *Bell Journal of Economics* 13:
        324–40.
HOROWITZ, RUTH
1983   *Honor and the American Dream: Culture and Identity in a Chi-
        cano Community*. New Brunswick, N.J.: Rutgers University Press.
HOWLAND, WILFRED G.
1979   "Redlining: Damned If You Do, Damned If You Don't." *United
        States Banker* (May): 109–10, 113.
HUEBNER, SOLOMON
1914   "History of Marine Insurance." In *Property Insurance: Marine
        and Fire*, edited by Lester W. Zartman and William H. Price. 2nd
        ed., 1–38. New Haven: Yale University Press.
Independent Agent
1978   "Redlining: Pro and Con," by S. V. d'A. *Independent Agent* (Au-
        gust): 49–50.
Insurance Advocate
1944   "Towner Rating Bureau Celebrates Its Thirty-fifth Anniversary."
        Insurance Advocate (September 30): 7–9.
1945   "N.Y. Department Files Decision on Towner Bureau and Ap-
        proves Rate Filing." *Insurance Advocate* (July 28): 10–11.
1979   "N.Y. Hearing on Implementation of Anti-Redlining Laws Finds
        Industry Critical of Proposed Regulation 90." *Insurance Advocate*
        (September 15): 5, 27–29.
INSURANCE CRIME PREVENTION INSTITUTE
n.d.   "Insurance Fraud: The $1.5 Billion Ripoff." Westport, Conn.: In-
        surance Crime Prevention Institute. Photocopy.
1979   "Three Years for Electrocuting Race Horse." *ICPI Report* 7 (May/
        June/July): 1.

INSURANCE INSTITUTE OF LONDON, THE
n.d.   *The History of Fidelity Guarantee*. Report H.R. 7 of the Historic
        Records Committee. London: Insurance Institute of London.
Insurance Marketing
1978   "Redlining: Curse of Urban Dweller." *Insurance Marketing* (Sep-
        tember): 24, 86–87.
JOHNSON, PETE
1963   "The Implied Warranty of Seaworthiness: A Study of Some Court
        Cases from Which This Warranty Has Evolved." The College of
        Insurance, New York, December. Photocopy.
Journal of Commerce
1977   "Marine Insurers Blame Fraudulent Claims for 'Skyrocketing'
        Premiums." *Journal of Commerce* (March 22): 2.
JOYCE, WILLIAM H.
1945   "Romance of Blanket Bonds and Various Other Forms." *Journal
        of Commerce* (January 15): 1A, 15A.
KEENY, HARRY
1979   "Loss Reduction Programs for Residential Properties: Pro-active
        Versus Reactive Considerations." In *25th Annual Workshop*,
        201–6. Boston: National Association of Independent Insurers.
KEETON, ROBERT E.
1971   *Basic Text on Insurance Law*. St. Paul, Minn.: West.
KELLY, AMBROSE B.
1956   "The How and Why of Factory Mutuals." *The Spectator* (Febru-
        ary): 30–31, 57–58, 61.
1957   "Insurance Buyers Hear of Services Available from Mutual Com-
        panies." *The Weekly Underwriter* (January 26): 248, 251–54.
1965   "Forms to Accompany the Fire Policy: Commercial." In *Property
        and Liability Insurance Handbook*, edited by John D. Long and
        Davis W. Gregg, 88–89. Homewood, Ill.: Richard D. Irwin.
KETCHAM, EDWARD A., AND MURRAY KETCHAM-KIRK
1922   *Essentials of the Fire Insurance Business*. Revised ed. N.p.: pub-
        lished by the authors.
KIORPES, A. A.
1979   "Loss Reduction Programs for Residential Properties." In *25th
        Annual Workshop*, 197–99. Boston: National Association of Inde-
        pendent Insurers.
KLIMON, ELLEN L.
1979   "An Attempt to Define Dishonesty." *The National Underwriter
        (Property and Casualty Edition)* 83 (May 18): 37–38.
KNAUTH, ARNOLD WHITMAN, AND CHRISTOPHER R. KNAUTH
1969   "Salvage Convention." In *Knauth's Benedict on Admiralty*, edited
        by Arnold Whitman Knauth and Christopher R. Knauth. 7th ed.,
        rev., 1249–53. New York: Matthew Bender.

KNIGHT, FRANK H.
  1971   *Risk, Uncertainty and Profit*. Chicago: University of Chicago Press. Originally issued in 1921.
LAVE, CHARLES A., AND JAMES G. MARCH
  1975   *An Introduction to Models in the Social Sciences*. New York: Harper and Row.
LAW, FRANK E. ("OBSERVER")
  1924   *Needed Improvements in the Methods and Practices of the Fidelity and Surety Business*. New York: National Surety Company.
LESY, MICHAEL
  1973   *Wisconsin Death Trip*. New York: Random House.
LONGLEY-COOK, L. H.
  1970a   "Rate Making: Manual Rates." In *Multiple-Line Insurers*, edited by G. F. Michelbacher and Nestor R. Roos. 2nd ed., 11–44. New York: McGraw-Hill.
  1970b   "Rate Making: Individual Risk Rating." In *Multiple-Line Insurers*, edited by G. F. Michelbacher and Nestor R. Roos. 2nd ed., 45–56. New York: McGraw-Hill.
LOVELL, BERNARD
  1980   "U.N. Aide Ties Open-Registry to Salem Loss." *Journal of Commerce* (January 11):8.
LUCE, R. DUNCAN, AND HOWARD RAIFFA
  1957   *Games and Decisions*. New York: John Wiley.
LUKER, KRISTIN
  1975   *Taking Chances: Abortion and the Decision Not to Contracept*. Berkeley and Los Angeles: University of California Press.
LUNT, EDWARD C.
  1940   "Corporate Suretyship: A Review of Mr. Crist's Book." *The Weekly Underwriter* (February 24):492–93.
MAATMAN, GERALD L.
  1965   "Loss Prevention in Fire Insurance." In *Property and Liability Insurance Handbook*, edited by John D. Long and Davis W. Gregg, 158–68. Homewood, Ill.: Richard D. Irwin.
MACAVOY, PAUL W., ED.
  1977   *Federal-State Regulation of the Pricing and Marketing of Insurance*. Washington, D.C.: American Enterprise Institute for Public Policy Research.
MAGRATH, JOSEPH J.
  1955a   "New York Insurance Rating Law and Rating Organizations." In *New York State Insurance Department: Examination of Insurance Companies*. Vol. 5, 265–79. Albany: State of New York.
  1955b   "Techniques of the Rating Process." In *New York State Insurance Department: Examination of Insurance Companies*. Vol. 5, 281–97. Albany: State of New York.

1955c "Insurance and Service Organizations." In *New York State Insurance Department: Examination of Insurance Companies*. Vol. 5, 299–317. Albany: State of New York.

MARCH, JAMES G., AND HERBERT A. SIMON
1958 *Organizations*. New York: John Wiley.

MARCH, JAMES G., AND ZUR SHAPIRA
1982 "Behavioral Decision Theory and Organizational Decision Theory." In *Decision Making: An Interdisciplinary Inquiry*, edited by G. R. Ungson and D. N. Braunstein, 92–115. Boston: Kent Publishing.

MARSHALL, GEORGE M., JR.
1965 "Types of Marine Insurance." In *Property and Liability Insurance Handbook*, edited by John D. Long and Davis W. Gregg, 269–84. Homewood, Ill.: Richard D. Irwin.

MARTIN, FREDERICK
1876 *The History of Lloyd's and of Marine Insurance in Great Britain*. London: MacMillan.

MASIMORE, RICHARD
1978 "Redlining: A Panel Discussion." In *24th Annual Workshop*, 265–67. Boston: National Association of Independent Insurers.

MASON, JARVIS W.
1924 *Radio Talks: Season 1923–1924*. New York: American Surety Co.

McDOWELL, CARL E.
1965 "Development of Marine Insurance." In *Property and Liability Insurance Handbook*, edited by John D. Long and Davis W. Gregg, 235–51. Homewood, Ill.: Richard D. Irwin.

McGUFFIE, KENNETH C.
1958 *Kennedy's Civil Salvage*. 4th ed. London: Stevens and Sons.

McKEAN, ROLAND N.
1970 "Products Liability: Trends and Implications." *University of Chicago Law Review* 38 (Fall): 3–63.

McKINLEY, JAMES
1979 "Fire for Hire." *Playboy* 26 (September): 110, 112, 170, 248, 250, 252, 253.

McKINNON, GORDON P., AND KEITH TOWER, EDS.
1976 *Fire Protection Handbook*. 14th ed. Boston: National Fire Protection Association.

McMAHON, JAMES P.
1944 "Corporate Suretyship." *Pittsburgh Insurance Day* (April 24): 1–6. Mimeo.

MELEWSKI, BERNARD, AND MOLLIE LAMPI
1978 *Where Do You Draw the Line?* Albany: New York Public Interest Research Group.

MICHELBACHER, G. F., AND NESTOR R. ROOS
   1970   *Multiple-Line Insurers: Their Nature and Operation.* 2nd ed. New York: McGraw-Hill.
MILLIKAN, A. C.
   1940   *Corporate Suretyship in the Probate Courts.* New York: Association of Casualty and Surety Executives.
MINGENBACK, C. F., AND S. G. MEAD
   1906   *Mutual Insurance Manual.* McPherson, Kans.: no publisher listed.
MOBLEY, NATHAN
   1961   "Corporate Surety." *Best's Fire and Casualty News* (January): 127–32.
MORGAN, WILLIS D.
   1927   "The History and Economics of Suretyship." *Cornell Law Quarterly* 12 (February): 153–71 and (June): 487–99.
MOSTERT, NOEL
   1974   *Supership.* New York: Knopf.
MOUNTAIN, H. M.
   1965   "The Standard Fire Policy." In *Property and Liability Insurance Handbook,* edited by John D. Long and Davis W. Gregg, 58–71. Homewood, Ill.: Richard D. Irwin.
MULLINS, HUGH
   1951   *Marine Insurance Digest.* Cambridge, Md.: Cornell Maritime Press.
MURRAY, L. A., JR.
   1964   "Fidelity Rates." *Best's Insurance News, Fire and Casualty Edition* 65 (September): 83, 90.
National Underwriter, The
   n.d.   *Analytic System for the Measurement of Relative Fire Hazard: A Course of Study.* N.p.: The National Underwriter. Correspondence course to train fire inspectors.
   1961   "Banking Paper Urges the Wisdom of Excess Fidelity Bond Coverage." *The National Underwriter* (May 5): 10, 34.
   1963   "Tells Why, When, and How to Use Accountant on Fidelity Claim." *The National Underwriter* (August 16): 8, 15.
   1967   "Bonding Ex-cons Proves a Success." *The National Underwriter* (Property and Casualty Edition) 71 (August 11): 1, 4.
   1973   "Surety Guarantee Program Seen Charted for Success." *The National Underwriter* (Property and Casualty Edition) 77 (July 20): 3, 13.
   1979   "Labor Department Program Bonding Ex-offenders Shows Less than 2% Loss." *The National Underwriter* (Property and Casualty Edition) 83 (January 12): 58.

NICHOLS, HENRY W.
1939   *On Personal Sureties.* New York: Association of Casualty and Surety Executives.

NORTH, DOUGLASS
1953   "Entrepreneurial Policy and Internal Organization in the Large Life Insurance Companies at the Time of the Armstrong Investigation of Life Insurance." *Explorations in Entrepreneurial History* (Spring): 138–61.

OKUN, ARTHUR M.
1981   *Prices and Quantities: A Macroeconomic Analysis.* Washington, D.C.: The Brookings Institution.

OLSON, MANCUR
1971   *The Logic of Collective Action: Public Goods and the Theory of Groups.* Cambridge: Harvard University Press. Originally issued in 1965.

OXFORD, GILBERT B.
1965   "Ratemaking, Underwriting, and Loss Adjustment in Marine Insurance." In *Property and Liability Insurance Handbook*, edited by John D. Long and Davis W. Gregg, 285–301. Homewood, Ill.: Richard D. Irwin.

PAGE, RICHARD H.
1970   "Underwriting." In *Multiple-Line Insurers*, edited by G. F. Michelbacher and Nestor R. Roos. 2nd ed., 57–78. New York: McGraw-Hill.

PAIGE, KAREN ERIKSEN, AND JEFFERY M. PAIGE
1981   *The Politics of Reproductive Ritual.* Berkeley and Los Angeles: University of California Press.

PARKER, KENT H.
1965   "Ratemaking in Fire Insurance." In *Property and Liability Insurance Handbook*, edited by John D. Long and Davis W. Gregg, 169–89. Homewood, Ill.: Richard D. Irwin.

PAULY, MARK V.
1974   "Overinsurance and Public Provision of Insurance: The Roles of Moral Hazard and Adverse Selection." *Quarterly Journal of Economics* 88: 44–54.

PERROW, CHARLES
1984   *Normal Accidents: Living with High-Risk Technologies.* New York: Basic Books.

PHELAN, JOHN D.
1965   "Business Interruption Insurance." In *Property and Liability Insurance Handbook*, edited by John D. Long and Davis W. Gregg, 119–29. Homewood, Ill.: Richard D. Irwin.

POPKIN, SAMUEL L.
1981   "Public Choice and Rural Development: Free Riders, Lemons, and Institutional Design." In *Public Choice and Rural Development*, edited by Clifford S. Russell and Norman K. Nicholson, 43–80. Washington, D.C.: Resources for the Future.
PORTER, DAVID
1966   *Fundamentals of Bonding: A Manual on Fidelity and Surety*. Indianapolis: Rough Notes.
POSNER, RICHARD A.
1973   *Regulation of Advertising by the FTC*. Washington, D.C.: American Enterprise Institute for Public Policy Research.
1977   *Economic Analysis of Law*. 2nd ed. Boston: Little, Brown. Originally issued in 1972.
POWELL, MILDRED S.
1944   "American Surety Celebrates Diamond Jubilee." *Insurance Advocate* (April 29): 13–16.
RABIN, ROBERT L.
1976   *Perspectives on Tort Law*. Boston: Little, Brown.
RETAIL CREDIT CO.
n.d.   *Character Inspection Services for Fire Insurance Companies*. Atlanta: Retail Credit Co. Circa 1932.
RISLER, GEORGE A.
1963   "New Faces for the Surety Bond." *The Journal of Insurance Information* (March-April): 27–30.
ROBERTS, WILLIAM S.
1965   "Try Forgery Insurance for Client-Depositors." *Rough Notes* (February): 47–48.
ROGERSON, WILLIAM P.
1982   *The Structure of Wage Contracts in Repeated Agency Models*. Technical Report no. 388, Institute for Mathematical Studies in the Social Sciences. Stanford, Calif.: Stanford University.
ROSS, H. LAURENCE
1970   *Settled Out of Court: The Social Process of Insurance Adjustment*. Chicago: Aldine.
ROSS, STEPHEN A.
1973   "The Economic Theory of Agency: The Principal's Problem." *American Economic Review* 63 (May): 134–39.
ROSS, WILLIAM B.
1969   "Friend or Foe: Federal Riot Reinsurance in Perspective." Address to the Insurance Society of New York, January 23.
ROSSER, LAWRENCE B.
1979   "Underwriting in the Current Environment: Homeowners Problems and Opportunities." In *25th Annual Workshop*, 173–79. Boston: National Association of Independent Insurers.

ROTHSCHILD, MICHAEL, AND JOSEPH E. STIGLITZ
  1976   "Equilibrium in Competitive Insurance Markets: An Essay on the
          Economics of Imperfect Information." *Quarterly Journal of Eco-
          nomics* 90:629–50.
Rough Notes
  1950   "A Manpower Shortage Increases Chance of Embezzlement Loss."
          Rough Notes (September):26. Advertisement.
RUSSELL, ALBERT H.
  1951   "Corporate vs. Personal Bonds." *Casualty and Surety Journal*
          (July):15–22.
SCHELLING, THOMAS C.
  1978   *Micromotives and Macrobehavior*. New York: W. W. Norton.
SCHERER, FREDERIC M.
  1964   *The Weapons Acquisition Process: Economic Incentives*. Cam-
          bridge: Harvard Graduate School of Business.
SCHMIDT, JOHN, JR.
  1931   "Bonding Protection for Banks." *The Weekly Underwriter and the
          Insurance Press* (October 24):903–5.
SEARL, EDWIN N.
  1965   "Forms to Accompany the Fire Policy: Personal." In *Property and
          Liability Insurance Handbook*, edited by John D. Long and Davis
          W. Gregg, 72–87. Homewood, Ill.: Richard D. Irwin.
SHAPIRO, CARL, AND JOSEPH E. STIGLITZ
  1982   "Equilibrium Unemployment as a Worker Discipline Device."
          Department of Economics, Princeton University. Princeton, N.J.
          Photocopy.
SIMON, HERBERT A.
  1976   *Administrative Behavior*. 3rd ed. New York: Free Press.
SINCLAIR, WARD
  1984   "Big California Farmers Harvest Federal Cash." *Washington Post*
          (National Weekly Edition) 1 (January 2):30.
SOHMER, HAROLD
  1955   "Fire and Allied Insurance Rates." In *New York State Insurance
          Department: Examination of Insurance Companies*. Vol. 5, 159–
          79. Albany: State of New York.
SPALDING, ALFRED
  1967   "Suretyship: Is It Insurance?" *Western Underwriter* (Property and
          Casualty Edition) (April):10–11, 16–17.
SPENCE, MICHAEL
  1973   "Job Market Signalling." *Quarterly Journal of Economics* 87:
          355–74.
SQUIRES, GREGORY D., AND RUTHANNE DEWOLFE
  1979   *Insurance Redlining: Fact Not Fiction*. Washington, D.C.: U.S.
          Government Printing Office.

STATE OF NEW YORK DEPARTMENT OF INSURANCE
1914   *Report on Examination of the Towner Rating Bureau.* Albany,
        N.Y.: J. B. Lyon.
1945a   "Report on Examination of the Towner Rating Bureau, Inc.: Part
        I." State of New York, Albany. Library, College of Insurance, New
        York. Carbon copy.
1945b   "Report on Examination of the Towner Rating Bureau, Inc.: Part
        II." State of New York Senate Standing Committee on Insurance,
        Albany. Library, College of Insurance, New York. Carbon copy.
1966   *Report of the Senate Standing Committee on Insurance for Inves-
        tigation, Study and Research of Varying Insurance Rates.* Legis-
        lative Department, no. 13. Albany: State of New York.

STEVENSON, GELVIN
1977   "Upsurge in Arson Calls for Insurance Reform." *New York Times*
        (September 11): 1, 8.

STINCHCOMBE, ARTHUR L.
1983   *Contracts as Hierarchical Documents.* Work Report no. 65. Ber-
        gen, Norway: Institute of Industrial Economics.

STONE, CHRISTOPHER D.
1975   *Where the Law Ends: The Social Control of Corporate Behavior.*
        New York: Harper and Row.

STROBEL, LEE PATRICK
1980   *Reckless Homicide?: Ford's Pinto Trial.* South Bend, Ind.: And
        Books.

SULLIVAN, HERBERT A.
1950   "The Interview." *Rough Notes* (September): 25, 83ff.

SURETY ASSOCIATION OF AMERICA
n.d., a *Construction: The Bonded Contract Is the Owner's Protection.*
        12th printing, February 1964. New York: Surety Association of
        America.
n.d., b *Contract Bonds: The Unseen Services of a Surety.* 3rd printing,
        November 1974. New York: Surety Association of America.
n.d., c *Corporate Fiduciary Bonds: A Safeguard of Estates.* October
        1955; 9th printing, April 1968. New York: Surety Association of
        America.
n.d., d *Fidelity Bonds: An Informative Review for Accountants and Au-
        ditors.* 12th printing, May 1967. New York: Surety Association of
        America.
n.d., e *How Much Honesty Insurance.* 16th printing, February, 1978.
        New York: Surety Association of America.
n.d., f *Is the Public Official Personally Liable?* 1946; 12th printing, 1975.
        New York: Surety Association of America.

n.d., g *Joint Control: Its Role in the Administration of Estates.* 10th printing, May 1978. New York: Surety Association of America.

n.d., h *License Bonds: An Aid to the Administration of License Laws.*
March 1961; 2nd printing, June 1961. New York: Surety Association of America.

n.d., i *The Public Official and His Surety Bond.* 6th printing, September
1964. New York: Surety Association of America.

n.d., j *Rate Manual of Fidelity, Forgery and Surety Bonds.* Includes revisions through December 1978. New York: Surety Association of
America.

n.d., k *Safeguards Against Employee Dishonesty in Business.* 12th printing, August 1971. New York: Surety Association of America.

n.d., l *The Surety Bond in Court Proceedings.* 12th printing, July 1967.
New York: Surety Association of America.

1946   *Corporate Suretyship: The Balance Wheel of American Business.*
New York: Surety Association of America.

SUTTON, CHARLES T.

1949   *The Assessing of Salvage Awards.* London: Stevens and Sons.

SYRON, RICHARD F.

1972   *An Analysis of the Collapse of the Normal Market for Fire Insurance in Substandard Urban Core Areas.* Boston: Federal Reserve Bank of Boston. Originally written as Ph.D. diss., Tufts
University.

THOMPSON, JAMES D.

1967   *Organizations in Action.* New York: McGraw-Hill.

TODD, A. L.

1966   *A Spark Lighted in Portland: The Record of the National Board of
Fire Underwriters.* New York: McGraw-Hill.

TOWNER, R. H.

1924   *The Scientific Basis of Fidelity and Surety Rates.* Address deliv-
ered at the Annual Convention of the International Association of
Casualty and Surety Underwriters, White Sulphur Springs, W.
Va., September 25. N.p.: no publisher listed.

TOWNSEND, ROBERT M.

1980   "Contract Length and the Gain from Enduring Relationship."
Pittsburgh: Carnegie-Mellon University. Photocopy.

TRAVELERS INSURANCE CO.

1956   "Fidelity Insurance." *Travelers' Home Study Course.* Hartford:
Travelers Insurance Co.

TRENNERY, C. F.

1926   *The Origin and Early History of Insurance.* London: P. S. King
and Son.

TRUNKEY, DONALD D.
1983   "Trauma." *Scientific American* 249 (August): 28–35.

UNITED NATIONS CONFERENCE ON TRADE AND DEVELOPMENT
1978   *Marine Insurance: Legal and Documentary Aspects of the Marine Insurance Contract.* Geneva: United Nations Conference on Trade and Development.

UNSWORTH, EDWIN
1980a   "UK, Liberia to Probe Sinking of the Salem." *Journal of Commerce* (February 11): 8.
1980b   "World Tonnage Lost Soars 64% in 1979." *Journal of Commerce* (February 12): 34.

UPSHAW, P. C.
1933   *Underwriting Character.* Address before the Insurance Library Association, December 19. N.p.: no publisher listed.

U.S. DEPARTMENT OF COMMERCE
n.d.   "Property and Casualty Insurance Services." In *Crime in Service Industries*, chap. 6. Washington, D.C.: U.S. Department of Commerce.

VANDERBEEK, WARD
1979   "Insurance Industry Response to the Challenge of 'Redlining' Allegations as to Availability of Personal Lines Packages." In *25th Annual Workshop*, 187–92. Boston: National Association of Independent Insurers.

VAN SLAMBROUCK, PAUL
1978   "Insurance Fraud: Fighting the 'Almost Acceptable' Crime." *The Christian Science Monitor* (October 13): 86ff.

VLACHOS, WILLIAM
1929   *Moral Hazard.* 2nd ed. N.p.: Vlachos and Company.

Weekly Underwriter, The
1934   "Towner Rating Bureau Observes Anniversary." *The Weekly Underwriter* (September 29): 620, 623.
1979a   "Fire Will Blaze on Tuesday in California to Show Saving Potential of Sprinklers." *The Weekly Underwriter* (August 4): 21.
1979b   "New Anti-Redlining Regulation Needs Major Overhaul to Avoid Problems: AIA." *The Weekly Underwriter* (September 22): 6–7.
1979c   "Insurance Industry Should Invest in Urban Areas, American Insurance Association Board Told." *The Weekly Underwriter* (October 13): 8.
1979d   "FAIR Plans' First Quarter Results Show Biggest Population Gains." *The Weekly Underwriter* (April 15): 8.
1980   "AIA Endorses NAIC's Availability Reforms, Hits 'Redlining' Practices." *The Weekly Underwriter* (April 15): 8.

WEESE, SAMUEL H.
1971   *Non-Admitted Insurance in the United States*. Homewood, Ill.:
        Richard D. Irwin.

WEICHELT, GEORGE M.
1934   "Legal Angles of Suretyship." *The Weekly Underwriter* (August
        25):343–45.

WEISS, ANDREW
1981   "A Sorting *Cum* Learning Model of Education." Murray Hill,
        N.J.: Bell Laboratories.

WHITFORD, GEORGE V.
1965   "Concepts Associated with Fire Insurance." In *Property and Lia-
        bility Insurance Handbook*, edited by John D. Long and Davis W.
        Gregg, 45–57. Homewood, Ill.: Richard D. Irwin.

WHYTE, WILLIAM FOOTE
1943   "A Slum Sex Code." *American Journal of Sociology* 49 (July):
        24–31.

WILLIAMS, C. ARTHUR, JR.
1974   "Attitudes Toward Speculative Risks as Indicators of Attitudes
        Toward Pure Risks." In *Insurance Insights*, edited by Mark R.
        Greene and Paul Swadener, 81–93. Cincinnati: South-Western.

WILLIAMSON, OLIVER E.
1975   *Markets and Hierarchies: Analysis and Antitrust Implications*.
        New York: Free Press.
1981   "The Economics of Organization: The Transaction Cost Ap-
        proach." *American Journal of Sociology* 87 (November):548–77.

WILLIAMSON, OLIVER E., AND WILLIAM G. OUCHI
1981   "The Markets and Hierarchies Program of Research: Origins, Im-
        plications, and Prospects." In *Perspectives on Organization De-
        sign and Behavior*, edited by Andrew H. Van de Ven and Wil-
        liam F. Joyce, 347–70. New York: John Wiley.

WILMOT, NICOLAS
1975   "The Contract of Marine Insurance in English and Norwegian
        Law." Bergen, Norway: Institutt for Privatrett, Universitetet i
        Bergen. Book-length manuscript, photocopy.
1976   "Oppgjør Mellom Ulike Sjoassurandørgrupper" ("Settlements
        Among Categories of Marine Insurers"). Marine Law Seminar,
        Fall 1976. Oslo: Scandinavian Institute for Maritime Law.

WINTER, WILLIAM D.
1952   *Marine Insurance: Its Principles and Practice*. 3rd ed. New York:
        McGraw-Hill.

ZIMMERMAN, PETER A.
1963   "Coverage and Changes in Corporate Surety Bonds." *Insurance*
        (April 20):37–38.

Index

Compositor: G & S Typesetters, Inc..
      Text: 10/12 Times Roman
   Display: Goudy